Analogue | A Field Guide

Analogue | A Field Guide
Deyan Sudjic

FRANCES LINCOLN

HASSELBLAD

Catalogue

500 C
——
SWC

VICTOR HASSELBLAD AKTIEBOLAG SWEDEN

Contents

Introduction | It's only now the analogue world is effectively over that we can grasp its extraordinarily rich legacy, see how different life was until recently, and appreciate the creativity that went into so many now-extinct objects. Analogue technology shaped the way that the world worked until the early years of the twenty-first century. That technology reflected the ingenuity of the engineers who developed it and the creativity of the designers who gave it form. Its social and cultural side effects, from Beatles album covers to Kodachrome colour slides, encapsulated the culture of the times. These were the objects that measured out our lives.

When the celebrated American science-fiction magazine *Astounding* changed its name in 1960, it chose to call itself *Analog*, partly because it sounded more scientific, and mostly because it was a word that seemed to represent the future. But the analogue era was already facing the early tremors of the digital revolution. The transistors that would eventually transform computers from isolated room-size goliaths into universal desktop machines were first used in computers in 1954. In the 1960s, the Department of Defense was funding the ARPANET project in the US, laying the foundations for the internet. But the effects of all these technological shifts had yet to filter into the public consciousness, and there was still plenty of analogue innovation to come, particularly in the recording of sound and video.

Magnetic tape, for example, had been used for video since the 1950s, but it was not until the 1980s that video recorders became widely available. Sony and other Japanese companies produced a stream of charismatic new products that depended on the miniaturization of analogue technology for the general consumer rather than the professional user.

Even if analogue technology once seemed like the future, in fact it has been a way of understanding the world for a long time. It is, in essence, a way of representing or measuring such physical phenomena as size, time, sound and light. Sundials, yardsticks and compasses dating back two millennia or more could be said to be the early analogue era.

From the beginning of the nineteenth century, a range of developments in analogue technologies, not all of them related to each other, introduced new ways to reproduce images and sounds, and even to transmit them. In 1839 Daguerre set in motion the beginnings of modern photography; facsimile became a possibility in the 1840s; telegraphs used Morse code as an analogue form of communication; Scholes and Gidden made commercially successful typewriters after 1874.

If these represent the middle period of the analogue age, its late period began with the development of the vacuum tube at the beginning of the twentieth century and was turbocharged by the transistor after 1947, making possible the mass adoption of television and portable radios.

Analogue technology had an impact that was social and cultural as well as economic and industrial. Photography was both a technical breakthrough and a new art form, which some believed was stealing souls when it was first developed in the nineteenth century. Radio in the 1930s was even more of a transformation of political life than newspapers had been in the 1830s. The vinyl record that could play seven three-minute recordings on each side created a modern musical form, the album, and triggered in turn a minor new art form: the album cover. Television introduced advertising, made stars and celebrities, and homogenized culture.

The 1960s and 1970s were the finale of the age of analogue and saw some of the most ingenious consumer artefacts ever produced, including the Polaroid SX-70 camera (see page 139) – the closest that analogue technology ever got to the weightless instant results of digital photography. In the same era, Sony produced the Walkman (see page 95), and Dieter Rams designed multiple radios for Braun, including the RT20 (see page 54).

The rate of change was accelerating at an extraordinary pace. The telephone was an analogue technology that depended on handsets with a microphone that turned the voice into an analogue signal and transmitted it down copper wires through a switch exchange to a receiver. It became the dominant form of long distance communication, until it was swept away in less than a decade. At the end of 1999 there were just 492 million mobile phone subscribers in the entire world – and quite a lot of these were first generation analogue mobile phones. Ten years later the number had reached almost five billion and they were all digital.

(1) The Algol portable television (see page 173), designed by Marco Zanuso and Richard Sapper for Brionvega and still in production – using updated electronic technology – today.

1

When the first smartphone was launched by Apple in 2007, it was a kind of mass extinction event for a vast range of analogue products, from maps to cameras, music players, tape recorders, radios and alarm clocks.

Digital technologies recorded the same physical phenomena as analogue had done, not by replicating a sound wave physically (as analogue recordings had done, in wax, for example), but by sampling it numerically, and storing the essential information that would allow it to be reproduced as speech or music.

In the last 15 years, the extent of the shift away from analogue has become clear. The US switched off analogue television signals in 2009. The BBC in Britain followed three years later. All new car radios are digital now. Many countries are preparing to switch off analogue wireless signals, if they have not already done so, in a shift that would make hundreds of millions of radios (and representing several generations of innovation) not only obsolete, but useless. Norway, for example, switched off all FM radio signals in 2017, although the BBC has postponed its switch off until at least 2030.

Analogue as a category is not completely dead. There are devices that use both analogue and digital technologies, such as modern cameras equipped with analogue image sensors that produce data that is then converted into digital signals. Certain everyday objects, such as the mechanical wristwatch, that should logically have been extinguished by their far cheaper, more reliable, and more accurate digital replacements, have in fact survived. Thanks to our custom of marking out our lives by the possessions that we own, and our continuing preference for passing them on to our descendants, the watch has taken on the character of jewellery. So many analogue technologies came to the premature end of an evolutionary road, but not watch mechanisms, which have gone on to adopt ever more baroque complications.

The continuing appeal of analogue is both aesthetic and emotional. Just as some musicians favour analogue reproduction techniques for the quality of sound it makes possible, so some film directors, notably Wes Anderson and Quentin Tarantino, still make their movies using film. This is because of the quality of light, colour and tone it offers in comparison to what they call the clinical quality of digital cameras.

The vinyl record has come back from the edge of extinction. This is in part the result of perceptions about quality, as LPs have come to be regarded as offering a more resonant sound than compact discs. Turntables, amplifiers and speakers have gone much the same way as the design of wristwatches, with ever more costly and elaborate equipment, and in some cases even resurrecting the thermionic valve for use in amplifiers rather than transistors.

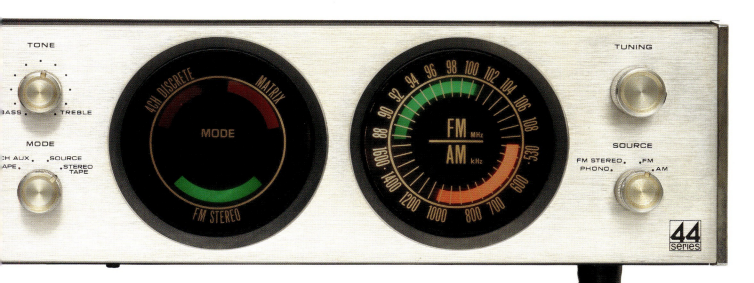

3

(2) Panasonic SA-504 four channel receiver radio (see page 63) – a briefly popular technological fad from the 1970s, which offered the possibility of so-called quadrophonic sound.

(3) The Polaroid SX 70 camera (see page 139), a culmination of Edwin Land's attempts to liberate photography from the dark room.

Perhaps as significant as its perceived sound quality, a vinyl record brings with it a sense of ownership that relying on an intangible streaming service cannot offer. In their nature, analogue machines of all kinds were more engaging than their digital successors. Analogue machines depended on tangible mechanical parts. There were buttons to press, dials to check, features that gave them a tactile quality; these became an essential part of their personality and the means with which we interacted with them. The distance a switch could travel, the sound that it made while doing so, the touch of the ridged edges of a knob to tune a station on a radio – these all added to the impression machines gave us that we controlled them, and that they were putting us in charge of something with a sense of purpose. Despite their utilitarian origins, controls became a kind of decoration – embellishments used by designers to flatter consumers as 'professional users'.

Analogue machines click and respond to the touch. They are configured in such a way as to suggest what they are for and to give their users an intuitive understanding of how to operate them. Digital ones beep and are much less involving or communicative, offering less physical interaction than their analogue predecessors. It is not surprising then that the age of analogue can seem so appealing to a new generation of users alienated by a world of intangible pixels.

James Laver, a curator at the Victoria and Albert Museum in London in the 1940s, half-jokingly formulated what he called Laver's Law to describe the arc that fashion goes through. A garment is indecent when it is too far ahead of its time. It is daring when it is just a little ahead of its time, and chic when it is of its time. It quickly becomes old hat, and then hideous. Inevitably it will then become amusing, then cute, and then charming, before it turns into beautiful. Many types of analogue objects have been through a similar process, from avante garde, to obsolete, to cute, to collector's items.

Tom Hanks, who famously has a collection of 250 manual typewriters, told the *New York Times* 'the tactile pleasure of typing old school is incomparable to what you get from a de rigueur laptop'. He captured the analogue experience, when pressing a button was to feel that something important was happening. 'Computer keyboards make a mousy tappy tap tappy tap, like ones you hear in a Starbucks – work may be getting done, but it sounds cozy and small, like knitting needles creating a pair of socks. Everything you type on a typewriter, the words forming mini-explosions SHOOK SHOOK SHOOK. A thank you note resonates with the same heft as a literary masterpiece.'

The age of analogue has left an indelible mark on the digital era. The QWERTY keyboard designed for the typewriter in 1874, for example, is still used for laptops. Typography began as wooden type, moved to metal, then to photosetting, and is now digital, but the idea of the serif letter has its origins in stone carving, and remained due to concerns about legibility and ink. The way that print is set in columns – justified or ragged – again is a hangover from calligraphy, a look that is still reproduced on a screen.

This book is an exploration of all things analogue, organized into four sections: sound, vision, communication and information. Each section has a chronological account of the development of every category of object, from record players and cameras, to watches and typewriters.

At a time when the enthusiasm for analogue has seen production of Polaroid film restart, and 50-year-old reel-to-reel tape recorders become valuable collector's items, *Analogue: A Field Guide* offers an insight into its continuing significance and its appeal. An understanding of its analogue roots tells us a lot about contemporary technology and the history of the present.

(4) Marcello Nizzoli's Lexikon 80 manual typewriter, designed for Olivetti, and a predecessor of the Lexikon 82 electric typewriter (see page 231).

Sound

Chapter One

Since the day in August 1877, when Thomas Edison recorded himself reciting a nursery rhyme by making physical marks on a metal cylinder wrapped in a sheet of tin foil, analogue technology has changed not only the way we listen, but also what we listen to. Edison experimented with cylinders of wax that when 'played' with a needle, and amplified through a diaphragm and a loudspeaker, could reproduce the sounds that he had previously recorded on a master from which he pressed copies. This marked the beginning of a procession of new analogue recording media, from wax and vinyl to magnetic tape of various kinds.

Edison's two-minute recording of *Mary Had a Little Lamb* was limited to the capture of a fragment of a performance. Later, a 30cm (12-in) diameter vinyl record, spinning at a steady 33⅓ revolutions per minute and offering 30 minutes of playing time on a turntable, became far more than a technical object. As the Beatles demonstrated in 1967, with the launch of *Sgt. Pepper's Lonely Hearts Club Band*, the LP (as the long player was known) emerged as a new cultural form in its own right. Recorded music now had the potential to draw a narrative arc, just as opera and novels had done in previous centuries. The sequence of songs was a vital part of the experience – an aspect that has become lost in the process of digital music streaming today. The album title and sleeve design were essential parts of the listening experience; the medium shaped the message.

Recording came first, but broadcasting developed alongside it, both technically and in providing content. Italian inventor and electrical engineer Guglielmo Marconi's experimental wireless broadcasts in the 1890s soon led to the first radio stations – in 1920 in the US, and two years later in the UK, when the British Broadcasting Company, the BBC's forerunner, began daily operations. Shortwave transmissions would reach across the world, beaming propaganda, or enlightenment, to small radio sets that could be concealed from the agents of authoritarian regimes.

The first commercial sound-recording machines became available in the US in 1903, making use of magnetized steel wire. Undergoing steady technical improvements, they continued in production until the end of the 1950s. They were primarily used in offices for dictation, and to record radio broadcasts – wire was impractical as a medium for home entertainment when an hour's recording time took up almost 2km (6,500 feet) of wire.

The German engineer Fritz Pfleumer later patented a process for coating paper with a magnetic stripe that would eventually replace wire. AEG, the pioneering manufacturer of electrical appliances, used it for the Magnetophon K1 launched in 1935, but tape recorders would not become a consumer product until the 1960s. Reel-to-reel tape recorders required a patient and relatively skilful user, as flimsy plastic-based tape had to be threaded through playback and recording heads, and onto a second spool. It made the process feel more like a craft than a simple loading operation.

(1) After years of research, Thomas Edison commercialized his first experiments with sound recording. His wax cylinders, sold in cardboard boxes, played music for two minutes and remained the dominant recording format from 1890 until around 1912, when they were overtaken by discs.

(2) Broadcasting technology developed in parallel with the growth of content. Across most of the world, radio stations operated as a government monopoly with networks of local transmitters. Radios were marked with the names of the stations to enable tuning.

(3) In the 1960s open reel-to-reel tape players, such as this Dieter Rams designed model manufactured by Braun (see page 87), competed with record player based audio systems, such as Brionvega's (see page 81). Each medium had an avid following among audio enthusiasts.

1

1878 The Edison Speaking Phonograph Company was established, allowing customers to record short messages on wax cylinders and play them back.

1898 The Danish engineer Valdemar Poulsen produced a wire recorder, which he marketed as a dictation machine that he called the Telegraphone.

1889 The forerunner of the jukebox, a coin-operated Edison phonograph in an oak cabinet, was installed in a San Francisco bar.

1922 The BBC began broadcasting from London, Birmingham and Manchester, offering news, weather, concerts, and the first children's programme, a reading of Oscar Wilde's *The Happy Prince*.

2

3

1924 Marconi made the first successful shortwave broadcast from Cornwall, which was picked up in Lebanon, demonstrating the reach of radio.

1930 The first commercial car radio, Motorola's 5T71, incorporated a tuner and speakers. In those days, theft from parked vehicles was not seen as a concern.

1933 The Nazi party launched the 'People's Radio', the cheap, newly designed Volksempfänger 301 (see page 39), as part of Joseph Goebbels' propaganda machine.

1935 Fritz Pleumer licensed his patented process for magnetic recording tape to AEG, which used it to launch the Magnetophon K1, aimed at professional broadcasters.

4

5

(4) Brionvega worked with architects such as Marco Zanuso – responsible with Richard Sapper for the Concetto record deck (see page 81) – on its distinctive range of audio and television equipment.

(5) Replacing fragile thermionic valves with the newly developed, much smaller transistors allowed for the development of pocket-sized portable radios, such as the Regency TR-1 (see page 44).

1951 Todd Storz used *Billboard* magazine's weekly survey of America's most popular records to provide the playlist for what became the first Top 40 music radio station.

1954 Regency produced the TR-1 (see page 44), the first portable transistor radio in the US, shortly before Sony manufactured its own product.

1958 The first commercially available stereo discs, pressed on vinyl, went on sale in the US. Among the titles available was an album by Johnny Puleo and his Harmonica Gang.

1966 Sony launched the TC-100, its first tape-cassette player, popularizing the compact cassette developed by Phillips, just six years earlier.

The equipment we use to listen to recorded or broadcast sound has shaped critical moments in many personal histories. The jukebox in the café and the transistor radio that relayed the records played by the pirate radio stations that overwhelmed Britain's state monopoly, provided the soundtrack to daily life. This equipment has also had a historical impact. As one example, a coup against the government in France by its colonial army in Algeria, in 1960, was thwarted when conscripts heard President Charles de Gaulle's broadcast ordering them back to their barracks on the transistor radios that they carried in their kitbags. This foreshadowed the role that social media has more recently played in the Arab Spring in the early 2010s. And the hidden machines that recorded the White House tapes had the unintended consequence of terminating the ill-fated Nixon presidency.

The objects that played music became significant in themselves. At first, technology was smuggled into the home in the guise of furniture in ornate cabinets. Later, audio systems flattered their owners with finishes and controls that suggested the technical precision of a laboratory, and implied that their owner had the expertise to match. The variety of approaches reflected every taste, from sober, high-minded modernism to colourful pop and gaudy kitsch. Radio sets, in particular, but also tape recorders and record players, have been designed by distinguished architects, as well as the anonymous marketing departments of Japanese electronics companies, prepared to offer their customers every kind of novelty. The timescale of change in technology and style has been almost as rapid as the fashion cycle in clothes, and as a result, analogue audio equipment provides a remarkably revealing history of taste and culture. Like clothing, a radio, a record player or a tape recorder is closely related to the rituals of our daily lives, from the way that a large wireless set was once the focus of the home around which families would gather, to the rituals of teenage courtship played out around an eight-track car-stereo player.

The Regency TR-1, the first US-made radio to use tiny transistors rather than valves the size of light bulbs, allowing the set to become small enough to be easily portable, went on sale in 1954. It was followed by Sony's smaller, cheaper TR 65 rival. Paradoxically, the unfeasibly large boom box the size of a suitcase, ostensibly devised to provide portable musical accompaniment, turned into a mobile style signifier in the 1970s. The Sony Walkman was not just portable, but also allowed users to withdraw from their surroundings into music. Machines like these become closely connected with the body. The way that they were carried and used, made them extensions of their owner's personality.

6

(6) Richard Sapper worked on the design of a number of distinctive radios. The TS 502 (see page 57), with its carrying handle and hinged structure, was particularly inventive.

1969 Samsung entered the field of consumer electronics, and was quickly able to undercut the dominance of Japanese manufacturers.

1976 The Yamaha YP 800/1000 record deck reflected the spread of the high-fidelity cult, which separated out the elements of a stereo system into individual components.

1979 Sony launched the first of its Walkman products (see page 95), offering personal listening with immersive sound through headphones, making music wearable.

1992 French-owned Thomson appointed Philippe Starck in a failed bid to revamp its product range with high-style radios, such as Moosk, and stave off Asian competition.

Product Directory

Records

Cylinder recordings date back to 1877 and Thomas Edison's foil-wrapped cylinders. Emile Berliner, the German American inventor, came up with a flat disc as a better alternative for a format that could carry sound recordings. In its earliest incarnation, the disc was a way to preserve a performance, as its name 'record' implied. It later turned into a consumable object – a way to buy a musical experience.

Record Players

The first record players were hand-cranked mechanical machines which played rotating discs. Electric motors and amplifiers transformed recorded music into a much more convincing representation of a live performance, improved still further by the development of stereophonic systems that could record on multiple channels. Many companies were able to offer both the hardware to play records, and also set up recording studios to produce the content they played.

Radios

The first generation of radios – known as wireless sets because they were not connected to the transmitting station – depended on fragile valves the size of light bulbs. This inevitably made them large objects that were too heavy and too delicate to be moved easily, but the introduction of the transistor in the post-war years transformed the radio into a personal and portable object.

Radiograms

The idea of combining a record player with a radio was less a technological innovation, than a marketing-led development. It was a more compact arrangement than having an individual radio side by side with a record player. It could be more economical, too, if the two elements shared a power source and a single loudspeaker. But it was

Brionvega's and Braun's designs that convincingly established the radiogram as a category in its own right.

Reel-to-Reel

Magnetic recording tape followed the development of wax cylinders as the preferred medium for broadcasters. Tape recorders began as machines aimed at professionals, which required a certain expertise to use. As the machines became more refined, operating them became simpler. Unlike machines designed to play wax records, they gave the user the chance to record sound for themselves, rather than relying on pre-recorded music sold to them by the manufacturer.

Cassette Tape Players and Recorders

Originally developed by the Philips company, the ambition behind the cassette was to combine the convenience of a record, with the sound quality offered by larger format magnetic tape played on a reel-to-reel machine. Increasingly sophisticated formulations of ferric-oxide coating for the tape promised better reproduction and sound quality. Portable cassette players allowed users to circumvent copyright restrictions and record radio broadcasts and LPs, which made them popular.

8-Track Cassette Players

The 8-track cassette format was both a mechanical and a technical innovation. It used a wider tape that allowed for a more accurate recording, and the cassette itself could play both sides of the tape without the need to eject it from the player and re-insert it. The 8-track was originally sold as a form of in-car entertainment, where it formed the musical background of the 1970s, but was less successful in the home.

Boom Boxes

Much in the way that certain kinds of sportswear were taken up as cultural signifiers, so the boom box – a portable radio combined with a cassette player – came to be an essential youth culture accessory. Originally presented as a battery-powered portable machine for outdoor use, the boom box developed an unexpected audience for whom it was the act of being seen carrying the machine that had the most appeal.

78 rpm record

Date: 1887

Designer: Emile Berliner

Manufacturer: United States Gramophone Company, Washington, DC, US

Dimensions: 25cm (10in) or 30cm (12in) diameter

Records have been manufactured since the last years of the nineteenth century, based on speeds that fluctuated around 78 revolutions per minute (rpm). They took over from the cylinders that Edison had invented. In the early days, it was not easy to be precise about the speed of a hand-cranked turntable. It was only after 1925 that 78.26 rpm became an industry standard, and it remained the dominant format for recorded music until the 1950s when new technologies introduced in 1949 supplanted it with the 33⅓ rpm long-playing record.

At first, the 78s were made from shellac, a natural resin, pressed from a wax master, which was the product of a recording that left an analogue version of the sound waves. They were made in either 25- or 30-cm (10- or 12-in) sizes, with the larger size offering up to six minutes of music. They mostly came in standard printed-paper envelopes, with an open window to show the label.

Vinyl LP

Date: 1948

Designers: Peter Goldmark, William Savory, William Bachman, Howard Scott

Manufacturer: Columbia Records, New York, NY, US

Dimensions: 30cm (12in) diameter

Vinyl was supplanting shellac for records even before Columbia launched the first long-playing record, Mendelssohn's Violin Concerto in E minor, played by Nathan Milstein with Bruno Walter conducting the New York Philharmonic Symphony Orchestra. It was the result of years of research into a technology that could offer a minimum of 20 minutes playing time, using slower speeds and alternative recording techniques. It allowed for a new musical format, the album, a sequence of up to six tracks per side, which was quickly adopted by Columbia's competitors such as Philips (pictured), Brunswick, the Anglo-German Parlophone label, and Decca. The album cover turned out to be equally fertile ground for designers' artwork (see page 32).

45 rpm single

Date: 1949

Designer: RCA Victor

Manufacturer: RCA Victor, New York, NY, US

Dimensions: 17.8cm (7in) diameter

The history of popular music was transformed by the launch of a record designed to play for three minutes at 45 rpm on a 17.8-cm (7-in) disc. It was smaller and offered less material than the LP, and seemed initially to offer less value, but it was cheaper. RCA's first release of seven singles covered the whole range of musical tastes, from the Delta Blues singer Arthur 'Big Boy' Crudup's *That's All Right*, which would later be recorded by Elvis Presley, to Saul Meisels, a Juilliard-trained singer who specialized in renditions of Yiddish folk songs.

The single really took off when musicians began to tailor their work to the format, to make the most of a three-minute explosion of sound. Bill Haley's *Rock Around the Clock* sold three million copies, demonstrating the power of the single, reinforced by the introduction of the hit parade, music radio DJs, and the juke box.

Airconditioning Curved Air vinyl record

Date: 1970

Designer: Mark Hanau

Manufacturer: Warner Bros Records,
Los Angeles, CA, US

Dimensions: 30cm (12in) diameter

One of the first picture discs, pressed by
Metronome records in a limited edition of
10,000, *Airconditioning* was issued in a
clear plastic sleeve. Contrasting patterns
on either side of the record produced a
dynamic, 'psychedelic' effect when the
disc was spinning. Curved Air's debut
album was designed by their manager
Mark Hanau; 'I loved Art Nouveau, and
the front cover art was my version of that
style,' he said later. It was produced by creating
one segment, which was then copied under a
25.4 × 20.3-cm (10 × 8-in) format DeVere copy
camera and re-exposed 16 times. The other
side was airbrush art intended to animate
when viewed using a strobe light. Sonja
Kristina, Curved Air's vocalist, was less certain
about the sound quality. 'The problem with the
picture disc was that it had the artwork under
clear vinyl and this kept on picking up static, so
the sound quality wasn't as good as on black
vinyl. But it was still a really good idea.'

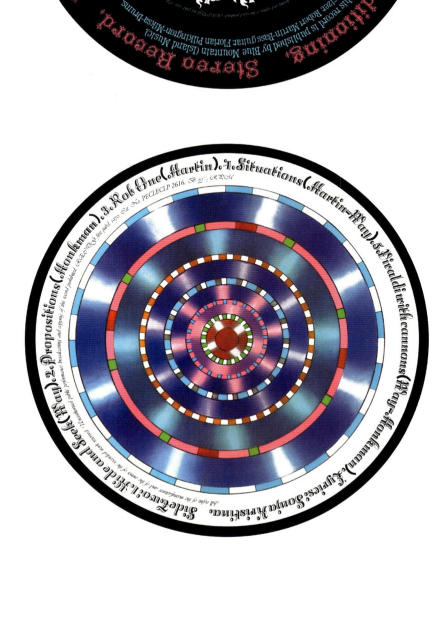

HMV 102 hand-cranked gramophone

Date: 1931

Designer: HMV

Manufacturer: HMV, Hayes, England

Dimensions: 42 × 29 × 16.5cm
(16½ × 11½ × 6½in)

In the 1930s, an HMV gramophone was a luxury item, expensive enough to be offered on hire-purchase terms. The basic black version cost £5 12s 6d, but it was also available in a choice of colours, or a deluxe red-leather case for 8 guineas, which allowing for inflation is the equivalent of £900 today. The gramophone used no electric components, but otherwise looked much like a contemporary record player, with an arm and a needle that tracked the grooves on a 25.4-cm (10-in) wax disc. The needles had to be changed after every second or third use to avoid damaging discs. A sound box was connected to the needle with a diaphragm, and the sound was amplified through an acoustic horn beneath the turntable, which was powered mechanically by means of a detachable wind-up handle. Inside the case was a tray designed to carry half a dozen records. The only way to adjust the volume was to muffle the horn with a cover.

Garrard 301 Transcription record deck

Date: 1954

Designer: Edmund Mortimer

Manufacturer: Garrard, Swindon, England

Dimensions: 64 × 48 × 21.5cm
(25 × 19 × 8½in)

Garrard, a company originally set up as an offshoot of the jewellery business of the same name, developed an enviable reputation for technical expertise and high-quality manufacturing. The 301 was one of the first record players to offer high-fidelity performance, addressing the shortcomings of early recording technology. In the 1950s, it had to be capable of operating at three different speeds, addressing the recently introduced 33⅓-rpm and 45-rpm formats. Garrard also made the tonearm, which carries

the stylus that turns the grooves on the record into sound. This, along with the cast aluminium turntable, still look modern. It is only the details of the controls, sitting on metal plates, that reveal it as a product of the early 1950s.

Garrard 301s were expensive machines, used by the British Broadcasting Corporation (BBC) and many European commercial broadcasters. To install one required the ability to add a plinth, since Garrard sold their turntables without either a plinth or an arm.

Dansette Conquest record player

Date: 1962

Designer: Dansette Products Ltd

Manufacturer: Dansette Products Ltd, London, England

Dimensions: 41 × 47 × 46cm (16 × 18½ × 18in)

The Dansette was a tradename that belonged to the J&A Margolin company, which became closely associated with British youth culture during the 1960s. Dansettes were to be found in student halls of residence and teenagers' bedrooms. The Dansette Conquest had an auto changer on which you could stack up to six discs that would play in sequence, although there was always the risk of damaging one as they dropped down the spindle on which they were positioned. The amplifier was valve driven and rather outdated. 'You'll love the tone of these smartly styled Dansettes, deep rich reproduction that makes your records sound twice as good' claimed the advertising. Mixing hyperbole with technical jargon, it suggested that 'the Conquest auto is the top of the line, truly luxurious with a high-quality two-stage amplifier, 17.8-cm (7-in) matching speakers, and a two-tone colour scheme'.

Goldring GL 75 record deck

Date: 1967

Designer: Goldring Manufacturing

Manufacturer: Goldring Manufacturing, London, England/Lenco, Switzerland

Dimensions: 46 × 15.8 × 36.5cm (18 × 6 × 14½in)

The Goldring GL 75 record deck was described as a transcription turntable, a term that derived from the BBC's practice of transcribing recordings onto discs for broadcasting, and implied a high degree of accuracy. The Goldring came with four speeds: 78 for older recordings, 45 for singles, as well as 33⅓ and 16 rpm. Getting the speed exactly correct was crucial to ensuring the sound was an accurate reflection of the original recording. Played too slow, and the record sounded deeper than the original, while moving too fast meant that the treble tones were over emphasized. Goldring used a stroboscopic light to provide an optical check that the turntable was revolving at the right speed. The light flashes rapidly, illuminating four rings of dots marked on the edge of the turntable, each corresponding to one of the four speeds. The stroboscopic effect makes the dots appear to freeze when the turntable is rotating precisely at one of those speeds.

P 40 amplifier

Date: 1969

Designers: Gordon Edge, Peter Lee,
Roy Gray (case)

Manufacturer: Cambridge Audio, St Ives,
England

Dimensions: 41.9 × 24.1 × 5.1cm
(16½ × 9½ × 2in)

Cambridge Audio would be called a start-up today. It emerged from the work of a group of young engineers associated with Cambridge Consultants that drew on the work of the tech cluster around the university. Engineer Gordon Edge joined the company from Pye, the long-established electronics company.

Edge assembled a team to design what eventually became a range of audio equipment, and which began with the P 40 amplifier – the designation referred to its output of 20 watts per channel.

The P 40 stood out by reconfiguring the electronic circuits needed to amplify the analogue signal from a record deck or a tape player. It incorporated a doughnut-shaped transformer that made it possible to reduce the size of the amplifier box, reduce the heat generated, and minimize noise. It was an innovation that would become a standard feature of high-end amplifiers.

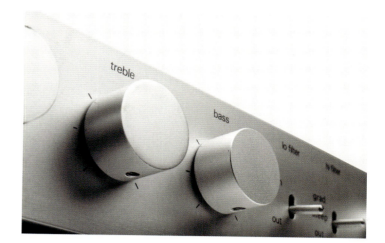

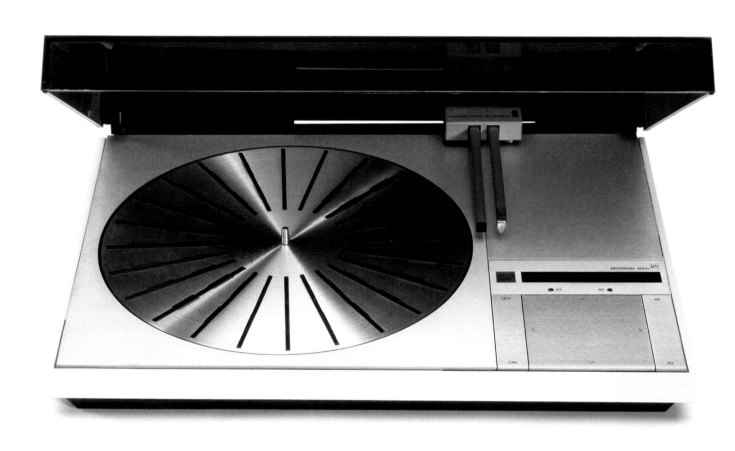

Beogram 4000 turntable

Date: 1972

Designer: Jacob Jensen

Manufacturer: Bang & Olufsen,
Struer, Denmark

Dimensions: 10 × 38 × 49cm (4 × 15 × 19¼in)

When it was launched, Jacob Jensen's record player was like no other – not purely for aesthetic reasons, although it was certainly an exceptionally refined design, but rather in terms of improved acoustic performance. Jensen and B&O's engineers went back to first principles to avoid acoustic distortions. Instead of the usual tracking arm balanced on a pivot, the Beogram 4000 had a pair of tangential tracking arms. The right-hand arm carried the stylus, while the one on the left used an optical tracking system to ensure the arm with the

stylus was always lowered in the correct place. This minimized the risk of damage to either the record or stylus. The aluminium-surfaced platter came framed in a choice of rosewood or teak, unmistakably rooting the record player in the carefully proportioned world of modern Danish design. It also reflected the refined and elegant approach of Jensen's other designs for B&O.

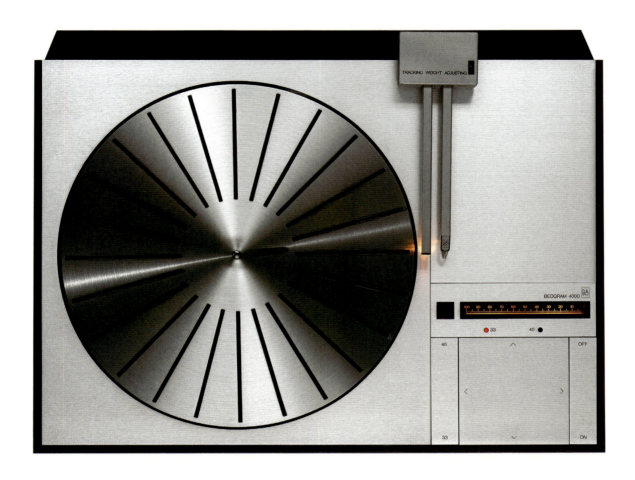

Album Art

The album-art genre began to emerge in 1938, when Columbia Records employed the poster designer Alex Steinweiss, who had trained at the Parsons School of Design in New York, as its first art director. He transformed what had previously been utilitarian paper sleeves into colourful album covers that had an immediate impact on boosting sales. When Columbia started pressing LPs after 1949, Steinweiss brilliantly demonstrated how an album cover could become an art form. He mixed illustration, collage and colour in his treatment of Columbia's recording of Bruno Walter conducting the New York Philharmonic in their performance of Beethoven's *Eroica*. It was the beginning of an intense burst of creativity that lasted over 50 years. Despite the tight restrictions of the format, usually 31.5 × 31.5cm (12 × 12in), the album cover was no longer merely humble packaging. Important artists such as Robert Rauschenberg and Richard Hamilton have conceived covers (respectively for Talking Heads' *Speaking in Tongues* and the Beatles' *White Album*). Andy Warhol put a banana on The Velvet Underground's debut album, and suggested to Mick Jagger that he should use the zip that features on The Rolling Stones' iconic *Sticky Fingers* album. Another important approach was photographic, a treatment that was particularly important for established recording stars. Richard Avedon photographed Paul Simon and Art Garfunkel for *Bookends*, for example, and Annie Liebowitz portrayed Bruce Springsteen for *Born in the USA*.

For some acts it was more important to create a mood or an atmosphere that could in some way suggest the kind of music that new listeners would discover, than a representation of the artist. Britain was particularly fertile ground for designers specializing in album covers. Designers Storm Thorgerson and Aubrey Powell set up a joint studio called Hipgnosis. Their first album cover in 1968, for Pink Floyd's *A Saucerful of Secrets*, was followed by a whole series of striking designs. Their approach was later supplanted by the Punk explosion and Jamie Reid's work for the Sex Pistols or Barney Bubbles' design for Elvis Costello and the Attractions' *Get Happy!!*.

The compact disc did not entirely kill off album art – as *Very*, the Pet Shop Boys' 1993 CD box in specially textured orange, demonstrated – but album art's last flowering was represented by the creative abstraction of Peter Saville's colour wheel design for the back cover of New Order's *Power, Corruption & Lies*, and Malcolm Garrett's work for Buzzcocks' *A Different Kind of Tension*.

1

(1) Graphic designer Alex Steinweiss, pictured here in c. April 1947, was working for Columbia Records at the time that the company started making the very first LP records.

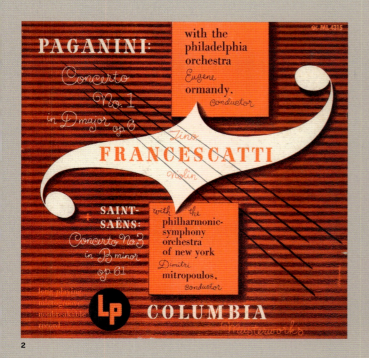

2

3

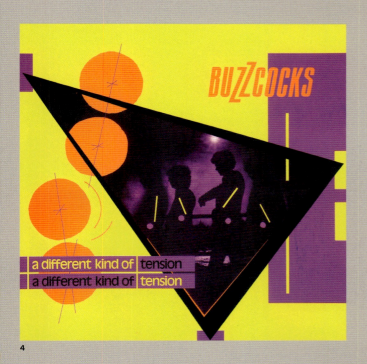

4

5

(2) and (3) Steinweiss had already created a distinctive look for the paper sleeves used to wrap 78 rpm records, but went on to use the cardboard LP sleeve as a canvas for what amounted to a new art form.

(4) The arrival of Britain's burgeoning New Wave musicians was signalled by the work of another generation of designers such as Malcom Garrett, who produced this cover art.

(5) Peter Saville's colour wheel design for New Order established a new graphic language for conveying the essence of an album.

Technics SL-1200 record deck

Date: 1972

Designer: Shuichi Obata

Manufacturer: Matsushita Electric Industrial
Co. Ltd, Osaka, Japan

Dimensions: 45.3 × 36.6 × 18cm
(18 × 14½ × 7in)

Panasonic's Technics division developed a
direct-drive record deck that was able to reach
playing speeds more quickly than belt-driven
models. The electric motor was positioned
directly beneath the turntable rather than to
one side, connected by a belt. The SL-1200
came with a diecast aluminium cabinet and
heavy platter, with a distinctive patterned
edge. It became unexpectedly popular in
the newly emerging DJ culture, where it was
used to achieve scratching and needle-drop
techniques that defined the hip hop and disco
style. Technics engineers worked to add new
features, and these turntables began to be
called musical instruments in recognition of
the creative part played by the DJ.

Sondek LP12 record deck

Date: 1972

Designer: Jack Tiefenbrun

Manufacturer: Linn Products, Glasgow,
Scotland

Dimensions: 44.5 × 14 × 35.6cm
(7½ × 5½ × 14in)

The Tiefenbrun family owned a precision-
engineering company that started building
high-performance turntables during the
1970s. Most previous attempts at getting
the best sound quality from gramophone
records concentrated on refining the speakers.
Tiefenbrun, however, believed that working on
the turntable could produce the best results.
The founder's son, Ivor Tiefenbrun, suggested
that 'Linn didn't invent the turntable, we simply
understood that there was more information
on an LP record than people were capable of
accessing, so we applied our understanding
of engineering to extracting it.' Accurate
speeds, steady power supply, and a well-
engineered tone arm are all critical factors.

Strathearn Audio SMA2 record deck

Date: 1973

Designers: Gordon Edge, Roy Gray

Manufacturer: Strathearn Audio Ltd,
Belfast, Northern Ireland

Dimensions: 37 × 32 × 13cm
(14½ × 12½ × 5in)

In the midst of a military confrontation, there were well-intentioned but misconceived attempts to modernize Northern Ireland's economy using government subsidies. Strathearn Audio was an unsuccessful attempt to jump-start a hi-fi manufacturing company. Government money paid for a new factory for Strathearn, which went to PA Technology, a Cambridge-based consultancy tasked with designing a new product range. They came up with a number of innovative ideas, including low-cost, direct-drive turntable motors and parallel-tracking tonearms. Strathearn manufactured two record decks. With a sleek design, the more ambitious SMA2 featured distinctive red dots on the direct-drive turntable and touch-sensitive buttons. It looked impressive, but a new factory and an inexperienced workforce could not meet the exacting expectations of the specialist hi-fi market, or make money from the limited number of units that they produced. Once government subsidies ended, the factory closed in 1978.

Ron Arad Concrete Stereo

Date: 1983

Designer: Ron Arad

Manufacturer: One-Off Ltd, London, England

Dimensions: Turntable and amplifier each:
41 × 51 × 11.2cm (16 × 20 × 4½in); Each
speaker: 91 × 20 × 20cm (35¾ × 8 × 8in)

Architect and designer Ron Arad has worked simultaneously with mass-produced items and limited-edition studio pieces. He began with the Rover armchair, using recycled seats salvaged from the Rover car, and went on to make sculptural furniture pieces from welded steel sheets, before turning to a more conventional design approach working with factories that could extrude plastic by the kilometre.

From the early part of his career, the Concrete Stereo was a kind of surrealistic contrast between the precision and fragility of a record player and the rough, hardness of the exposed concrete in which it was set. Arad took off-the-peg electronic components and dropped them into cast concrete bases. They included a turntable, amplifier and two floor-standing speakers. Arad allowed fragments of the reinforcing steel on which the concrete was poured to protrude from the edges of the components. Of the ten or so examples made by Arad's studio, most are now in museum collections around the world, including the V&A in London.

Muon loudspeakers

Date: 2007

Designer: Ross Lovegrove

Manufacturer: KEF, Maidstone, England

Dimensions: 200 × 60 × 38cm
(80 × 23½ × 15in)

Every analogue sound system needs a source
(a record, tape deck or radio), along with an
amplifier, and either loudspeakers in some
form or headphones. In the early days of radio,
speakers were concealed within the cabinet.
Early transistor sets miniaturized them to be
as compact as possible, at the cost of sound
quality. Now that analogue music systems
have become more focused on sound quality,
as much attention is paid to the form and
performance of the loudspeakers as to the
engineering of every other element in the
system. KEF's 2-m- (80-in-) high Muon
speakers are a particularly extreme example
of the tendency to produce larger and larger
speaker systems. Lovegrove has used
superformed aluminium to create a pair of
architecturally scaled sculptural objects that
were conceived as an edition limited to 100
pairs, and at $225,000 priced accordingly.

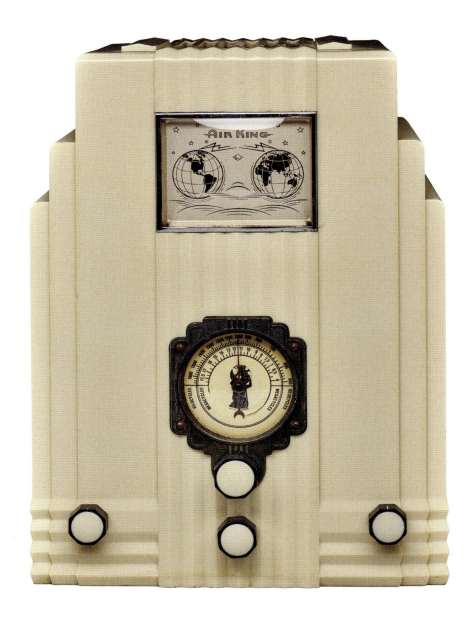

Air King 66 radio

Date: 1933

Designers: Harold van Doren, J. G. Rideout

Manufacturer: Air King, Brooklyn, NY, US

Dimensions: 30 × 23 × 18cm (12 × 9 × 7in)

Originally trained as an art historian, Harold van Doren set up one of the first design consultancies in the US with John Rideout, after a spell as a museum curator. He took a more restrained approach than some of his extrovert contemporaries, who presented themselves as responsible for every aspect of a product. Van Doren published a book on industrial design in 1940, in which he argued for an approach that integrated design, engineering and manufacturing skills. He worked for the Air King company for several years, producing a range of designs for radios that went through rapid stylistic changes. The Bakelite 66 model, known for obvious reasons as the 'skyscraper', went through a number of different versions and was available in startling mint green, as well as other colours. Valve-driven radios from this period have enjoyed a second life as collectors' items, sought after enough for one Air King 66 to be sold at auction, in 2021, for $44,000.

Volksempfänger VE 301 radio

Date: 1933
Designers: Walter Maria Kersting,
Otto Griessing
Manufacturer: Statssfurter Rundfunk
Gmbh, Staßfurt, Germany
Dimensions: 39 × 27.7 × 17cm
(15¼ × 11 × 6¾in)

Conscious of the power of broadcasting
in political propaganda, the Nazi party set
out to produce a radio for a mass audience.
The original price was one-third of the cost of
conventional models, and the state made the
designs available to 28 manufacturers across
the country, who produced it with minor
variations. By 1941, more than two in three
German households had one. Simplifying
the set served a political purpose, as well as
making it cheaper to produce. It could only
receive medium-wave signals, which reduced
its range to German stations only. Hitler's
architect, Albert Speer, suggested that through
the use of 'technical devices like the radio
and the loudspeaker, 80 million people were
deprived of independent thought'.

Ekco AD-65 radio

Date: 1934
Designer: Wells Coates
Manufacturer: EKCO, Southend, England
Dimensions: 40 × 39.5 × 20cm
(15¾ × 15¼ × 8in)

Eric Kirkham Cole used his initials to name his
wireless manufacturing company. EKCO stood
out from its competitors through its early use
of Bakelite, the first synthetic plastic, to make
the cabinets for its valve radios. Architect
and furniture designer Wells Coates designed
several of its models. Coates' radio sets
were somewhere between Art Deco and
modernism. They looked very different from
the timber cabinets of their contemporaries.
They were certainly impressive – once
the valves had warmed up, they glowed,
suggesting a visitation from the future in
traditionally furnished homes. And they
powerfully convey an era when the family
would gather around a radio to listen to news
and entertainment together, a function that the
television set would later serve in the 1950s.

Cristallo radio

Date: 1938, reissued by Cassina in 2021
Designer: Franco Albini
Manufacturer: Franco Albini, Milan, Italy
Dimensions: 66 × 28 × 72cm (26 × 11 × 28¼in)

In the early days of consumer electronics, most radios, record players and television sets were housed in timber cabinets that presented them as if they were pieces of domestic furniture. Franco Albini was one of the first to produce an alternative approach with the Cristallo radio. Albini was responsible for the architecture of the first stations on Milan's subway system and the Rome branch of the Rinascente department-store chain. He designed and made a radio for himself in 1938 by dismantling a conventional set that he had been given as a wedding gift. Removing the traditional timber case, he reconfigured the components within two heavy sheets of toughened glass. The resulting radio was selected for display in 1940 by the pioneering Swiss company Wohnbedarf in Zurich. Cassina, which also manufactures Albini's intricate shelving system (Veliero and Infinito), made its own version of the radio in 2021 as part of its collection of re-editioned historic pieces of furniture.

Phonola 547 radio

Date: 1940

Designers: Livio Castiglioni, Pier Giacomo,
Luigi Caccia Dominioni

Manufacturer: FIMI, Saronno, Italy

Dimensions: 20.5 × 24.5 × 26.5cm
(8 × 9¾ × 10½in)

FIMI, set up in 1931, began by importing
electrical components from the US to build
its first radio sets. From 1939 they began to
work with the Italian architect and designer
Livio Castiglioni, his brother Pier Giacomo,
and Luigi Caccia Dominioni on a new range of
products. The most striking of the three radios
that they designed together was the 547
model, which reflected the aesthetics of
rationalist architecture – the Italian version
of modernism. Castiglioni went back to first
principles of what a radio should look like,
reducing the case to pure geometric forms –
a square base, a circular loudspeaker, and a
rectangular tuning display. It was designed
either to hang on a wall and broadcast fascist
propaganda, or to sit on a table. To achieve the
sculptural form, FIMI worked with Bakelite, the
tradename for phenolic resin. Production was
halted after Italy entered World War II, when
FIMI's factory was turned over to supply the
military, but Livio returned to work for the firm
on subsequent products in the 1950s.

The New Super De Luxe TRANS-OCEANIC

Zenith Portable Radio Model L600

Zenith Trans-Oceanic L 600 portable radio

Date: 1954

Designer: Robert Davol Budlong

Manufacturer: Zenith Radio Corporation, Chicago, IL, US

Dimensions: 43.2 × 27.9 × 20.3cm (17 × 11 × 8in)

Zenith branded the last of its valve radios the 'Super Deluxe Trans-Oceanic', a reflection of the close connections between American industrial design and the advertising industry. Its designer, Robert Budlong, a long-standing consultant to Zenith, began his career in an advertising agency. He styled up the Trans-Oceanic in gold, cream and brown Bakelite. The name was intended to signal the capacity of the set to tune into shortwave transmissions – 'the wave magnet' as it was called, to suggest precision and performance.

It was equipped with slide-rule tuning and a back-lit dial. While the Japanese were busy developing the transistors that represented the future, Zenith was still making Trans-Oceanics loaded with features that were unnecessary from a functional point of view, but which offered their owners the chance to play at being intrepid seafaring navigators with the built-in log books and charts. It represented the end of the valve-radio era, both technically and stylistically.

Regency TR-1 transistor radio

Date: 1954

Designers: David Painter, James Teague,
Victor Petertil

Manufacturer: IDEA, Indianapolis, IN, US

Dimensions: 7.6 × 12.7 × 3.2cm (3 × 5 × 1¼in)

Texas Instruments had the technical expertise
to make transistors, but in the early 1950s did
not have an obvious market for its products.
One promising area seemed to be in replacing
valve components with much smaller
transistors to miniaturize radios. After
being rebuffed by a range of established
manufacturers, Texas Instruments signed an
agreement to supply Industrial Development
Engineering Associates, an Indiana-based
start-up, with the transistors to manufacture
the world's first commercial transistor radio,
narrowly ahead of Sony in Japan. IDEA
commissioned David Painter, James Teague
and Victor Petertil to work on the industrial
design of what became the Regency TR-1.
It came in a plastic box with a choice of
colours and had a leather carrying case,
because that is what cameras had. While its
sound quality was not great, it was compact
and portable. For the first time, wireless
technology was freed from the scale of a
valve-driven radio.

Braun G11 radio

Date: 1955

Designers: Hans Gugelot, Otl Aicher

Manufacturer: Braun AG, Frankfurt, West Germany

Dimensions: 54 × 35.5 × 33.5cm (21¼ × 14 × 13in)

Early wireless sets used either Bakelite, to create sculptural shapes for the cabinet, or dark wood, to suggest traditional furniture. In the early post-war years, before moving on to aluminium and ABS (Acrylonitrile Butadiene Styrene) plastic, Braun explored lighter-coloured timbers, to suggest a more contemporary look for their products. These were substantial machines, powered with mains electricity. They were dependent on valves that demanded a sizeable cabinet to allow the heat that they gave off to be dissipated.

The G11 radio receiver was the beginning of a new approach, with its case made of light maple wood. It had a clear scale made of plastic that was developed by the graphic designer Otl Aicher, who was enough of a purist to view the use of capital letters as mildly immoral. He was the co-founder of the Hochschule für Gestaltung design school in Ulm, whose austere functionalist principles became closely associated with Braun's products.

Braun SK1 radio

Date: 1955

Designers: Artur Braun, Fritz Eichler

Manufacturer: Braun AG, Frankfurt, West Germany

Dimensions: 23.4 × 15.2 × 13cm (9 × 6 × 5in)

Braun's reputation as a company with a unique design language that represented the essence of modernity dates from 1951 when the two Braun brothers took over the running of the company that their father, Max Braun, had established before World War II. Working with the art historian and critic Fritz Eichler as a creative director to advise on the look of Braun's products, its packaging and advertising, they set out to develop a new identity that seemed to reflect the spirit of post-war Germany.

The SK1's form, with its radiused corners, reflects the potential of moulded plastic, and is a clear departure from the aesthetics of earlier timber-cabinet models. The SK1 sits on two unobtrusive ridges that make the cabinet appear to float weightlessly. The controls are reduced to the bare minimum, with just three elements: a tuning dial, an on/off switch, and a volume control.

Libelle 4D61 radio

Date: 1955

Designer: Funkwerk Halle

Manufacturer: Funkwerk Halle, Halle, East Germany

Dimensions: 30 × 23.5 × 12.5cm (11¾ × 9¼ × 5in)

The story of Germany's audio manufacturing in the post-war era was shaped by Europe's military and political history. Existing German industries were the subject of seizures by both Western and Soviet regimes in the name of war reparations. The Soviet Union commandeered entire production lines, shipped goods back to its own territory, and began making German-designed products under new brand names.

After 1949, the newly installed Communist regime in East Germany expropriated all privately owned businesses, and took charge of the Soviet-run factories. The Libelle 4D61 valve radio was a product of this period, and reflected its heritage of German engineering expertise, even though the Cold War conflict meant that the factory would have no access to the latest transistor technology. The Libelle ('dragonfly', in German) has much personality, with the graphic treatment of the loudspeaker opening in its case, and the carrying handle, implying a degree of portability.

Braun T3 radio

Date: 1958

Designer: Dieter Rams

Manufacturer: Braun AG, Frankfurt,
West Germany

Dimensions: 15.1 × 8.4 × 4.1 cm
(6 × 3½ × 1½ in)

The T3 was one of Braun's few pocket-sized transistor radios. Dieter Rams claimed that his approach to its design was based on clarity. Yet deciphering the tuning dial required a certain level of expert knowledge. Black numbers were used to represent medium wave, red numerals were for long wave, and the two scales were mixed together in a circular form with a black triangle pointer mid-way between two plastic ridges.

The T3 was pointing the way toward the closer relationship that electronics could have with their user when they moved from the floor or the tabletop to a bag or pocket. Although the T3 had a far more restricted range of uses, its tactile qualities foreshadowed the symbiotic relationship we now have with the smartphone.

Sony TR-610 radio

Date: 1958

Designer: Kozo Yamamoto

Manufacturer: Sony, Tokyo, Japan

Dimensions: 6.3 × 10.6 × 2.5 cm
(2.5 × 4.2 × 1 in)

Sony's work with transistor radios marked its transformation from a start-up in a burnt-out department store basement to a worldwide industrial success. Akio Morita, one of Sony's founders, had been interested in the potential of the transistor to replace valves in radio sets from as early as 1953. He licensed the technology from the American patent owner, but the Regency TR-1 (see page 44) was released in 1954. Sony followed with its own model, the TR-55, and then the smaller TR-63, but it was the TR-610, the first product to carry a Sony typographic logo, that was the company's definitive transistor radio. Small enough to fit in a shirt pocket, as the marketing campaign claimed, it was the beginning of truly personal electronics. The case was available in a black, green or red moulded plastic.

Sony

The Sony Corporation began with nothing more than a few fragments of surplus equipment from World War II, salvaged by its two scientist founders, Akio Morita and Masaru Ibuka, from the ruins of a country in which many were going hungry. Its success became an emblem of the emergence of a sophisticated new Japan, competing internationally with premium-priced, technically and creatively innovative products, rather than low-budget copies of machines that had their origins in Europe or North America.

Sony's history is inextricably linked with the emerging history of contemporary design. Through a sequence of Sony products, from its first, huge, reel-to-reel tape recorders, to its miniature shortwave radios, the company has defined the evolution of mass-produced technological consumer products. It has drawn on the earliest days of Japanese modernism for the imagery of its products, but it has also explored the aesthetics of American conspicuous consumption.

Perhaps the most impressive thing about Sony is the sheer range of projects that it was able to bring to the market simultaneously. In 1987, for example, the company firstly redefined what a television set could look like with the Profeel Pro. The Profeel is no more than a monitor, with the screen housed in an open cube formed from moulded black plastic. The back is as carefully considered as the front. In the same year, Sony launched lightweight folding stereo headphones, styled by Luigi Colani. They also developed their Sports sub brand, characterized by vivid yellow, moulded-plastic casings with black accents. There was a portable cassette player, a record-only video camcorder (splash-resistant, rather than the deep-sea-diving kit perhaps suggested by the yellow Sports colour scheme), a Walkman with Dolby sound, a built-in solar cell/rechargeable battery, an AM/FM radio, and the Kando portable radio in grey and black ABS plastic with elegant radiused corners. Yet another new launch in the same year was the Watchman; with the proportions of an early brick-sized mobile phone, it was a handheld television set with a 5-cm (2-in) screen.

Sony became synonymous with the modern world. One thing that the company never did was follow the post-modernism of its Japanese competitors, or explore the playful retro styling of Olympus's Écru (see page 147) or O cameras (see page 145). When Sony was being playful, it needed a functional excuse. So the ABS case of the second generation Walkman used decorative accents of colour to signal stop–start functions, and vivid orange sponges turned the accompanying headphones into a statement.

Norio Ohga, who had previously trained as a professional musician, consolidated the place of design in Sony's management structure: 'I suggested to Mr Morita that our designs needed be consistent and that we should bring the designers together all in one place. My belief was that if products were to be produced with the Sony name, the design must be governed by an overarching philosophy and have consistency, irrespective of which department was making the product.'

(1) Akio Morita (left) and Masaru Ibuka (right), January 1973.

(2) Sony prided itself on innovation in its engineering and new product development. The Walkman range repackaged existing technology to create a new approach to personal experience that was followed by its competitors.

(3) Though it was early in developing video, offering its first camera in 1981, Betamax Sony's proprietary system (see page 194) was a rare corporate failure.

(4) The Profeel Pro monitor (see page 188) was Sony's adaptation of the component approach used for audio systems to video equipment. It could be coupled to a VCR, a tuner or a camera.

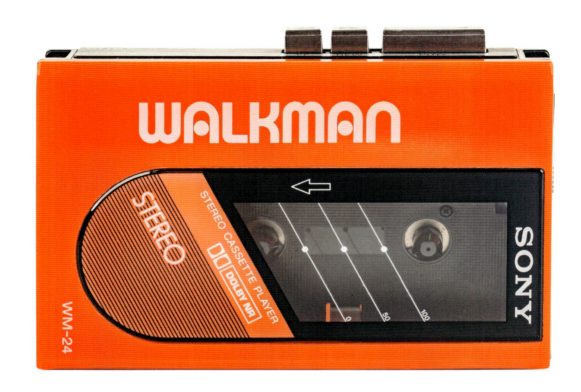

2

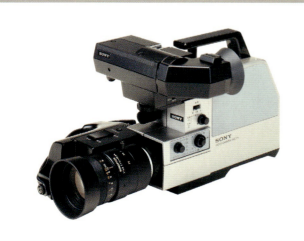

3

4

Transmaster 7 transistor radio

Date: 1959

Designer: Richard Sapper

Manufacturer: La Rinascente, Milan, Italy

Dimensions: Approx. 15 × 8 × 4cm
(6 × 3 × 1½in)

Richard Sapper's work reflects a softer version of the aesthetics of the functionalist Ulm School of Design. Before joining the Italian architect Marco Zanuso and collaborating on a series of memorable television and radio designs, Sapper worked briefly for La Rinascente, the Milanese department store that developed a reputation for talent spotting. The young Giorgio Armani was another employee at the time.

While he was there, Sapper produced designs for own-brand electrical products whose manufacture would have been outsourced. The most striking was an early transistor radio. Sapper told one interviewer it 'was a very early transistor radio that explored a modern look. It was related to the design of Braun products that were appearing on the market at the same time.'

Stern 2 radio

Date: 1960

Designer: VEB Stern

Manufacturer: VEB Stern, Rochlitz,
East Germany

Dimensions: 27 × 18 × 9cm (10½ × 7 × 3½in)

As East Germany attempted to modernize its economy in the 1960s, it worked hard to compete with the more prosperous and successful western half of the then-divided state. In practice, East German electrical products came to look increasingly like paraphrases of what designers saw through privileged access to Western magazines.

The remains of the nationalized electronics industries were reorganized to create the Stern conglomerate, in an attempt to build a corporation that could compete with rivals such as Sony or Braun. With a controlled domestic market, East Germany could keep out imports, but it was looking to build its export presence by introducing more ambitious designs and incorporating new technologies.

Match transistor radio

Date: 1962

Designer: Richard Sapper

Manufacturer: Telefunken Italia, Milan, Italy

Dimensions: 16 × 6 × 3cm (6½ × 1¼ × 2½in)

Richard Sapper's unusual format for what Telefunken called a 'pocket', and sometimes also a 'miniature', radio was successful enough to be updated a year later in a second version. Sapper gave it a shape that was designed to fit into the palm of the hand and to feel good to the touch. To create the sense that this was a precious object, it was sold inside a royal blue cardboard box and had a brown leather case with a carrying strap.

Sapper gave the two plastic tuning wheels a vivid red colour – in sharp contrast to the brushed aluminium body – set into a satisfyingly tactile groove. The resulting radio felt good in the hand and looked impressive on a tabletop. Sapper used the same sharp red tone for the switch on the matt-black Tizio desklight and on the keyboard of his ThinkPad IBM laptop.

Braun RT 20 radio

Date: 1963

Designer: Dieter Rams

Manufacturer: Braun AG, Frankfurt,
West Germany

Dimensions: 26 × 50 × 19.5cm
(10¼ × 19¾ × 7¾in)

Dieter Rams gave the RT 20 radio a wedge form, shaped from beechwood veneer with a steel control panel painted in either dark or pale grey. The control panel was an extraordinarily refined graphic composition, with contrasting circles of four different diameters, sized according to their function and relative importance.

The largest of the four twisting controls, which is used to tune the radio, is positioned underneath a rectangular transparent window that displays an illuminated tuning scale.

Three smaller controls are aligned vertically in parallel to the rectangular window, and are used to adjust volume and tone. A second row of five push buttons are used to select wave bands or to activate a socket to connect a record player to the radio's loudspeaker. Unlike the other buttons, which have a flat surface, these are indented, to indicate how they should be used. The circular speaker grill is defined by 26 straight incisions cut into the surface of the radio's case.

National Panasonic Super Sensitive 10 Transistor R-307 radio

Date: 1963

Designer: National Panasonic

Manufacturer: Matsushita Electric Industrial Co. Ltd, Osaka, Japan

Dimensions: 6.4 × 14 × 5.4cm (10¼ × 5½ × 2in)

During the Cold War, different markets and political cultures had diverging requirements of their radios. Shortwave reception, that could pick up broadcasts from extreme distance, was a minority interest in Western Europe, where local stations provided a full range of viewpoints. However, it was not the same on the other side of what was called the Iron Curtain. In some parts of Eastern Europe and Asia, with tight restrictions on broadcasting, shortwave radios were the only way to hear a different point of view. The R-307 might not

have the sensitivity of a large valve-driven shortwave receiver, which would appeal to a hobbyist in London or New York, but they were small enough to be more readily concealed, if necessary. And they could be easily moved, to find the right spot for good reception to pick up distant stations, without large and conspicuous aerials that drew attention.

Braun T1000 radio

Date: 1963

Designer: Dieter Rams

Manufacturer: Braun AG, Frankfurt, Germany

Dimensions: 36 × 26 × 13.5cm
(14 × 10 × 5¼in)

In the 1960s, the T1000 was a new departure for Braun – a radio designed to pick up shortwave broadcasts. Dieter Rams created a distinctive new look for the format – an aluminium case, rather than one made of wood. This was a machine that required a certain level of expertise to operate, so there was a built-in slot in which to store the instruction manual.

Rams designed the set with a fold-down front panel to conceal the controls to allow the user to tune to a particular station, adjust volume and tone, and then close it up to listen undistracted by the visual clutter of knobs and dials. He used a strictly limited colour palette, with just one vivid splash of orange reserved for the FM selector button. It was a reflection of the approach that Rams used for all his products for Braun.

TS 502 radio

Date: 1963
Designers: Richard Sapper, Marco Zanuso
Manufacturer: Brionvega, Milan, Italy
Dimensions: 13 × 22 × 13cm (5 × 8¾ × 5in)

Marco Zanuso, one of Italy's most gifted architects in the 1960s, worked with Richard Sapper on two different versions of the TS radio, the 502 followed by the 505 in 1977. Both versions were based on a hinge that in a fully open position formed a rectangle, and when closed became a cube. The loudspeaker was housed in one half, with the controls in the other. The main difference was the alignment of the dials. The original version positioned the tuning dial centrally, but for the 505 it was repositioned to the side.

With its retractable carrying handle, the TS 502 could perhaps be considered a predecessor of the boom box in its format, and also of the generation of folding-screen smartphones. Under new ownership, Brionvega brought the TS 502 back into production with modern electronics half a century after its original launch.

National Panasonic R-8 radio

Date: 1965

Designer: National Panasonic

Manufacturer: Matsushita Electric Industrial
Co. Ltd, Osaka, Japan

Dimensions: 17.7 × 6.7 × 7.75cm (7 × 2½ × 3in)

The R-8 was a miniature radio, but styled as if it were a larger table set – the world's smallest, as Matsushita claimed– a trick that gave it a toy-like quality. It was this element of playful novelty that the company emphasized in its advertising, where the R-8 was presented as an 'exciting gift idea'. To play up the gift aspect, the R-8 incorporated a hidden compartment with a hinged lid that could be used as a cigarette box. 'Even when you see and hear it, you will hardly be able to believe that such full sound comes from such a tiny radio,' ran the adverts. To underscore the point, Matsushita photographed the set held on the palm of a hand, demonstrating its diminutive size. The bold graphic treatment used contrasting colours and materials, playing a perforated metal grille for the speaker off against the clean metal of the control panel.

The Gadabout Model R-1326 portable radio

Date: 1965

Designer: Panasonic

Manufacturer: Matsushita Electric Industrial Co. Ltd, Osaka, Japan

Dimensions: 3 × 10 × 7cm (1 × 4 × 3in)

The Panasonic company marketed the Gadabout radio (with a name implying movement) as a miniature portable radio in 1965, when the miniaturization of wireless technology made possible by reliable transistors was still an attractive novelty. It was small enough to fit in the hand, but to reassure customers that small did not mean any loss of quality, Panasonic's advertisements used the word 'powerful', and promised what they called 'superb reception'. They called the Gadabout 'beauty packed and power packed' and promised 'slide rule tuning and an earphone'. Slightly mysteriously, Panasonic were also keen to tell customers that the Gadabout was styled to look like a camera.

Micromatic radio

Date: 1967

Designer: Clive Sinclair

Manufacturer: Sinclair Radionics Ltd, Cambridge, England

Dimensions: 4.5 × 3.4 × 1.5cm (2 × 1¼ × ½in)

Before he ushered in the era of affordable personal computing and cheap digital watches, Clive Sinclair had a business manufacturing consumer electronics. He mixed technical ingenuity with a certain showmanship and bargain-basement prices.

One of his obsessions was miniaturization. First he marketed the Transrista – which came with a strap and could be worn on the wrist – as the world's smallest radio, followed by the Micromatic radio. The size of a matchbox, it was available pre-assembled or in kit form for hobbyists to put together with a soldering iron. The Micromatic was an example of the tendency of miniaturization to become an end in itself. Once the controls are so small as to be impossible to manipulate, and the object itself becomes hard to find, it's time to rethink the concept.

Stern Camping R130 portable radio

Date: 1968

Designer: Michael Stender

Manufacturer: VEB Stern Radio, Berlin, East Germany

Dimensions: 27.2 × 16.8 × 7.9cm (10¾ × 6½ × 3in)

The relatively sophisticated-looking R130, with its gently tapered plastic case, showed how far Stern products had come since the obsolete-looking Stern 2 (see page 52) produced just eight years earlier.

Stern's products achieved a ready export market in the command economies of the Soviet Union, as well as with East Germany's other Warsaw Pact allies. Here, there was little competition from Western manufacturers and long waiting lists for consumer products, which depended on strictly rationed components.

Nevertheless, East German designers such as Michael Stender were able to achieve a distinctive identity for their products, though they were most often inferior to what was on offer in the West. As soon as Communism collapsed and East Germany was open to Western products, Stern's factories closed. Stern's products have subsequently taken on a nostalgic appeal for what now seems like a more innocent time – when designers did not have to make products that had to sell hard, because there were no alternatives.

Panasonic Toot-a-Loop R-72S radio

Date: 1969

Designer: Kajiwara Daisuke

Manufacturer: Matsushita Electric Industrial Co. Ltd, Osaka, Japan

Dimensions: 6.4 × 14.9cm (2½ × 6in)

In addition to its high-priced, high-quality audio equipment, Panasonic developed a series of more playful budget products such as the Toot-a-Loop – which was also called the Sing-O-Ring in some markets. This range relied on using bright colours and toy-like shapes. The set has a hinge mechanism: when it is fully closed, the Toot-a-Loop takes the form of a bangle with an off-centre circular opening, but twisting it open reveals the controls and the speaker.

The Toot-a-Loop represented a clear distinction between the approach that consumer electronics manufacturers took for products designed for specialist users, as opposed to the wider public. It was playful and colourful as opposed to focused on the idea of precision and performance.

Panasonic Panapet R-70 radio

Date: 1970

Designer: Panasonic

Manufacturer: Matsushita Electric Industrial Co. Ltd, Osaka, Japan

Dimensions: 11 × 11 × 11cm (4¼ × 4¼ × 4¼in)

In 1970, the Matsushita corporation invested in a prominent pavilion at Osaka's spectacular world fair, Expo 70. The pavilion featured a globe-shaped time capsule containing an array of objects intended to portray daily life from 1970 in the future. Panasonic, one of several brand names used by Matsushita, produced a spherical AM radio to commemorate the event. It came in a choice of colours including red, yellow, white, blue and avocado green. The two control discs were painted in a contrasting silver, with the tuning dial set into the plastic globe. It was equipped with a little chain with a ring, like a yo-yo. This exercise in cuteness carried through to the name, 'Panapet', and the advertising campaign that suggested: 'Don't listen to squares, your next radio can really be a ball.'

Beolit 400 radio

Date: 1970

Designer: Jacob Jensen

Manufacturer: Bang & Olufsen, Struer, Denmark

Dimensions: 36 × 22 × 6cm (14 × 8¾ × 2½in)

Jacob Jensen, one of Denmark's leading designers, began working for Bang & Olufsen in 1964. Over the course of 27 years he was responsible for 200 of their products, from radios and television sets to record players. Denmark's approach to design is rooted in the country's traditional crafts: woodworking, metalwork and glass. Jensen himself began as a cabinet maker, and designed everything from chairs to typewriters. As Jensen once explained, 'Constructing a fountain pen, writing a poem, producing a play or designing a locomotive, all demand the same components, the same ingredients: perspective, creativity, new ideas, understanding and first and foremost, the ability to rework, almost infinitely, over and over. That "over and over" is for me the cruellest torture.' The Beolit radio, with its tuning dial in the form of a scientific-looking slide rule, certainly lived up to Jensen's explanation of his approach which was 'to be different but not strange'.

Rotel RX-150A receiver

Date: 1972

Designer: The Rotel Co. Ltd

Manufacturer: The Rotel Co. Ltd, Tokyo, Japan

Dimensions: 41.5 × 13.3 × 17.3cm
(16¼ × 5¼ × 7in)

The widespread adoption of component-system hi-fis led to a reconsideration of the possibilities of radio. A radio receiver could be used in conjunction with the high-quality loudspeakers of an audio system rather than requiring its own. Many manufacturers designed products that could be used to provide radio input for a system. Some of them were offered as part of an amplifier, others were simply receivers. They were styled to match the format of the system, most often as part of a set of stacked boxes.

Rotel's RX-150A model used a 122-cm (48-in) wire antenna to pick up radio signals. The front was dominated by the illuminated green tuning strip set into a brushed-metal panel. Complex connections to speakers, tape recorders and power were positioned on the rear of the teak-framed box.

Panasonic SA-504 four channel receiver radio

Date: 1972

Designer: Panasonic

Manufacturer: Matsushita Electric Industrial Co. Ltd, Osaka, Japan

Dimensions: 42 × 29.2 × 10cm (16½ × 11½ × 4in)

The brushed-aluminium front panel of the SA-504 is dominated by two large circular openings, deep set like a pair of eyes. They draw attention to what the receiver claims to be capable of doing. One is for tuning, the other shows the mode of operation. Both backlit dials are embellished with cosmetic splashes of colour in vivid green and red. One of the dials, somewhat mysteriously, carries the words, Matrix, 4CH and Discrete.

The 4CH, which stands for four channel, refers to a briefly popular technological fad

from the 1970s, which offered the possibility of so-called quadrophonic sound – four speakers positioned in the four corners of a space, placing the listener in the middle. Audio enthusiasts were unimpressed, pointing to the built-in speakers on the SA-504, which suggested that it was fundamentally a table radio, although it had the circuits to allow it to be wired up to four speakers.

Panasonic Cougar No 7 RF-877

3-band radio

Date: 1973

Designer: Panasonic

Manufacturer: Matsushita Electric Industrial
Co. Ltd, Osaka, Japan

Dimensions: 23 × 22 × 9cm (9 × 8¾ × 3½in)

For the majority of users, listening to a radio is a passive experience – the machine may be portable, but it mostly stays in the same position, and is tuned to just one or two stations. But in the 1970s, a generation of Japanese consumers developed a fascination for shortwave radio. They took as much pleasure in the number of exotic stations that they could find by carefully tuning the radio, as in the actual content of the transmissions that they could hear.

The design development of such radios was a two-way process: Panasonic created the Cougar No 7 to appeal to this shortwave subculture and the charm of the radio was designed to expand its audience. Styled in matt black with a web of carrying straps to suggest a certain military-like ruggedness, it came with an external whip aerial as well as a ferrite rod, which Panasonic called the Gyro Antenna, to help find far-distant international stations.

National Panasonic R-1045 AM portable radio

Date: 1974

Designer: National Panasonic

Manufacturer: Matsushita Electric Industrial Co. Ltd, Osaka, Japan

Dimensions: 7 × 11 × 3.6cm (2¾ × 4¼ × 1½in)

As one of Japan's largest creators of consumer electronics, National Panasonic built a product range that spanned the entire spectrum, from sophisticated and extraordinarily costly shortwave receivers, to the most modest pocket-sized transistor radios. It tailored the look of its products to appeal to its multiple audiences. Metal came to suggest high performance, while bright colours were for fashion-conscious younger consumers.

For a pocket-size portable radio as small as the Panasonic R-1045, there wasn't much scope. It was designed with a strongly graphic pattern in the metal front, held in place by a moulded plastic body.

Panasonic R-1330 7 transistor radio

Date: 1975

Designer: Panasonic

Manufacturer: Matsushita Electric Industrial Co. Ltd, Osaka, Japan

Dimensions: 10.6 × 8.9 × 3.5cm (4 × 3½ × 1¼in)

Konosuke Matsushita's first major business success was a battery powered bicycle lamp housed in a bullet-shaped casing. It had a continued impact on the company's subsequent approach to product design as it grew into a corporate giant with a global reach. Panasonic started making valve radios in the 1930s and was exporting them after 1954.

The R-1330 had an eccentric shape, designed to make it stand out, rather than for functional purposes. Many radios emphasize the loudspeaker, but the R-1330 reverses this: it is on the back of the machine in subdued black plastic. The Panasonic brand name, elaborately rendered in metallic finish, is positioned next to the tuning control on the front of the machine, while the volume control is awkwardly positioned to one side, at an angle.

National Panasonic GX600 RF-1150 radio

Date: 1975

Designer: National Panasonic

Manufacturer: Matsushita Electric Industrial
Co. Ltd, Osaka, Japan

Dimensions: 24.6 × 23.7 × 10cm
(9¾ × 9¼ × 4in)

The GX600 RF-1150 was National Panasonic's attempt to compete with Sony in the market for shortwave radio receivers designed to appeal to hobbyist and enthusiast consumers. The RF-1150 is distinguished from many portable radios capable of tuning into shortwave frequencies by the adjustable ferrite-rod antenna positioned on top of its case. Ferrite is a magnetic iron-alloy that is able to concentrate the magnetic component of radio waves, and so offers a much greater degree of sensitivity than conventional aerials.

The rod is positioned on a pivot, which allows for the antenna to be adjusted to achieve optimum reception. The Panasonic can pick up Citizens Band – short-range transmissions popularized by America's truck drivers – and amateur radio, as well as the full range of broadcasting stations. The black-and-silver aesthetic and bold geometry is relieved by an illuminated tuning dial.

Sony ICF-5900 Skysensor shortwave radio

Date: 1975
Designer: Sony
Manufacturer: Sony, Tokyo, Japan
Dimensions: 22 × 23 × 10cm (8¾ × 9 × 4in)

Sony made a version of the ICF-5900, called the Skysensor, for its domestic Japanese market, catering for the 1970s craze for shortwave broadcasts. For the export market, the ICF-5900 was tailored to a different range of frequencies appropriate to non-Japanese stations (in Japan, FM stations were allocated a different part of the spectrum). Although they had different technical capabilities, the two machines were visually similar, with an olive-green, utilitarian or military aesthetic.

The precision tuning dial was positioned at the centre of the machine. To address radio interference, Sony included a dual-conversion circuit. The Skysensor was also equipped with beat-frequency oscillators – circuits that allowed amateur radio and morse transmissions to be audible. Yet, given the way these sets were marketed, this was perhaps a conspicuously redundant capacity.

National Panasonic GX 300 radio

Date: 1975
Designer: National Panasonic
Manufacturer: Matsushita Electric Industrial Co. Ltd, Osaka, Japan
Dimensions: 23 × 19.5 × 6.5cm (9 × 7¾ × 2½in)

The GX 300, available in serious black or attention-grabbing red, was styled to look as if it could offer much more than conventional radios. The front, sides and top were each given a different character. The impression of capability was underscored by a broad carrying strap clipped to metal angles positioned on each side of the machine, rather than the more flimsy-looking wrist straps typically tacked onto the side of a transistor radio. The front was characterized by an arrangement of concentric circles moulded in black plastic typical of Panasonic's approach. The top had the character of the front elevation of a component hi-fi system. It offered shortwave and UHF frequencies, as well as FM, with a recording jack built into one side to allow for a microphone.

Grundig Satellit 2100 shortwave receiver

Date: 1976

Designer: Grundig

Manufacturer: Grundig, Nuremberg, Germany

Dimensions: 46 × 27 × 12cm
(18 × 10½ × 4¾in)

In the early days of broadcasting, shortwave frequencies were seen as useful only for amateur radio until Guglielmo Marconi developed a curtain array aerial transmitter that was an economical way of transmitting over long distances. Shortwave radio broadcasting was used by governments during World War II and in the Cold War period to reach overseas audiences. The subsequent rapid growth of the internet has made shortwave broadcasts much less significant as a means of communication.

Grundig's Satellit 2100 shortwave receiver had the capacity to reach ten shortwave bands, including amateur broadcasters, ships and aircraft, as well as the long- and mediumwave broadcasts. This was a German-made machine, but one which reflected Japan's approach to styling, and represented the peak of Grundig's production. Grundig subsequently found it impossible to resist Asian competitors, who were able to innovate more quickly and undercut on price.

Stern Garant R2130 radio

Date: 1977

Designer: Stern

Manufacturer: VEB Stern Radio, Quedlinburg, Berlin-Treptow, East Germany

Dimensions: 22.7 × 24.7 × 8cm (9 × 9¾ × 3in)

Stern's product designers moved beyond toy-like bright colours during the late 1970s, at a time when Braun and Sony had made matt black synonymous with technological sophistication. The Garant R2130 did its best to provide its own take on technological fetishism, although it clearly owes a debt to the look created by Panasonic for their radios and shortwave receivers. Stern even went so far as to launch a hesitant advertising campaign, producing posters that showed the Garant photographed in a natural setting. These had no commercial purpose – there was no need to stimulate demand for its products since they were in short supply at home – but its Western rivals used advertising, so Stern did the same, in an attempt to make a 'real' product.

Panasonic RF-2900 shortwave radio

Date: 1979

Designer: Panasonic

Manufacturer: Matsushita Electric Industrial
Co. Ltd, Osaka, Japan

Dimensions: 38 × 25 × 12cm (15 × 10 × 4¾in)

The RF-2900 had the capacity to receive amateur broadcasts, so-called 'ham' radio shortwave frequencies. The two business-like, chrome-plated carrying handles, which also double as protective bars when in transit, were a tribute to the sort of equipment found in a ship's radio room, and gave a strong hint of the machine's potential. It had the words 'Double Superheterodyne System' printed across it, enough to suggest to even those who had only the vaguest understanding of the reference that this was a radio to be reckoned with.

It was backed up by an array of knobs, dials, switches, and a blizzard of numbers, culminating in a fluorescent digital read-out of the selected reception frequency. The tuning knob was designed to be pulled out to allow for fine tuning. The set was either battery or mains powered.

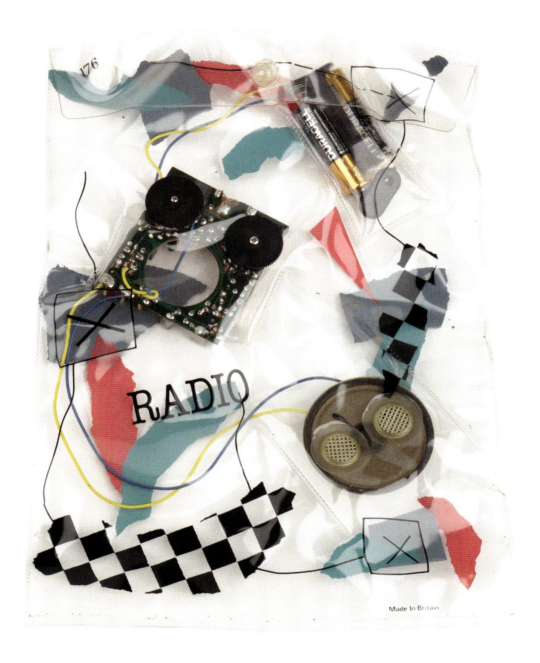

Bag radio

Date: 1981

Designer: Daniel Weil

Manufacturer: Daniel Weil, London, England

Dimensions: 29 × 20.7 × 3cm (11½ × 8 × 1in)

In the mechanical era, machines had moving parts that gave clues to their purpose and how they operated. Transistors and processors offer fewer clues. Daniel Weil is a designer who turned an idea that began as a student project when he was at the Royal College of Art in London into a commercial radio. He put electronic components inside a printed PVC bag. The bag radio was an exploration of a new language for design. When a machine has no mechanical parts, then the designer has no functional clues to follow in giving it shape –

it can be made to look like anything, and the electronics can be turned into decorative motifs. Weil's radio was a critique of the idea that form follows function. He was also trying to give a glimpse inside the black box that had come to represent most electronic appliances.

BayGen Freeplay radio

Date: 1995

Designers: TKO (Andy Davey), Trevor Baylis

Manufacturer: BayGen Power Company Ltd, Johannesburg, South Africa

Dimensions: 20.3 × 20.3 × 29.2cm
(8 × 8 × 11½in)

The Freeplay was invented by Trevor Baylis, who had the idea of an off-grid radio, with a hand-powered generator taking the place of both batteries and mains supply. Winding the clockwork spring for just 30 seconds generated enough power to give the radio 30 minutes of listening time. Baylis saw BayGen as a philanthropic project, aimed at reaching communities where regular supplies of mains electricity could not be taken for granted, but where the radio could be an important means of communication.

He assembled a working prototype and then looked for investment to get it manufactured. His idea was given an attractively styled case by the industrial designer Andy Davey. The robust form reflects the needs of its original target market, but it was made available in a range of colours, including a clear plastic tinted red, and various other styles to appeal to a wider audience.

Hyperbo 5 RG Steel radiogram

Date: 1934

Designer: Peter Bang

Manufacturer: Bang & Olufsen, Struer, Denmark

Dimensions: Approx. 107 × 70 × 43cm (42 × 27½ × 17in)

Peter Bang and Svend Olufsen began building radios in 1925. They broadened their product range into radiograms (a combined record player and radio) with the Hyperbo range. They were housed in elaborate timber cabinets that took the form of substantial pieces of furniture with carved legs and decorative flourishes. An exception was the Hyperbo 5 RG Steel, which in retrospect can be seen as a forerunner of the purist design language adopted by the company for all its later products. It had the proportions of a filing cabinet rather than a chair, with the turntable in a covered compartment on top and a sliding drawer in the side for storing gramophone records. At the time it was made, it was understood as an experimental one-off. It was still more like furniture than a piece of electronic equipment, but it reflected the cantilevered tubular steel chairs of Marcel Breuer of the Bauhaus era and its fascination for the aesthetics of machinery, rather than traditional carpentry.

Braun SK 4 radiogram

Date: 1956

Designer: Hans Gugelot, Dieter Rams

Manufacturer: Braun AG, Frankfurt, West Germany

Dimensions: 58 × 24 × 29cm (23 × 9½ × 11½in)

The idea of a transparent Perspex cover for Braun's combined record player and radio was mocked by the company's competitors when it was unveiled, who called it 'Snow White's coffin'. Yet Dieter Rams, the industrial designer who shaped Braun's identity for two decades, had created a model that became universal for record players long after Braun had given up manufacturing audio equipment. The wooden sides of the case were the last vestige of the idea that household electronics should be domesticated by treating them as if they were pieces of furniture. This was one of the first products that Rams worked on for Braun. The neutral colour scheme and simple geometric forms were the personification of Ram's philosophy. His strategy, he used to say, was to make products that, like a traditional English butler, were invisible when not required but would perform with effortless efficiency when called upon.

Braun TP 1 transistor radio/portable record player

Date: 1959

Designer: Dieter Rams

Manufacturer: Braun AG, Frankfurt, West Germany

Dimensions: 4.5 × 15.2 × 23.5cm (1¾ × 9¼ × 6in)

With the TP 1, Dieter Rams produced an unusual and conceptually interesting combination of a transistor radio with a record player. The pocket-sized radio could be used on its own, and showcased Rams' dedication to purist geometry. When plugged into the record player, the TP 1 also served as its amplifier and loudspeaker. Combined, both components were carried in an anodized aluminium tray with a leather strap. The record player was designed for singles, the 45 rpm vinyl discs that served to define pop music in the 1960s, and – unusually – the stylus played the record from underneath. The stylus was positioned not in the usual record arm but in a compartment set into the deck, concealed beneath a sliding cover. Panasonic tried to do something similar with the SwingWay, which it sold as a portable radio that produced a fold-out record deck at the touch of a button.

Brionvega RR126 Radiofonografo radiogram

Date: 1966

Designers: Achille Castiglioni, Pier
Giacomo Castiglioni

Manufacturer: Brionvega, Milan, Italy

Dimensions: With speakers on top: 92 × 62
× 35cm (36 × 24½ × 13¾in); With speakers
attached to sides: 92 × 121 × 35cm
(36 × 47½ × 13¾in)

The two Castiglioni brothers introduced a
playful element to Italian design in the 1960s.
The main body and speakers of this radiogram
are made from laminated plywood. The body
is an elongated cuboid and its controls are
arranged on the front to suggest a face.
The design plays up its anthropomorphic
characteristics – the face has two eyes in the
form of twin AM and FM circular dials. They
are each fringed by 'eyebrows', suggested by
the shape of the tuning scales. A prominent
line of push-button controls is a subliminal

suggestion of a mouth. On top of the unit,
located toward the proper left end, is the
turntable sourced by Brionvega from
Garrard in the UK, with a removable clear
polycarbonate cover, following the precedent
set by Dieter Rams for Braun (see page 75).
Underneath the unit is a painted wooden flex
winder for the electrical cable.

Mario Bellini

Like many Italian designers, Mario Bellini trained to be an architect. He joined the team of designers working for Olivetti not long after Ettore Sottsass and, during the two decades that the two spent consulting for the company, they represented two radically different approaches.

If Sottsass asked questions about what objects ought to be, Bellini had a gift for making those objects look desirable. He added buttons that had tactile qualities to typewriters and calculators, to give touching them an irresistible appeal. Bellini's career did not end with Olivetti, and it spanned both the analogue and the digital eras. He was responsible for electric typewriters and mechanical calculators, as well as for the Programma 101 from 1964, the machine behind Olivetti's claim to have produced the first desktop computer.

Bellini's special skill has been an ability to give mechanical objects distinctive sculptural forms. He uses a formal language that is warmer than the cool logic of Max Bill and the Ulm School of Design. In the course of his long career, he has moved from controlled curves to a sharp, wedge form.

What sets his work apart is his ability to bring the shape-making of his architectural background to the scale of objects and to give them a historical resonance. In a lecture that he gave at the Aspen Design Conference in 1981, he followed an image of a finger pressing the button of one of the keyboards that he had designed with a detail taken from a Renaissance painting that showed the Madonna and Child with a finger in contact with a nipple.

'What's interesting for me,' he said, 'is to design the first portable electric typewriter, not the fifth version of the same basic idea.' Steve Jobs was in the audience at Aspen, and came to see him in his studio afterward, but the project that they worked on for Apple didn't reach production.

Bellini made his mark on hi-fi design with Totem, for Brionvega. To call it a radiogram hardly does the project justice. Designed in 1971, and reissued with modern electronics in 2021, Totem closes up to form an immaculate white cube. The top half is formed by twin speakers that pivot outward and reveal the record deck, the radio tuner, and a simple control panel set inside the lower half of the unit.

Bellini's cassette-tape deck for Yamaha was an equally pure geometric form, and a striking departure for the type – wedge-shaped rather than a box.

1

(1) Mario Bellini at Salone Internazionale Del Mobile during the 2014 Milan Design Week.

(2) Brionvega commissioned Bellini to design a complete stereo system. The resulting Totem RR130 (see page 80) was a piece of sculptural purist geometry.

(3) The idea of making a record player as portable as a pocket transistor radio has been attempted by a number of manufacturers. Bellini's 1969 Pop GA was one of the more convincing. It could play a 45 rpm single while being carried by the handle.

(4) Yamaha wanted Bellini's signature on its cassette-tape deck in both the literal and the figurative sense (see page 83). He put his name on the case, which reflected his distinctive approach to geometry.

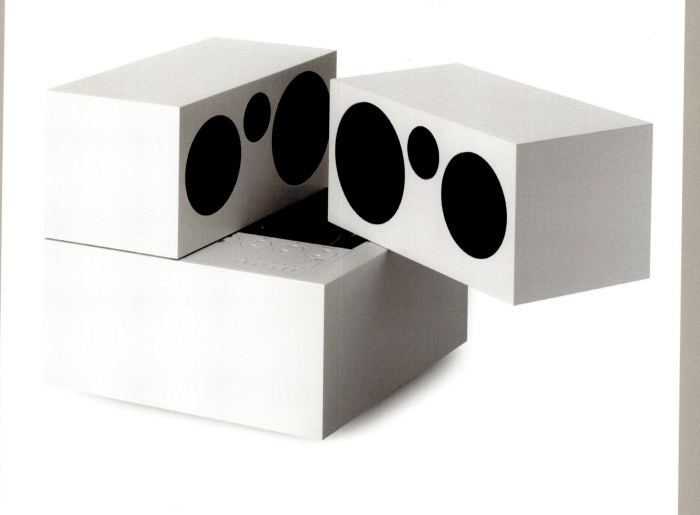

2

3

4

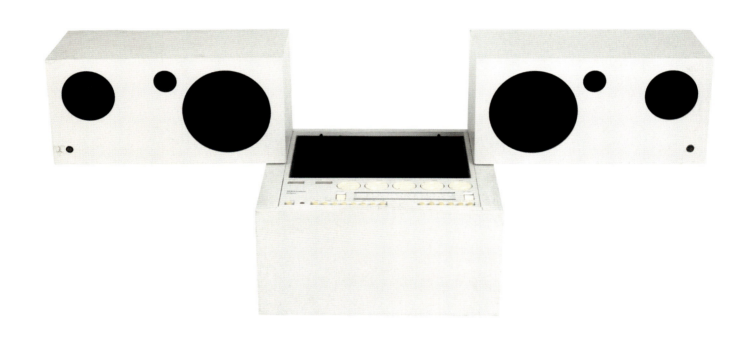

Totem RR130 music system

Date: 1971

Designer: Mario Bellini

Manufacturer: Brionvega, Milan, Italy

Dimensions: 52.5 × 52.5 × 52.5cm
(20½ × 20½ × 20½in)

Rather than expressing each component of an audio system as separate elements, Bellini, who also designed a television set for Brionvega, conceived the Totem as a single, integrated form. The base accommodates a turntable, cassette player and radio. The speakers sit on pivoting plates that allow them to fold out when in use, revealing the concealed turntable and operating controls. The pivoting speakers each reveal a single black circle that covers the grille. They can also be detached from the base unit and positioned where needed. Folded back, they form a piece of pure geometry, a snow-white sculptural cube that gives no obvious sign of its function and purpose. As with several other of their products, Brionvega has released a new version of the Totem, which has modern electronics within a replica of the original cabinet. The company has changed hands several times since it commissioned Bellini, Castiglioni and Zanuso, but continues to manufacture technologically updated versions of their designs.

Concetto 101 record deck and amplifier

Date: 1974

Designers: Richard Sapper, Marco Zanuso

Manufacturer: Brionvega, Milan, Italy

Dimensions: 20 × 45 × 34.5cm
(7¾ × 17¾ × 13½in)

The Concetto took an unconventional approach to the familiar pattern of audio systems, combining a record deck with an amplifier, and giving it an idiosyncratic mix of geometries. Instead of the usual transparent cover for the player, Zanuso and Sapper designed a lid that conceals it completely when closed. The base of the record player is a simple rectangle, but the cover has an organic, curved shape, reflecting the arc taken by the tonearm as it tracks the record, and as a result reduces the overall bulk of the machine. The interior of the lid is finished in a high-gloss, rich red colour to contrast with the matt-black exterior. The speakers designed to be paired with the system have a similar formal approach, combining a rectangular cabinet with an organic profile to the front face.

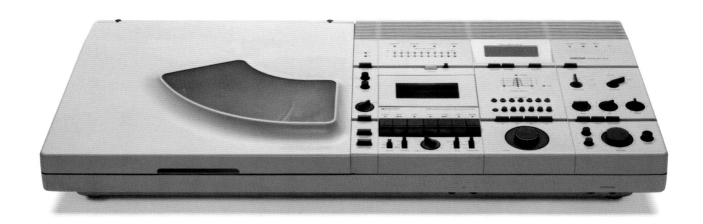

Wega Concept 51k sound system

Date: 1976

Designer: Hartmut Esslinger

Manufacturer: WEGA (Wuertermbergische
Radio Gesellschaft), Stuttgart, West Germany

Dimensions: 15.2 × 83.8 × 40.6cm
(6 × 33 × 16in)

At different times, WEGA commissioned both
the visionary Danish furniture designer Werner
Panton and the German industrial designer
Hartmut Esslinger to give its products a
striking new look before the long-established
German company was taken over by Sony in
1976. Esslinger, founder of the Frog design
consultancy, was responsible for some of
the look of Apple's early personal computers.
WEGA worked with him in an attempt to create
a distinctive identity that would suggest that its
products could command a premium.

WEGA's Concept sound system was
launched after the takeover by Sony. It put
a record deck, tape player, tuner and an
amplifier within a single wedge form. The
turntable lid had a crescent-shaped window.
Esslinger's design took a line between
complexity and careful organization, with
enough sliders and buttons to suggest mission
control while still making their purpose and
use comprehensible.

Aiwa M301 audio component system

Date: 1980

Designer: Aiwa

Manufacturer: Aiwa, Tokyo, Japan

Dimensions: Power amp: 21 × 7.1 × 21.7cm (8¼ × 2¾ × 8½in); Preamp: 21 × 7.1 × 22.8cm (8¼ × 2¾ × 9in); Stereo tuner: 21 × 7.1 × 25.4cm (8¼ × 2¾ × 10in); Stereo cassette deck: 21 × 7.2 × 22.9cm (8¼ × 2¾ × 9in)

In the early days of high fidelity, audio enthusiasts made a point of assembling their own systems, with a record deck purchased from one manufacturer, loudspeakers from another, and amplifier from a third. For the larger manufacturers, it was a lost sales opportunity, so they started to produce their own, visually coordinated systems.

The mini system was a development of this, with advances in manufacturing technology making it possible to reduce the size of components considerably. In fact, the Aiwa

M301 successfully shrank each component, without a loss in sound quality, so that it occupied no more space than a boom box. Aiwa's designers were able to give the four basic components the same width and height, only 21 × 7.1cm (8¼ × 2¾in), although with minor variations in their depth. The system also offered a record player that was just a little larger.

Grundig TK 24 reel-to-reel tape recorder

Date: 1959

Designer: Grundig AG

Manufacturer: Grundig AG, Neulsenburg, West Germany

Dimensions: Approx. 35 × 32 × 18cm (13¾ × 15½ × 7in)

Max Grundig, who owned a stake in a radio shop before World War II, started his own company, Grundig, in 1945. Grundig initially manufactured radio sets before branching out into reel-to-reel tape recorders.

At first, Grundig worked hard in their advertising campaigns to explain some of the uses of their machines, in order to persuade customers to buy them. This apparent lack of confidence in the abilities of contemporary consumers to grasp the purpose of a tape recorder was matched by a worry that, even having bought a Grundig machine, customers would not understand how to use it. The chromed buttons and knobs on the control panel were accompanied by detailed written instructions and diagrams, along with the company's red three-leaf clover logo.

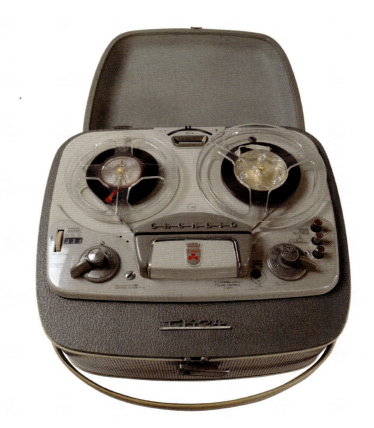

Uher 4000 Report monitor tape recorder

Date: 1961

Designer: Uher

Manufacturer: Uher, Munich, West Germany

Dimensions: 26 × 39 × 12cm (10¼ × 15½ × 4¾in)

Primarily intended for use by broadcasting companies to record interviews and to edit material in the field, the Uher 4000 was light and easily portable. Powered by rechargeable batteries and fully transistorized, it came in a carrying case with a plug-in microphone suitable for news gathering and simple editing. It was workmanlike and well-priced, at least in comparison to Nagra's alternative, the Nagra III. Uher did not need to seduce its customers, opting instead for a kind of public-service aesthetic that promised sturdy reliability. Later versions of the machine offered four-track and then stereo recording, rather than the two-track mono of the original. The Uher company also manufactured the equipment used to record the notorious White House tapes.

Revox A77 reel-to-reel tape recorder

Date: 1967

Designer: Willi Studer

Manufacturer: Studer-Revox, Loffingen, West Germany

Dimensions: 41.5 × 35.9 × 18cm (16¼ × 14 × 7in)

Revox reel-to-reel tape recorders have their origins in a business founded by Willi Studer in Switzerland to manufacture oscilloscopes that could measure voltage. Studer went on to manufacture high-performance, specialist tape recorders in the 1950s. He switched production to Germany in the 1960s, where the A77 was manufactured, and went on to dominate the market for studio recording equipment for two decades.

Revox's output was limited by a shortage of skilled craftsmen, who built each machine virtually by demand. The A77, supplemented by matching FM tuners and an amplifier, was its bestselling model. Nearly 400,000 were manufactured over the course of seven years, before it was superseded by the Revox B77.

Nagra IV-S reel-to-reel tape recorder

Date: 1971

Designer: Stefan Kudelski

Manufacturer: Nagra Audio Technology, Lausanne, Switzerland

Dimensions: 33.3 × 24.2 × 11.3cm (13 × 9½ × 4½in)

The word *nagra* is Polish for 'will record', but the company, established in Lausanne in 1951, is Swiss. Stefan Kudelski, Nagra's founder, was a brilliant inventor who left Warsaw as a child refugee at the time of the German invasion. He made his first tape recorder as a student project, combining his expertise in engineering and acoustics, and set up his own company shortly after. Nagra tape recorders have a reputation for scientific precision that is reflected in their no-nonsense appearance, which has the

flavour of medical equipment built to last rather than a consumer item – a Ferrari rather than a Ford. Their robustness and high performance was aimed at professional broadcasters and sound engineers – these recorders were used extensively in the film industry. The designation IV reflects the fourth generation of Nagra's evolving recording technology. The IV-S was the company's first stereo recorder.

Braun TG 1000 reel-to-reel tape recorder

Date: 1975

Designer: Dieter Rams

Manufacturer: Braun AG, Frankfurt, West Germany

Dimensions: 45 × 32 × 14cm (17¾ × 12¾ × 5½in)

Reel-to-reel tape recorders were developed for their efficiency as recording instruments. They acquired a reputation with audiophiles for offering better sound quality than early gramophone records. The dexterity required to work with tape helped to underpin their status – these were not machines for beginners, they were for professionals. The result was a format designed for recording sound that was used by enthusiasts for listening to music. Its usefulness was limited by the restricted availability of pre-recorded tapes. Recording stereo radio broadcasts using a receiver was a cumbersome alternative. Playing tapes of birdsong or steam engines, recorded on small portable machines, was for hobbyists. Braun's TG 1000 was the finale of the company's twelve-year history with reel-to-reel tape recorders. It was designed for the consumer rather than the professional market, but Dieter Rams and his team gave it a calm, authoritative quality that still gives it a presence.

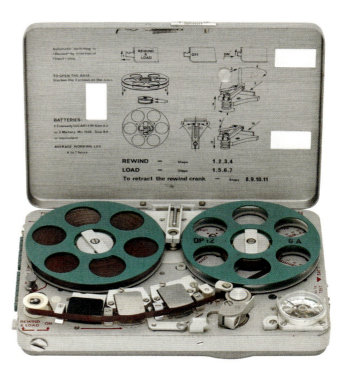

Nagra SNST-R miniature tape recorder

Date: 1977

Designer: Stefan Kudelski

Manufacturer: Nagra Audio Technology, Lausanne, Switzerland

Dimensions: 14.6 × 10.1 × 2.6cm (5¾ × 4 × 1in)

Stefan Kudelski designed a miniaturized tape recorder as a product that would be useful both to sound recordists working on film sets, who could record simultaneous dialogue with an all-but-invisible machine, as well as to various security and law enforcement agencies engaged in covert surveillance. The machine is milled from a solid block of aluminium using a computer numerical-controlled cutter. The result is both hard-wearing and beautiful to look at, a kind of functionalist sculpture that looked like the

natural outcome of its purpose and the materials from which it was made. Nagra were one of the first industrial companies to use the technique. Thirty years later, Apple began making its laptops carved from solid aluminium, partly for sustainability reasons, and partly to avoid the way that fingerprints leave marks on plastic surfaces. For Nagra it was about robustness and utility, which resulted in an authoritative piece of unselfconscious design.

Pioneer RT-707 reel-to-reel tape recorder

Date: 1977

Designer: Pioneer Corporation

Manufacturer: Pioneer Corporation, Tokyo, Japan

Dimensions: 32.4 × 48.3 × 22.2cm (12¾ × 19 × 8¾in)

By the time that Pioneer launched its RT-707, the audio tape cassette was already a well-established format. As a result, most reel-to-reel machines were understood as being aimed squarely at the enthusiast. To appeal to the hobbyist market, they grew in size and complexity. Pioneer saw a gap in the market for an open reel machine that was straightforward to use and more affordable than a professional machine; because of the inherent limitations of cassette recording, tape could offer better sound performance than even top-of-the-range cassette players. The RT-707 offered an automatic reverse, although for those who could do without, there was a cheaper option. Early tape machines had twin spools on top. The 707 positioned them on its front, with a simplified set of controls, allowing it to be used as part of a stack of audio components.

TDK audio tape cassette

Date: 1966

Designer: Tokyo Denki Kagaku Kogyo

Manufacturer: Tokyo Electric Chemical
Industry, Tokyo, Japan

Dimensions: 10 × 6.3 × 1.3cm (4 × 2½ × ½in)

Before Philips abandoned consumer
electronics and lighting, it produced both
the means to play recorded sound and the
recordings to play on them. It pioneered the
compact cassette format as a commercial
product in 1963. Cassettes saved users
the trouble of threading tape through the
mechanism of a playback machine. When Sony
licensed the technology, Philips' version using
a magnetized metal-coated polyester tape
became the dominant format for recorded
music, overtaking vinyl records in the 1980s.

TDK had specialized in manufacturing
magnetic recording tape since the 1950s.
It invested in new ferric-oxide tape coatings that
could offer higher-quality sound reproduction.
TDK offered a range of recording times, while
also ensuring the build quality of the cassette
did not distort sound quality.

**National Panasonic RS-275 US
cassette player**

Date: 1971

Designer: National Panasonic

Manufacturer: Matsushita Electric Industrial
Co. Ltd, Osaka, Japan

Dimensions: 44.1 × 12.1 × 30. 2cm
(17¼ × 4¾ × 11¾in)

Cassettes were initially regarded as a cheap
and low-quality method of listening to music.
Panasonic's first attempt to make cassette
players integral to a serious domestic
audio-component system involved giving them
a personality that could dispel the negative
connotations and justify premium prices.

The RS-275 had no speaker, and was
configured as a kind of jewel casket with the
cassette placed in a compartment on the top
of a timber-framed box. A pair of dials marked
VU (Volume Units) – one for the left-hand audio
channel and one for the right – measure the
level of sound intensity. Anything above the
zero decibel mark shows that the sound is
being distorted. The arrangement encouraged
users to treat cassettes with respect.

Stern R160 casette player

Date: 1972

Designer: Stern Radio

Manufacturer: VEB Stern Radio, Berlin, East Germany

Dimensions: 38 × 22 × 10.5cm (15 × 8¾ × 4in)

The R160 was the first cassette player to be manufactured in East Germany. It came with a radio, with both elements housed in a plywood case. The R160 remained in production for six years. It offers some evidence that the style difference between Western and Eastern European products was dwindling by the early 1970s. Yet, for the discerning eye, Stern products' slight air of nostalgia still betray their origins.

TEAC A 450 stereo cassette deck

Date: 1973

Designer: Tokyo Electro Acoustic Company

Manufacturer: Tokyo Electro Acoustic Company, Tokyo, Japan

Dimensions: 44.5 × 17.6 × 27cm (17½ × 6¾ × 10½in)

The development of the compact cassette could not have happened without a simultaneous exploration of the forms that the machines it would be played on should take. At the budget end of the spectrum, speaker, amplifier and recording functions were all contained in a single case. For more expensive products, designed to appeal to audio-enthusiasts, the tape deck was conceived as part of a components system with discreet speakers, amplifier and tuner. The dimensions of the record player, which had to be wide enough to accommodate an LP disc and a tonearm, became the determining factor. The first decks, such as the TEAC A 450, were configured for the cassettes to be placed flat on the top of the machine. The TEAC A 450 had a compartment to store a limited number of cassettes and adopted a black and brushed-aluminium aesthetic, framed by teak veneer.

Yamaha TC-800GL stereo cassette deck

Date: 1976

Designer: Mario Bellini

Manufacturer: Nippon Gakki Co. Ltd,
Hamamatsu, Japan

Dimensions: 9.8 × 31.2 × 31.2cm
(3¾ × 12¼ × 12¼in)

Yamaha commissioned Mario Bellini (see page 78) to create a distinctive identity for what it wanted to sell as a premium product at a time when the cassette deck was only just emerging. The TC-800GL was intended to be portable and came with a carrying case. The sliding controls suggest the precision of a recording studio mixing deck.

It was available in black or ivory coloured ABS plastic. The wedge shape is a form that Bellini used for several of the calculators and typewriters that he designed for Olivetti.

The shape helped it stand out from its competitors, which were either front or top loading, but compromised its ability to form part of a stack of stereo components.

Sony EL D8 cassette player

Date: 1978

Designer: Sony

Manufacturer: Sony, Tokyo, Japan

Dimensions: 32.2 × 10 × 29.8cm
(12½ × 4 × 11¾in)

The Elcaset, an acronym for 'large cassette', was an unsuccessful attempt to devise an alternative to the conventional compact cassette that could achieve the sound quality of a reel-to-reel tape recorder. It has the same format as a compact cassette but, at twice the size, is large enough for a wider 0.5-cm (¼-in) tape that moved at 9.5cm (3¾in) per second, considerably more quickly than a standard cassette. During playback, the tape was drawn out of its container, avoiding any sound distortion caused by build quality, unlike compact cassettes. Sony produced two models designed for home use. The EL D8, a battery-powered portable version, came with a built-in monitor speaker. It was styled to suggest professional quality precision with its circular dials. The format did not deliver the performance required to achieve the wide acceptance needed to support pre-recorded music tapes and was withdrawn from sale in 1980.

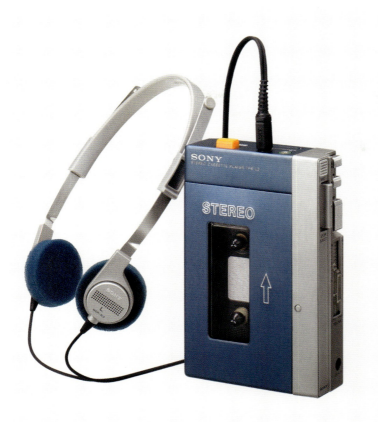

Sony TPS-L2 cassette player

Date: 1979

Designer: Kozo Ohsone

Manufacturer: Sony, Tokyo, Japan

Dimensions: 15 × 9 × 3.5cm (6 × 3½ × 1½in)

Sony was founded by Akio Morita and Masaru Ibuka, two talented engineers who were also astute marketeers. They invariably launched their most successful products by giving them a memorable origin story. If it was not that Sony were making the world's smallest version of something, it was that they were meeting a previously unfulfilled need. In the case of the TPS-L2, the machine that was the starting point for what became the Walkman, Ibuka is said to have asked for a product for his personal use to listen to music on, while on long flights. The head of the tape-recorder division, Kozo Ohsone, modified an existing miniature recorder, the Pressman, to do the job. The blue and silver TPS-L2 had the look of its business-like origins, but was equipped with two headphone jacks for shared listening, suggesting the needs of the new audience that the Walkman would soon find.

Sony WM2 Walkman

Date: 1981

Designer: Sony

Manufacturer: Sony, Tokyo, Japan

Dimensions: 29.5 × 10.9 × 8cm
(11½ × 4¼ × 3in)

'Mind blowing sound in your own private world. When you strap it on and turn on, you feel only the weight of the music,' or so claimed one of Sony's early campaigns for the WM2, the first of its products to carry the Walkman brand name. The idea of retreating to a private world caught the essence of what made the Walkman so different from anything that had gone before, and it signalled the arrival of the universal ear bud. The technology itself was not that much of a leap from the dictaphone, but the way it was used represented a major shift in behaviour. It turned sound into a personal experience. Sony's silver-and-black case, embellished with a green dot and orange-coloured sponge rubber headphones, was one of the first examples of an industrial designer treating an electrical product as if it were jewellery.

Nakamichi Dragon cassette deck

Date: 1982

Designer: Niro Nakamichi

Manufacturer: Nakamichi Corporation, Tokyo, Japan

Dimensions: 45 × 30 × 13cm (17¾ × 11¾ × 5in)

The Nakamichi Corporation was established by Etsuro Makamichi in 1948 after his wartime service in the Japanese navy working with sonar systems. Working with his brother, Niro, the company started building components for tape recorders after 1951. It was Niro who designed the Dragon cassette deck, launched in 1982, shortly after Etsuro's death; a machine that remained in production for 11 years. For audio enthusiasts it remains a benchmark for quality, which is reflected in the high price it continues to command in the collector's market. In 2023, vintage models in good condition were priced at £3,500 ($4,320). Nakamichi addressed the distortions in playback frequency that were inherent in the mechanisms of a tape player with several technical innovations; for example, the auto azimuth correction, which allowed for an accurate playback of a cassette even when it wasn't perfectly aligned with the tape heads.

Sony WM-F5 portable cassette player

Date: 1984

Designer: Sony

Manufacturer: Sony, Tokyo, Japan

Dimensions: 12.5 × 10 × 4.2cm (5 × 4 × 1½in)

When Sony's managers saw the dramatic success of the Walkman format, they worked hard to find ways of persuading customers to buy more than one. If people were ready to wear a different watch with a suit to the one that they would put on to go sailing, why not offer a Walkman tailored for outdoor pursuits? Walkman was not just a product, it became almost as strong a brand as Sony itself. Most, although not all, Sports Walkmen were coloured a vivid yellow, a subliminal reference to underwater diving equipment that

suggested, but did not definitively claim, to be waterproof. The case, which was noticeably more robust than the rest of the range, came with rubber seals around its edges and had membranes to cover its controls. But, in practice, they would not do more than repel a modest drizzle and would be unlikely to survive total immersion.

Marantz PMD 430 cassette recorder

Date: 1984

Designer: Marantz

Manufacturer: Marantz, Los Angeles, CA, US

Dimensions: 24.1 × 15.2 × 5cm (9½ × 6 × 2in)

With its compact dimensions, low weight and rechargeable battery-pack option, the PMD 430 was aimed at enthusiasts looking to make high-quality live recordings in the field. Unlike many portable recorders, the Marantz PMD 430 has separate channels to record left and right, offering stereo sound. It has two types of noise reduction, suitable either for speech, or for music, and an attenuator to guard against the risk of overload in extremely loud environments, such as recording onstage at a rock concert. The styling, with twin, circular VU (Volume Unit) meters, makes it look more like a reel-to-reel tape recorder than most cassette decks, which was an attempt to suggest that it offers high performance. Cassettes are top loaded. While there is a built-in speaker to monitor recordings, the machine was designed to be used at home as part of a stereo system.

Toshiba KT AS10 Walky cassette player

Date: 1985
Designer: Toshiba Corporation
Manufacturer: Toshiba Corporation, Tokyo, Japan
Dimensions: 12 × 8.4 × 3.5cm (4¾ × 3¼ × 1¼in)

Since Sony had trademarked the word 'Walkman', Toshiba could not use it for its products. Instead, it called its range of personal cassette players the Walky and, in order to differentiate them, it set out to make the world's smallest. The KT AS10 was barely larger than a compact cassette.

Toshiba's claim might have been technically accurate, but its measurements did not include the cassette itself, which protruded from the machine when placed inside. As did the plug-in tuner, in the form of a cassette, which allowed the Walky to function as a radio, but needed to be carried separately when not in use. Toshiba's designers also contrasted their cassette players by flattening surfaces and giving them sharp rectangular edges, unlike Sony's softer radiused curves.

Olympus Pearlcorder S950 Microcassette recorder

Date: 1995
Designer: Olympus Corporation
Manufacturer: Olympus Corporation, Tokyo, Japan
Dimensions: 12 × 2.4 × 6cm (4¾ × 1 × 2¼in)

Olympus entered the sound-recording market in 1969 when it launched the Microcassette, the product of an extended period of research. It was considerably smaller than Philips' compact cassette patented a few years earlier, but nevertheless offered reasonable capacity by operating at slower speeds. The slower speed compromised the quality of the recording and meant that it was used mainly for recorded speech by journalists, interviewers, and for dictation. The machine itself had a similar aesthetic to the careful detailing of Olympus cameras. The 1995 Olympus Pearlcorder S950 is a voice-activated Microcassette recorder with Auto Date/Time Memory for convenient recall of recordings.

8-track audio cartridge and Learjet stereo 8

Date: 1964

Designers: Bill Lear, Richard Krauss

Manufacturer: RCA Victor, New York, NY, US (from 1965)

Dimensions: 13.3 × 10.2 × 2cm (5¼ × 4 × ¾in)

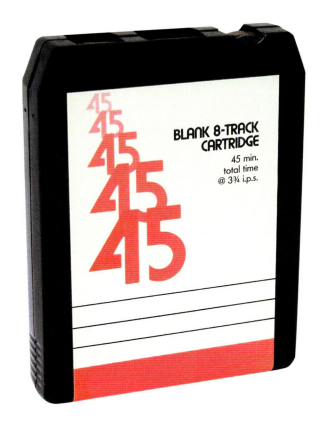

The 8-track tape cartridge became an essential part of American auto-culture when Ford began to offer cassette players as an optional extra for its upmarket models after 1966. The format was developed by Bill Lear, a serial entrepreneur, who had built up the Lear Corporation as a manufacturer of small jet aircraft.

In response to the demand for pre-recorded tapes that could be played in cars, music companies began producing 8-track versions of their new releases on vinyl. When manufacturers started building playback machines designed for domestic use, such as the Learjet stereo 8, 8-track migrated from the car to the home. The cartridge mechanism allowed for the continuous movement of the tape, with no need to turn it over to play the complete recording. But there were drawbacks: as the tape unwound, there was an audible fade and click as it moved from one track to the next and, if there was a misfeed, the result was a hopeless spaghetti-like tangle of tape.

Weltron 2001 8-track tape player and radio

Date: 1970

Designer: James Pratt Winston

Manufacturer: Weltron, Durham, NC, US.
Made in Japan.

Dimensions: 30cm (12in) diameter

By the start of the 1970s, low-cost manufacturing was moving to Asia from American and European factories. One of the first examples of this shift was the rise of US companies, such as Weltron, who used a range of anonymous Asian factories and suppliers to source products that they sold under their own brand names. By and large they succeeded with products that grabbed attention with their striking, often outlandish, looks, rather than building a consistent brand identity through a coherent image or a reputation for reliability.

The Weltron 2001, a name clearly intended to resonate with Stanley Kubrick's 1968 film *2001: A Space Odyssey*, had an 8-track tape player, radio and built-in speakers housed inside a white, canary yellow, green or red spherical helmet.

Audiovox C-902A 8-track portable player

Date: 1971

Designer: Shintom Industries Co. Ltd, Japan

Manufacturer: Audiovox Corporation,
Hauppauge, NY, US

Dimensions: Approx. 4 × 13 × 15cm
(1½ × 5 × 6in)

Before European and American electronics companies started to move their manufacturing to Asia, there was already a significant number of entrepreneurs sourcing products from overseas to their own specifications, and importing them to sell under their own brands. Import trading company Audiovox was one such business. In 1965, after founder John Shalam found a ready market for 2,000 imported car radios, he began to specialize in audio equipment designed for use in cars. There was never a domestic manufacturing base, but the Audiovox brand was able to establish itself on the basis of budget pricing. It was significant that it drew attention to its 'designed in Japan' connection, which was seen as a positive attribute in the development of audio equipment at this time.

Panasonic RS 833S 8-track player

Date: 1976

Designer: Panasonic

Manufacturer: Matsushita Electric Industrial
Co. Ltd, Osaka, Japan

Dimensions: 30.5 × 22.9 × 8.9cm
(12 × 9 × 3½in)

Following the same colourful design language
established by the unabashed pop sensibility
that Panasonic developed for its Panapet and
Toot-a-Loop radios (see page 61), its portable
8-track cassette player was commonly
described as the 'Swiss Cheese' player.
It came in bright red or ivory, and could also
be compared to a handbag, designed to be
carried in public, closer to a boom box than
the silent Walkman. Yet, unlike a handbag,
which is designed to be shown off from all
angles, the technical side of the RS 833S

seemed like a visual afterthought. It had
a more toy-like character than the usual
technocratic imagery of brushed-steel
instrument panels derived from scientific
equipment. It shared the flamboyant Pop Art
typography of other Panasonic models, visible
in large-scale numerals on the tuning dial.
Less impressive was the unresolved slot in the
side of the machine, which was used to insert
a cassette.

Sony CF-1980 boom box

Date: 1974

Designer: Sony

Manufacturer: Sony, Tokyo, Japan

Dimensions: 37.6 × 24.5 × 10.6cm
(14¾ × 9¾ × 4¼in)

The official designation that Sony came up with for this portable cassette player, recorder and radio combination was 'cassette corder'. It was one of the early examples of what came to be known as the boom box or ghetto blaster. Beyond passive listening to broadcasts or recordings, the CF-1980 had the technology to be used for performances and to create new musical work. Sony described it as offering authentic studio-mixing functions, such as 'wireless mixing', which enables tape mixing from a distance of approximately 100m (330ft)

using an FM wireless microphone. The design is reminiscent of a studio adjustment table.

Sony counts the CF-1980 as a corporate milestone, recognizing its place as a category definer. Its restrained design, its face formed with minimal geometry – a simple rectangle and two circles – and a subdued metallic finish, would soon give way to much more flamboyant decorative schemes for popular boom boxes.

JVC RC M-90 boom box

Date: 1981

Designer: JVC

Manufacturer: Matsushita Electric
Industrial Co. Ltd for Japan Victor
Corporation, Tokyo, Japan

Dimensions: 66.8 × 35 × 17.7cm
(26¼ × 13¾ × 7in)

When *Solid Gold Hits*, the Beastie Boys'
greatest-hits compilation, was launched in
2005, the JVC RC M-90 boom box that was
featured prominently on its cover was already
obsolete enough to qualify as a piece of
sought-after vintage electronics. It had a
radio and could play tapes, but didn't have the
capacity to handle the compact disc, the digital
harbinger of the end of the analogue age.

The machine was the embodiment of a
very particular moment in musical culture –
reflected by the cover of LL Cool J's 1985
debut Rap album, *Radio*, which was filled
almost entirely with an image of the M-90.
The portable recorder player format has its
roots in a Philips battery-powered product
from 1963, the EL 3300, that could be used
outdoors. Adopted as a symbol of urban youth
culture, it took on a very different meaning
when hoisted shoulder-high, rather than
sedately positioned on a garden table.

Sony CFS 500 boom box

Date: 1983

Designer: Sony

Manufacturer: Sony, Tokyo, Japan

Dimensions: 53.3 × 29.2 × 15.2cm
(21 × 11½ × 6 in)

Just as sneakers began life as athletic wear and were quickly adopted as cultural signifiers, so the boom box, originally designed for use at picnics, was put to uses never envisaged by its original designers. If the Walkman had the effect of privatizing space, insulating the listener from their surroundings, the boom box, a less dismissive name for what some people called a ghetto blaster, turned out to be a means to colonize urban space. Once the marketeers understood this unexpected new audience, they briefed their product

developers to respond with new designs that played up to this new identity. By the flamboyant styling standards of the boom box, Sony's CFS range, with a radio, tape player and built-in speakers, was relatively restrained visually, a reflection of the company's somewhat high-minded approach to design. It had the shiny aluminium skin that characterized the type, but it maintained manageable proportions.

Philips Le Cube D-808002 boom box

Date: 1985

Designer: Philips

Manufacturer: Philips, Singapore

Dimensions: 29 × 27 × 27cm
(11½ × 10½ × 10½in)

Philips has had a long history of technical innovation in recording technology. Yet, despite the establishment of an international design team in its corporate headquarters in Eindhoven, the visual identity of its products did not keep up with that of Sony, a company with which it collaborated over the years, or of its direct rivals.

Le Cube was a self-conscious attempt to redefine the boom box as a much less aggressive-looking object. Rather than adopt the suitcase configuration, as popularized by

LL Cool J, Le Cube came in a different format. Available in vivid yellow, white or green colours with black contrast, it was intended to suggest a close connection with an unthreatening ice box you might take to a barbecue. It made for a striking object, but none of its rivals followed the precedent.

Sharp HK 9000 boom box

Date: 1986

Designer: Sharp Corporation

Manufacturer: Sharp Corporation, Osaka, Japan

Dimensions: 86 × 29 × 23cm (34 × 11½ × 9in)

Even without the ten batteries needed to power it in the absence of mains electricity, the Sharp HK 9000 weighed a hefty 15kg (33lb). It was styled to look like an audio system made up of individual components, even though it was, in fact, a single unwieldy object the size of a suitcase rather than a portable radio. Demonstrating that you could carry it with confidence was something of a statement in itself.

Sharp crammed a bewildering array of features into the box. There were two tape players and a graphic equalizer, ostensibly a means for boosting hi-fi quality by adjusting the relative prominence of selected frequencies, but also offering a visually impressive array of sliding controls that emphasized the sense of power. There was even a jack into which you could plug an electric guitar for an impromptu jam session. It was the kind of super abundance that could be considered conspicuous redundancy.

Sharp QT-50 boom box

Date: 1986

Designer: Sharp Corporation

Manufacturer: Sharp Corporation, Osaka, Japan

Dimensions: 24 × 58 × 29cm (9½ × 23 × 11½in)

Sharp, a company that took its name from the 'Ever-Sharp' propelling pencil that it manufactured in its early days in the 1920s, set out to differentiate itself from its competitors in the 1980s by embracing post-modern aesthetics. Sony was more restrained and Panasonic went for pop, but Sharp proclaimed, 'Suddenly, everything with style is plugged into pastels. And now Sharp is first with pastels that you can plug in all around you. Get ready for the shock of vibrant, pulsating color in places where it's never been before:

microwave ovens, clock radios, stereo radio cassette players, telephones, calculators, vacuum cleaners, and televisions with color inside out, all with the intense heat of a tropical sunset. It's lifestyle in living color. High tech turned hot tech. Sharp pastels. There is absolutely nothing neutral about them.' The QT-50 mixed art deco style with ice-cream colours – a look that got it into the design collections of trend-spotting museums.

Vision

Louis Daguerre, the celebrated French artist, diorama painter and photographer, built on the discoveries of Joseph Niépce, who is credited with the world's first photograph, to produce the Daguerreotype in 1839. It was an innovation often described as the first commercial photographic process. Daguerre designed a camera based on Niépce's methods, and later devised a silver-plated copper sheet that, when exposed to light and treated with the right mix of chemicals, left a permanent image. Daguerre patented his discoveries and licensed their use to others. Although this was not quite open-source technology, it had the effect of galvanizing a burst of innovation in making photography simpler and more economical. It was a process involving art as much as science, which culminated 50 years later in Thomas Eastman's roll film, and his affordable and simple-to-use Kodak cameras. A whole new industry had come into being, initially centred in France, Germany and the US, where much of the initial research was carried out, and then in Japan and the Soviet Union. It employed hundreds of thousands of people, from film processors to lens makers.

The long-term impact of Daguerre's work was as much cultural as commercial. The development of a method of apparently accurately portraying the world triggered a fundamental reassessment of the meaning and purpose of art. Members of the French Academy described the lifelike quality with which Daguerre could depict reality as

miraculous. The influential Victorian critic John Ruskin initially welcomed photography as the most 'truthful' form of representation, but later changed his mind, suggesting that it could never be considered 'art'. It is a view that artists such as Thomas Struth and Christina Hofer, who work with photography as a medium, have convincingly overturned. Their work hangs in museums of contemporary art and attracts seven-figure bids at auctions.

Long before Struth and Hofer, photographers as varied as Man Ray, Rodchenko and Cartier-Bresson had shown the range and depth of the cultural impact of the camera. Photography became both a means of artistic self-expression, and a tool with which photojournalists could communicate everything from the brutality of modern warfare to the sugar-coated excess of celebrity. Still photographs turned out to have a remarkable capacity to encapsulate historical turning points. The raising of the American flag by US marines on Iwo Jima in 1945, near the end of the Pacific war against Japan, won a Pulitzer Prize for the Associated Press photographer, Joe Rosenthal. Photojournalist Nick Ut's horrifying image of Phan Thi Kim Phúc, the Vietnamese child running in agony after a napalm attack in 1972, was another photograph that circulated the world.

The camera became an object that carried meaning in itself. When raised to eye level, half hiding the face as an unconscious barrier, it could

1

(1) Metal film cannister from Kodak, dating from the 1950s and designed to hold 35mm film.

(2) Louis Daguerre devised his own camera, pictured, to speed up the process of making images.

2

1826 The first photograph was taken by Joseph Nicéphore Niépce, titled *View from the Window at Le Gras*.

1878 The first moving images were created by Eadweard Muybridge.

1888 The first successful roll-film hand camera, the Kodak, was released.

1927 *The Jazz Singer*, the first feature-length movie with synchronized dialogue, or 'talking picture', was released.

3

(3) Daguerre's 1838 photograph of the Boulevard du Temple in Paris is considered the first to show a human being (the figure in the bottom left-hand corner).

(4) Like his pioneering predecessors, Edwin Land wanted to simplify film processing. He brought his Polaroid instant film, and the cameras to use it, to the market in 1948 (see page 120).

4

1929 John Logie Baird produces the first commercial television set, the Model B Televisor.

1935 Kodachrome is launched, the first successful, mass-market colour film (see page 118).

1948 Edwin Land's Model 95 (see page 129), the first instant camera, went on sale at a department store in Boston. It sold out within minutes.

1953 NBC and CBS networks began regular colour-television transmissions, using the National Television System Committee's 'compatible color' system.

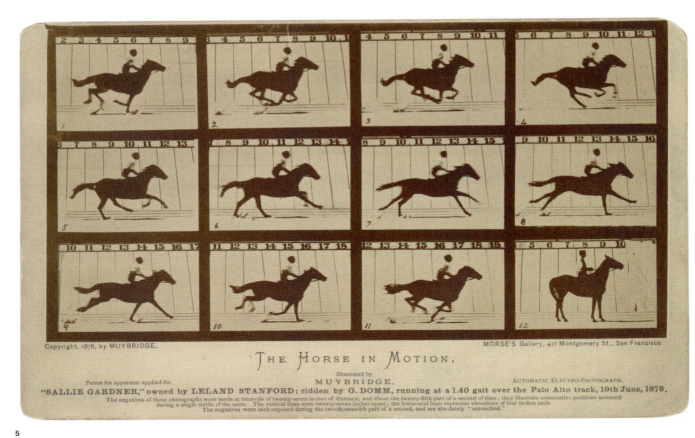

5

6

(5) Eadweard Muybridge's particular contribution to photography was his exploration of movement in animals and humans. As seen here, he captured motion in a sequence of still images, using multiple cameras with high-speed shutters.

(6) The early history of both still photography and then cine film was shaped by professionals. Equipment for amateur users, such as this Filmo cine camera (see page 149), followed.

1959 One of the most historically significant cameras ever made, the Nikon F SLR (see page 138), launched, redefining modern professional photography.

1960 The release of the Sony TV8-301 (see page 168), notable as the world's first all-transistor television.

1963 Release of the Kodak Carousel-S slide projector, featuring a round tray holding 80 slides.

1975 Sony launch Betamax, a consumer-level video-cassette recorder (see page 194). Betamax recorders continued to be sold until August 2002.

(7) Cathode ray television sets were necessarily bulky. They were designed either to look at home in a domestic setting as a piece of furniture, or, like this Panasonic 1973 Orbiter model (see page 178), to stand out.

insulate the user from his or her subject. Worn around the neck to hang at waist level, it became part of the body.

The use of multiple-exposure cameras to create moving pictures was pioneered by the English photographer Eadweard Muybridge in the 1880s. He was followed by the Lumière brothers in France, who devised the equipment necessary to make short documentary outdoor films. Simultaneously, Thomas Edison was working on silent films portraying circus acts in the US. Photography changed the way that people saw the world, and transformed news reporting. Cinema created perhaps the most powerful new cultural form of the twentieth century. It became one of the dominant forms of popular culture, and led to the Hollywood system, later also replicated in Mumbai.

Cinema's impact, in its most powerful period, was as a social activity – an experience shared in a darkened, cigarette-smoke-filled, 1,000-seat auditorium. The Golden Age of film is reflected in the spectacular cinema buildings of the 1930s and 1940s. Their architecture, evoking every exotic style, from the Moorish Alhambra to the Chinese

pagoda, was as escapist as the subject matter of the films that distracted the masses from the trauma and deprivation of the Great Depression.

Cinema was later to be challenged by the development of television, launched in the 1940s as a medium that could transmit moving images from a broadcast studio into the home. The screen was much smaller and the experience was less immersive but, in the context of the domestic living room, television became a particularly intense medium. With the passage of time, television itself was undermined, when Sony and Philips developed the home video. It undercut the advertising-based broadcasting model and the idea of a sequential, curated experience.

Film and video were treated simultaneously as both amateur and professional activities. Kodak, for example, made film for Hollywood cameramen, but also for hobbyists. The format, the equipment, the results and the barriers to entry were different, even if they depended on the same basic techniques. It was the same for video in the 1970s. The Japanese companies mostly began by manufacturing large and expensive video cameras that only broadcasters or film studios could afford, and later came out with simpler and cheaper domestic versions. In the early days, these innovations were often presented as democratizing technology, opening the way to citizen journalism and creative self-expression outside the commercial Hollywood system. Yet, such hopes, in many cases, proved short-lived. With the possible exception of the burgeoning market for pornography, home movies and video were never a real challenge to the production values and budgets of the big commercial studios.

Analogue photography and filmmaking still survive as a specialist craft, much like book binding or letterpress printing, embraced by those who admire the subtlety and craft of the pre-digital world.

7

1976 JVC launch the VHS home video. The number of VHS recorder sales outstripped sales of Beta-format recorders, despite their head start to market.

1985 Panasonic produce the first VHS camcorder, the NV-M1, to meet a mounting need for an easy-to-use video with a built-in camera.

1986 Sony launch the Profeel Pro (see page 188), completely redefining what a television set could look like, with the screen housed in an open cube formed from moulded black plastic.

2012 Kodak filed for a £5.49 ($6.75) billion bankruptcy. The company was given an emergency loan from Citibank.

Product Directory

Photography

Making a photograph is a complex process that involves a long, drawn-out sequence of actions. It starts with ensuring that the camera is adjusted to take account of the light conditions at the time that the film is exposed. The film is sensitive to light until it is processed in a developing tank in a dark room. The image on the negative film is projected onto light-sensitive paper with an enlarger, then fixed in a chemical bath.

Cameras

Early cameras using roll film had either a twin-lens system or a range finder. Twin-lens cameras used one to expose the film and the other to compose the image, looking down at it with the camera held at the waist. Range-finder cameras were held at eye level. Single-lens reflex cameras use a mirror that gives a view through the lens. Opening the shutter to take the picture swings the mirror out of the way.

Cine Film

Cine cameras began as a product for professionals, then became available in a simplified and more affordable form for amateur use. The film itself was costly, which encouraged manufacturers to offer increasingly narrow formats, cutting film down from 35mm to 8mm, and in 50-m (164-ft) lengths that gave no more than four minutes of running time. Home viewing for an audience required a projector and a screen. Analogue video cameras that connected to a television screen were more convenient.

Televisions

For the half a century after 1955, television became the most pervasive form of domestic technology on the planet. Initially, a cathode-ray tube, accommodated in a more or less elegant box, was an important status symbol. It soon became a universal object, with at least one to be found in almost every home.

Video

Video was the offshoot of audio-recording technology based on magnetic tape. From the 1950s, many American and Japanese companies explored its potential. The issue was to refine ways to capture images, and at the same time to develop ways of broadcasting them. It took some time to determine if the format was best suited for consumers to create their own content, or to use the same equipment to play back pre-recorded material.

35mm black-and-white film

Date: 1896

Designers: William Kennedy Dickson,
Thomas Edison

Manufacturer: Eastman Kodak, Rochester,
NY, US

Dimensions: 8.9 × 8.9cm (3½ × 3½in)

George Eastman simplified the process of taking individual pictures in a still camera by replacing single plates with a continuous supply of light-sensitive film. Dickson and Edison saw that it could be used to create moving pictures, too. Perforating the edges of the film with sprocket holes made it possible to advance it at a steady pace through a specially designed camera to capture multiple still images. Projecting them in sequence created the illusion of movement.

Edison tailored Eastman's standard film stock, cutting four perforations to each picture frame, and then worked with Dickson to use it to make images for his new invention, the Kinetoscope. The 35mm format with four perforations per frame became the worldwide professional cinema standard.

Kodachrome colour slide film

Date: 1935

Designers: Leopold Godowsky,
Leopold Mannes

Manufacturer: Eastman Kodak, Rochester,
NY, US

Dimensions: 5.1 × 5.1cm (2 × 2in)

Kodachrome was initially marketed as a 16mm movie film in 1935, the same year that saw the release of the first Hollywood full-length colour feature film. Kodak followed with the launch of a 35mm version, designed for use in still cameras. It had a significant impact on how people looked at images and how they were stored – while conventional prints were kept in photographic albums or in individual frames, Kodak started making projectors to view Kodachrome images.

Initially, Kodak left its customers to make their own slide mounts. Later, they switched to putting them in glass, and subsequently introduced the ubiquitous cardboard mount with its familiar logo and date stamp.

Type 40 instant film

Date: 1948

Designer: Edwin Land

Manufacturer: Polaroid Corporation,
Cambridge, MA, US

Dimensions: 8.3 × 10.8cm (3¼ × 4¼in) prints

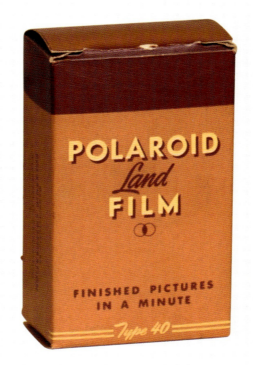

Edwin Land began working on instant film in 1943, when his daughter asked him to explain why she couldn't immediately see the pictures that he was taking on his camera. The whole roll had to be exposed before you saw a picture, either after mailing it to a processing lab or in a lengthy session in a home dark room. It took five years for Land to perfect a roll film, designated as the Type 40, that could produce a completed print in less than a minute. Land applied a photographic backing paper to a chemical-coated negative. Once the silver halide film was exposed to light, the chemicals began the process of fixing the image on the paper. The first version produced sepia prints, rather than true black and white, which took a couple more years to achieve. Type 40 was sold in boxes of six rolls that could each make eight prints.

Ikophot Rapid exposure meter

Date: 1956

Designer: Zeiss Ikon

Manufacturer: Zeiss Ikon, Stuttgart,
West Germany

Dimensions: 7.62 × 6.35 × 1.9cm
(3 × 2½ × ¾in)

In marketing its exposure meter, Zeiss Ikon was careful to reassure its customers that it would not be difficult to use. The Ikophot Rapid was 'an instrument as perfect as modern scientific knowledge can make it'. Yet, consumers could also be confident that 'positively no calculations are required'.

Exposure meters use a selenium cell that generates electric current when exposed to light and so has no need of a battery. In order to calculate the shutter speed and aperture size, the user sets the type of film that they are using on the meter's dial. The selenium cell generates a current, which moves a marker needle to indicate the settings needed for the specific light conditions. The Ikophot Rapid was set in a cream-coloured plastic housing.

Gossen Sixtino exposure meter

Date: 1960

Designer: Paul Gossen

Manufacturer: Paul Gossen, Nuremberg, West Germany

Dimensions: 4.8 × 5.6 × 3cm (1¾ × 2¼ × 1in)

The Sixtino exposure meter was small, compact, and looked like a more modern piece of equipment than its competitors. It relied on selenium to react to light exposure to drive a marker needle. For years, the exposure meter was the sign of an expert photographer at work, even as many manufacturers offered built-in light meters with their cameras, gradually making the product redundant. The Gossen company, originally established in 1919, continues to manufacture light-measuring equipment today. A tribute, perhaps, to its motto 'tradition is good, innovation is better', as the underlying technology on which they depend has changed completely.

Instamatic cartridge film

Date: 1963

Designer: Hubert Nerwin

Manufacturer: Kodak, Rochester, NY, US

Dimensions: 8.5 × 5.5 × 4.9cm (3¼ × 2¼ × 2in)

Hubert Nerwin was a senior member of the group of scientists running Zeiss Ikon in Dresden during the 1930s. After helping to re-establish Zeiss in post-war West Germany, Nerwin was one of a number of German experts shipped to the US by the American government as part of Operation Paperclip (the same scheme that took Wernher von Braun from the V2 rocket programme to NASA). Nerwin joined Kodak in 1955, and had the idea for the Instamatic cartridge, a device which allowed for what he called foolproof drop-in loading. It turned out to be one of the most successful products in the company's history, allowing Kodak to continue its domination of amateur photography for two more decades. The mountains of waste resulting from disposable plastic cartridges was not a consideration at the time.

Kodak Carousel-S slide projector

Date: 1963

Designers: Hans Gugelot, Reinhold Häcker

Manufacturer: Kodak AG, Stuttgart, West Germany

Dimensions: 15.2 × 28.6 × 27cm (6 × 11¼ × 10½in)

In the twentieth century, with the growth of amateur photography, and especially after the development of the colour slide, projectors became an increasingly popular way of sharing images. The first models depended on a straight slide tray. Kodak were offered the patent for a more convenient circular alternative by Louis Misuraca, an Italian-American inventor. Gugelot transformed it into a particularly well-proportioned machine that exemplified the Ulm School of Design's approach to poetic functionalism.

The projector allowed a new approach to lectures, with academics bringing their pre-sorted carousel of slides, in much the same way later generations saved a PowerPoint presentation to a USB stick. Often multiple projectors were deployed to marshal stronger visual arguments by making provocative juxtapositions.

Paterson System 4 developing tank

Date: 1968

Designer: Donald Paterson

Manufacturer: Paterson Products Ltd, London, England

Dimensions: 14.1 × 14.1 × 16.5cm (5½ × 5½ × 6½in)

Given that the vast majority of photographers found the process of loading a camera with roll film too demanding, and opted instead for Instamatic cartridges, its impressive that a substantial number of amateurs were ready to tackle the far more difficult task of loading exposed film in complete darkness into a tank to develop it. Donald Paterson, who had originally trained as a dentist but was a keen photographer, patented has own design for a self-loading film metal spiral that in the conditions of a dark room would make it easier to unspool an exposed film. Once the exposed film is in position, it is inserted into a light-tight developing tank and then filled with chemicals that fix the light-sensitive silver halide crystals. Paterson continued to refine the basic product over many years and the company sold more than eight million spirals.

Leica 1 Model C camera

Date: 1930

Designer: Oskar Barnack

Manufacturer: Ernst Leitz, Hesse, Germany

Dimensions: 6.6 × 13 × 6cm (2½ × 5 × 2¼in)

Ernst Leitz inherited his father's engineering firm, which had specialized in optical instruments and microscopes. It turned to making cameras when Oskar Barnack, one of Leitz's employees who was a gifted photographer as well as an inventor, devised a new approach to taking pictures with a lightweight camera, using the same 35mm film that Kodak had developed for cinematic purposes. It allowed for 36 exposures before the photographer needed to change the roll. The first model had all the features that came to define 35mm photography in the analogue age. The film moved through the camera horizontally rather than vertically. The Model C introduced an interchangeable lens, offering a more versatile approach to taking pictures.

The Leica allowed photography to become a more spontaneous process. It was the camera that Robert Capa used for his epochal photograph, *The Falling Soldier*, capturing the moment that a Spanish Civil War Republican militia man was shot dead.

Baby Brownie camera

Date: 1934

Designer: Walter Dorwin Teague

Manufacturer: Eastman Kodak, Rochester, NY, US

Dimensions: 7.1 × 7.1 × 8.4cm (2¾ × 2¾ × 3¼in)

Walter Dorwin Teague was a major figure in the development of the industrial design profession. He studied painting at the Art Students League in New York, then began his career as an illustrator and graphic designer. He spent four years working at the pioneering advertising agency Calkins & Holden. The agency's founder, Earnest Elmo Calkins, had formulated the concept of built-in obsolescence. As Calkins saw it, the job of the designer was to make products desirable to consumers, and then to create something

even more desirable the following year, in order to persuade the buyer to discard their original purchase in favour of its replacement. In the course of his long career working for Kodak, this was certainly Teague's strategy, and he worked hard to give the company's products attractive colours and shapes. The Art Deco Baby Brownie, with its Bakelite case, was one of his most successful cameras, and its shape became inseparably connected with the Kodak brand.

Kodak

George Eastman bought his first camera in 1877, as a young man with very little scientific background, still working in a bank. He learned how to take and process images, initially using the wet-plate method, laboriously preparing each glass plate with a mix of chemicals immediately before taking a picture. Each image had to be developed before the coating dried.

Eastman's first innovation was to build and patent a machine that could produce ready-made 'dry' plates, simplifying the development process. Over the next 20 years, Eastman and the company that he named Kodak (after the first camera that he sold) did for photography what Steve Jobs and Apple would do a century later for computing. He turned photography from a complex scientific process reserved for experts, into an activity that was made clear enough for anybody to attempt. Eastman worked both on the technology of photography – finding a way to replace glass plates with celluloid-roll film, which was much lighter and far easier to handle, and later to produce colour film – as well as the cameras that would use his films.

Before Eastman, cameras were enormous and required the use of what amounted to a portable darkroom. He found a way to make a camera small enough to be unobtrusive and intuitive to use. The first Kodak Brownie camera was introduced in 1900 and, at $1, was an instant success, selling more than 150,000 units in its first year on the market. The Brownie remained Kodak's bestselling brand for many years, transformed from the original black-cardboard-box format to a streamlined, Art Deco icon in moulded Bakelite by the great American industrial designer Walter Dorwin Teague. Teague started working for Kodak in 1929, and produced a whole sequence of Brownie cameras for the company.

Eastman had a natural gift for marketing, as well as for technology. He came up with the slogan: 'You push the button, we do the rest.' Under Eastman, Kodak became a huge success worldwide, with production in Britain and Germany as well as the US, and at its peak hiring 78,000 employees. The bulk of the company's income came not from the cameras that it manufactured, even though they were made in their millions, but from the film that they used. After perfecting celluloid-roll film, Eastman started manufacturing a 35mm film that was initially aimed at the movie industry. Kodak went on to make colour film generally available.

Following Eastman's death in 1932, the company grew into the dominant global force in cameras, film, and film processing. In the post-war years, the Instamatic camera and cassette films proved to be even more successful than the Brownie had been.

Kodak was well aware of the potential of digital photography – it had been experimenting with the necessary technology since the 1970s – and collaborated with Steve Jobs in the early stages of the development of the Quick Take, Apple's first consumer digital camera. However, the company was unable to negotiate the massive disruption to its business model represented by the end of film. From being the dominant company in the marketplace for photography, Kodak virtually disappeared, to re-emerge as a much smaller, specialist company.

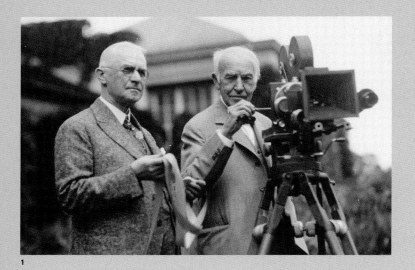

1

(1) George Eastman (left) seen with Thomas Edison (right), demonstrating the use of Kodachrome cine film. Eastman launched his first camera, the Kodak, in 1888.

(2) Successive generations of Brownie cameras, such as the Hawkeye (pictured) designed by Arthur Crapsey, were styled differently, but the brand remained alive until the 1980s.

(3) The original Brownie camera was designed by Frank Brownell in 1900 to be sold as cheaply as possible. Kodak used the playful name to suggest that the cameras were not intimidating pieces of technological equipment, but were affordable and simple to use.

(4) From 1951, Kodak used the Brownie brand for its range of cine cameras. The first cameras were followed by the improved Model 2 (pictured) five years later.

2

3

4

Minox Riga subminiature camera

Date: 1938

Designer: Walter Zapp

Manufacturer: VEF, Riga, Latvia

Dimensions: 8 × 2.7 × 1.6cm (3 × 1 × ½in)

Walter Zapp's initial concept was to make a camera small enough to carry everywhere as a personal, multi-functional tool. In its shape and details, the Minox Riga was a precedent for the smartphone, designed 70 years later and intended to be equally ubiquitous. Inevitably, its tiny size attracted the attention of the world's espionage agencies, whose agents used it for covert photography of documents. In the 1930s, the SLR 35mm camera was still described as miniature format, so the Minox was designated as subminiature with a stripped down film, just 9.2mm wide. Zapp contracted a factory in Latvia to begin production. The camera body was originally made of brass, with a stainless steel shell. Sliding the cover open revealed the lens, closing it advanced the film. Zapp restarted Minox production in the West German town of Wetzlar in 1948. Those cameras were outwardly similar to the original Riga models, but were made using aluminium.

Polaroid 95 Land camera

Date: 1948

Designers: Edwin Land, Walter Dorwin Teague

Manufacturer: Polaroid Corporation,
Cambridge, MA, US

Dimensions: 26 × 14 × 21cm
(10¼ × 5½ × 8¼in)

Edwin Land was a brilliant scientist who started his first business in the 1930s, exploiting his patents to manufacture affordable polarizing film that was used for sunglasses and microscopes. In 1948, he finally realized his long-term ambition to produce a self-developing photographic film. In fact, the first version, using the Polaroid 95 camera, took about a minute after the shutter button was pressed to deliver a completed print of the image. Compared with the hours it took for an amateur to develop and print their own work, let alone the week it could take to send it off for professional processing, it was quick enough to justify its description as an instant camera.

While Land invented the camera, the industrial design came from Walter Dorwin Teague who, after a career in advertising, had started working for Eastman Kodak, where he designed a version of the Brownie camera. Teague had a retainer with Polaroid for the rest of his life.

Asahiflex 1 SLR camera

Date: 1952

Designers: Nobuyuki Yoshida, Ryohei Suzuki

Manufacturer: Asahi Optical Co. Ltd,
Tokyo, Japan

Dimensions: 14.7 × 7.3 × 4.8cm
(5¾ × 2¾ × 1¾in)

The Asahi company was set up as a lens manufacturer, initially producing spectacles and then optical lenses used by Japanese camera makers. It began to explore design concepts for its own cameras in 1950. Japan's economic success in the years following World War II depended on copying Western products, and cameras were no exception. As the name suggests, Asahi based its first prototype on the Praktiflex, a German-made camera designed in 1939. It used a single-lens reflex (SLR) format for the first time in Japan. There was a waist-level viewfinder with a mirror, giving the user a view through the lens to allow them to compose the image. The mirror was connected to the shutter button, so that it moved up out of the way when the camera took a picture.

Zenit E 35mm camera

Date: 1952

Designer: Krasnogorzki Mekhanischeskii
Zavod

Manufacturer: Krasnogorzki Mekhanischeskii
Zavod (KMZ), Krasnogorsk, Moscow,
Soviet Union

Dimensions: 13.7 × 9.2 × 5.3cm
(5½ × 3½ × 2in) (without lens)

While the Soviet photographic industry used German technology that it had appropriated when its forces occupied what became East Germany, and the production equipment that it had seized as war reparations, the Zenit E was an early entrant in the field of 35mm single-lens reflex cameras. The Zenit was based on the Soviet Zorki rangefinder, which had itself used ideas taken from German-made Leica cameras.

Nikon S2 camera

Date: 1954

Designer: Nippon Kogaku KK

Manufacturer: Nippon Kogaku KK,
Tokyo, Japan

Dimensions: 13.6 × 7.9 × 4.4cm
(5¼ × 3 × 1¾in)

Nikon has its roots in Nippon Kogaku, which was originally an optical equipment company that moved on from producing microscopes to making lenses for Canon's cameras. It designed its first prototype camera, the Nikon, in 1946. It was a project that finally reached the market in Japan two years later. The Nikon was based on ideas taken from the Contax camera, a model made in Dresden by Zeiss Ikon more than a decade earlier. It was coupled with the rangefinder designed by Zeiss's rival, Leica, to help focus the lens.

Camera design developed quickly in this period in Japan, and the original Nikon was followed by a succession of newer models that continued to learn from what European manufacturers were doing. The body of the S2 was made using an aluminium alloy and it had a lever that advanced the film forward, rather than requiring a winder.

Hasselblad 500 C camera

Date: 1957

Designer: Victor Hasselblad

Manufacturer: Victor Hasselblad AB,
Gothenburg, Sweden

Dimensions: 17 × 10.9 × 10.4cm
(6¾ × 4¼ × 4in)

Hasselblad designed its cameras to work as a system of interchangeable components that users could configure to reflect their own preferences. Some photographers compose a picture by holding the camera at waist level and work with a viewfinder from the top. Others prefer to work with an eye-level viewfinder, made possible by the decision to locate the shutter within the lens. Hasselblad viewfinders, film magazines and camera bodies could be quickly swapped around, even in the middle of a shoot. The Hasselblad 500 C had no built-in electronics, and so no need of batteries. Light-level readings required an external light meter. The large-format film, 5.7 × 5.7cm (2¼ × 2¼in), allowed for larger negatives and so the potential for higher-resolution images and sharper prints. Almost 80,000 bodies were manufactured between 1957 and 1970, and astronaut Walter Schirra took one with him on his journey into Earth's orbit on the 1962 Mercury rocket.

Rolleicord Va camera

Date: 1957

Designer: Franke & Heidecke

Manufacturer: Franke & Heidecke,
Braunschweig, West Germany

Dimensions: 10 × 9.9 × 14.2cm
(4 × 3¾ × 5½in)

Frank & Heidecke initially started out as a
manufacturer of specialist precision optical
equipment, one of several such German
companies that would later become important
camera makers. It was known for the success
of its twin-lens reflex cameras, whose
professional models were branded with the
Rolleiflex name. Photographers including
Helmut Newton, Diane Arbus and David Bailey
used them. The consumer models were
instead designated as Rolleicord cameras,
but were similar in the way that they worked.
The twin-lens arrangement uses one lens
to focus light on the film to take an image.
The second lens, just above the first, allows
the user to compose a picture. Unlike an SLR
camera, with a viewfinder that allows for the
camera to be held at eye level, a twin-lens
reflex camera, likely supported by a neck strap,
is held at the waist. The image seen through
the second lens is reflected up to a viewfinder
on top of the camera.

Asahi Pentax SLR camera

Date: 1957

Designer: Asahi Optical Co. Ltd

Manufacturer: Asahi Optical Co. Ltd,
Tokyo, Japan

Dimensions: 14.5 × 9.2 × 5cm (5¾ × 3½ × 2in)

Asahi's Pentax was Japan's first single-lens reflex camera, launched two years before its two largest competitors – Canon and Nikon – could produce a rival product. It was successful enough for the company to rebrand itself as Pentax. The problem with using a system of mirrors inside a single-lens reflex camera to give the user an image on the viewfinder is that it inverts the image. Asahi Optical was not the first company to use a five-sided prism to turn the upside down image the right way up; this innovation came from Germany. But, when Asahi adopted the pentaprism for its cameras, it had a visible impact on the way that SLR cameras looked and worked, which set the model for others to follow. Asahi also produced such other early innovations as a lever to advance the film and a microprism device to help focus the lens.

Tochka 58-M subminiature camera

Date: 1958
Designer: All Union Optical Institute
Manufacturer: Krasnogorzki Mekhanischeskii Zavod (KMZ), Krasnogorsk, Moscow, Soviet Union
Dimensions: 8.3 × 2.8 × 2cm (3¼ × 1 × ¾in)

In the Soviet Union, every factory's basic function was to supply the equipment that its armed forces depended on. At the same time, they would produce a stream of products aimed at satisfying the demands of consumers at home and raising hard currency through export markets.

The Tochka 58-M was an example of this dual-aspect production. Its subminiature format was based on the Minox camera, and was initially manufactured to meet the needs of Soviet spies working for the KGB security service. Unlike the Minox, which placed the lens at the front of the camera, the Tochka's lens is positioned on top, and required an internal mirror to project the image onto the film inside.

Instamatic 100 camera

Date: 1963
Designer: Frank Zagara
Manufacturer: Eastman Kodak, Rochester, NY, US
Dimensions: 10.8 × 6.2 × 5.4cm (4¼ × 2½ × 2in)

George Eastman wanted to make the camera as simple to use as the pencil. The 1900 Brownie camera was a vital first step. Walter Dorwin Teague transformed the original wooden-box Brownie into a piece of Art Deco sculpture in Bakelite. The Instamatic 100 was its stripped down, modern replacement: a point-and-shoot camera that was even easier to use, though it rarely created impressive pictures. The film came in plastic cartridges that could be loaded anywhere without needing to worry about daylight ruining it. It was a very successful formula, and the Instamatic sold more than 50 million units.

Zenit Photosniper FS-3 camera

Date: 1965

Designer: State Optical Institute (GOI)

Manufacturer: Krasnogorzki Mekhanischeskii Zavod (KMZ), Krasnogorsk, Soviet Union

Dimensions: 14 × 23.5 × 56cm (5½ × 9¼ × 33in)

The Zenit Photosniper was a particularly exotic incarnation of a basic SLR camera, the Zenit E, which was popular because it was cheap, simple and hard wearing. The Photosniper FS-3 made a few modifications to the Zenit E's viewfinder and shutter control, and teamed it with a pistol grip and a stock, along with a telephoto lens, a standard lens and some lens filters. These were clipped in place inside a steel briefcase, like an assassination kit – the kind of thing that might have been supplied to James Bond.

The Photosniper had a heritage that lived up to this fantasy, with its origins in World War II. The State Optical Institute designed the first version for surveillance use in military contexts, and just a few hundred were manufactured. The production version, the FS-3, still appealed to Soviet intelligence agencies, but also added a certain glamour to the stolid Zenit E on which it depended. Its peacetime uses were to avoid camera shake while using a long lens.

Nikon F Photomic camera

Date: 1967

Designers: Masahiko Fuketa,
Yusaku Kamekura

Manufacturer: Nippon Kogaku KK,
Tokyo, Japan

Dimensions: 14.6 × 10.2 × 9.5cm
(5¾ × 4 × 3¾in)

The Nikon F range dates back to 1959 and was the subject of continuous development for many years. The Photomic version, with a light meter in the prism, was part of a system offering a wide range of lenses and accessories, including one for perspective correction and a motor drive that could expose four frames per second. Nikon F Photomic cameras had two qualities that made them popular with photojournalists: they were easier to use than the Leica; and they had a reputation for being extremely reliable and robust. They were ubiquitous during the later years of the war in Vietnam and made memorable appearances in films that evoked the era, including *Apocalypse Now* and *Full Metal Jacket*. Some image-conscious photographers taped over the Nikon brand. With extended heavy use, the black finish would eventually show signs of wear, revealing traces of the aluminium and brass body beneath – an effect that gave them the same kind of charm as faded denim.

Polaroid SX 70 camera

Date: 1972

Designers: Edwin Land, Henry Dreyfuss

Manufacturer: Polaroid Corporation, Cambridge, MA, US

Dimensions: 25.4 × 12.7 × 17.8cm (10 × 5 × 7in)

After half a century, Edwin Land's instant camera is still a beautiful and contemporary-looking object; its leather inset panel and brushed-steel case gives it the look of a cigar case. Launched in 1972, the SX 70 was the culmination of Land's attempts to liberate photography from the darkroom. This was the closest that analogue came to the instant gratification of the digital experience. Using the SX 70 was like performing magic. Press the button, hear the whoosh as the film cartridge emerged, and see the image take shape.

At its height in the 1980s, Polaroid had a £2.4 ($3) billion turnover and 21,000 employees. It was bankrupted less than 20 years later, unable to adjust to the digital explosion. Remarkably, Polaroid film, and cameras to use it, are being manufactured once again, to satisfy a hunger for things that people can touch and feel as an antidote to the slippery elusiveness of pixels.

Asahi Spotmatic F SLR camera

Date: 1973

Designer: Asahi Optical Co. Ltd

Manufacturer: Asahi Optical Co. Ltd,
Tokyo, Japan

Dimensions: 14.3 × 9.3 × 4.9cm (5½ × 3½ × 2in)

If the language of modern camera design had its roots in Germany with Leica and Zeiss, its most sophisticated expression came in the 1960s and 1970s, when Japanese manufacturers took the lead. They introduced both technical innovations, as well as the refinement of Japan's traditional attention to detailed design.

Asahi began manufacturing cameras with a built-in light meter in 1964. The Spotmatic name came from an initial concept of using a through-the-lens exposure system that would take spot readings, but, before the Spotmatic was launched, Asahi opted for a simpler method of metering light, deciding to keep the original name. Spotmatic cameras were distinguished by the refined quality of the detailing on the controls.

Olympus XA compact camera

Date: 1979

Design: Yoshihisa Maitani

Manufacturer: Olympus Corporation,
Tokyo, Japan

Dimensions: 10.2 × 6.4 × 4cm (4 × 2½ x 1½in)

One of the first Japanese companies to specialize in manufacturing cameras, over the course of many years Olympus addressed every aspect of the market – from professionals to casual amateurs. The XA was the culmination of chief designer Yoshihisa Maitani's long pursuit of the goal to make a 35mm camera small enough to fit into a shirt pocket, without compromising on quality.

The XA was cute to look at and, with its sliding cover protecting the lens, was as smooth as a matt-black egg. It had a piezo-electric shutter that took the place of a mechanical button. The reduced size is made possible by Maitani's ingenious reconfiguration of the lens array, with an internal focusing mechanism that does away with the need for a bulky lens barrel.

Sony Mavica still video camera

Date: 1981

Designer: Sony

Manufacturer: Sony, Tokyo, Japan

Dimensions: 13 × 8.9 × 5.3cm (5 × 3½ × 2in)

Sony entered the camera market only after its development of home video, relying on expertise based in its long dominance of magnetic recording tape. The Mavica (a name deriving from Magnetic Video Camera) started out as an analogue machine, even though it did not use photographic film. Instead, it stored analogue visual signals collected by a sensor on a floppy disk. To view the images, a special attachment was required that allowed the Mavica to be plugged into a television.

The Mavica was the product of a period of rapid transition in data technologies, at a time before the development of handheld digital cameras at the end of the 1980s, but when newspapers were already going online, and their journalists had started to use personal computers to communicate. Sony saw the camera as a bridge between the two technologies, allowing for photographic images to be readily transmitted to print and broadcast.

Polaroid Sun 660 instant camera

Date: 1981

Designer: Polaroid Corporation

Manufacturer: Polaroid Corporation, Cambridge, MA, US

Dimensions: 18.8 × 17.8 × 17.8cm (7½ × 7 × 7in)

The Sun 660 cameras combined an autofocus system patented by Polaroid that used sound waves to measure the distance to the subject and automatically adjusted the focus to achieve a sharp image, using its new 600 high-speed film type and a built-in flash. The flash is contained in a hinged element that folds down to cover the lens when the camera is not in use.

The Sun had a multi-element lens mounted on a rotating disc. The sonar autofocus, in the form of a gold circle on the front of the camera, detects the object the camera is pointed at, measures the distance, and selects one of five options for the lens focus that range from 5cm (2in) to infinity. It was the most sophisticated of Polaroid's many innovative products, capable of producing images instantly, but also of unusual quality.

Kodak Disc 4000 camera

Date: 1982

Designer: Eastman Kodak

Manufacturer: Eastman Kodak, Rochester, NY, US

Dimensions: 12 × 7.9 × 3.2cm (4¾ × 3 × 1¼in)

The Disc 4000 was meant to be Kodak's future. After relying on the Instamatic for the bulk of its consumer-market sales for two decades, Kodak needed something new and different to refresh its appeal in the 1980s. It came up with a miniature film, housed in a flat disc, holding just fifteen 10 × 8mm exposures, which would only work in a new purpose-made camera. At the time, Kodak still had the clout for other manufacturers to follow its lead, but disc cameras turned out to be a failure almost from the outset. They certainly looked sleek and modern, with a slim, rectangular format in a brushed aluminium fascia, but the minimal size of the negative meant that the quality of the prints was poor. *Forbes* magazine called it 'a flop – a humiliating Edsel of a product', referring to Ford's disastrous car. By 1999, Kodak abandoned production of the film, having given up on the camera years earlier.

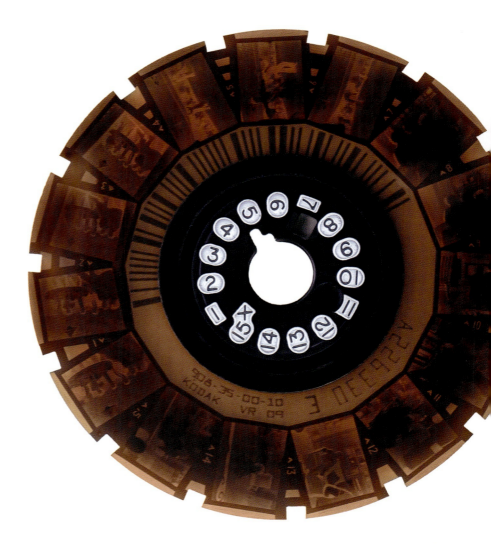

Canon T90 SLR camera

Date: 1986

Designers: Luigi Colani, Kunihisa Ito

Manufacturer: Canon Inc., Tokyo, Japan

Dimensions: 15.3 × 12.1 × 6.9cm

(6 × 4¾ × 2¾in)

Luigi Colani worked in a succession of German car-styling studios, before turning his attention to furniture and industrial design. He was fascinated by naturally occurring organic forms that he believed offered economy of means, as well as a powerful aesthetic language. He was introduced to Canon during the 1980s by Kunihisa Ito, and came up with a wide range of concept studies that pushed camera design toward shapes derived from the natural world. Colani proposed an underwater camera with a form suggestive of a sea creature. Canon asked him to explore shapes for what became the T90, intended to be a high-end camera, and launched it with Colani's signature. The injection-moulded body allowed for much more fluid forms than conventional manufacturing techniques at the time. Ito turned Colani's ideas into a shape that Canon were ready to put into production.

Konica KC-400 still video camera

Date: 1987

Manufacturer: Konica, Tokyo, Japan

Dimensions: 18.6 × 11.3 × 10.5cm
(7¼ × 4½ × 4in)

While the idea of still video cameras originated with Sony, other companies followed its lead, including Konica, a long-established Japanese camera maker. The KC-400 was aimed at professional users, such as photojournalists, who could afford to pay £3,250 ($4,000) for a complete system. It included purpose-made 5-cm (2-in) floppy disks, on which images were stored in the form of analogue scan lines. With its long-barrel lens and box-like projection to one side, the Konica-400 had little in common with the form of a conventional still camera. It was a transition between two entirely different categories of object, not quite a still camera, but not quite a fully formed video camera either. With its matt-black, unresolved collection of forms, the Konica-400 was bulky and technical-looking, rather than a seductive consumer-orientated object.

Olympus O-Product camera

Date: 1988

Designer: Naoki Sakai

Manufacturer: Olympus, Tokyo, Japan

Dimensions: 9.8 × 8.3 × 4.9cm (3¾ × 3¼ × 2in)

The concept of 'limited edition' comes from the art world, where lithographs, wood-cut prints, engravings on copper, or bronze casts were traditionally issued in editions of a dozen or fewer, to ensure that there was no loss of quality. By conceiving of the O-product as a limited edition, Olympus were playing with the nature of mass production, which by its nature is about the democratization of the object by making an unlimited number of perfect copies. Production was restricted to 20,000.

Olympus brought in Naoki Sakai as an outside consultant to create a striking new identity for one of its more pedestrian products. He took the working components of the Infinity Jnr, a basic point-and-shoot 35mm camera, and wrapped them in an aluminium body that, with its purist geometry, suggests nostalgia for the early days of modern cameras.

Canon Photura 35mm camera

Date: 1990

Designer: Canon Inc.

Manufacturer: Canon Inc., Tokyo, Japan

Dimensions: 10 × 7.4 × 15.6cm (4 × 3 × 6in)

The last days of analogue photography in the 1990s were marked by a wave of new forms and formats. It was like a final burst of baroque ideas of what cameras could be, even as film was facing its inevitable extinction. The Kyocera Samurai and the Canon Photura were both influenced by the impact made by the innovative form of Sony's Handycam in 1989, even though neither of them offered the ability to take moving pictures. They simply adopted the form of Sony's cameras, which could be operated using a single hand.

The Photura, known as the Epoca in Canon's European markets, and the Jet Boy in Japan, was a particularly striking object. It had a moulded-plastic tubular shape with a side strap. It was an object that offered users some of the playful qualities of a toy, with a push-button zoom that deployed a new lens and a clever autofocus function.

Olympus Écru camera

Date: 1991

Designers: Naoki Sakai, Shunji Yamanaka

Manufacturer: Olympus, Tokyo, Japan

Dimensions: Approx. 4 × 10.6 × 8.8cm
(1½ × 4¼ × 3½in)

The Écru, which is based on the working parts of a mass-produced Olympus compact film camera, the µ [mju:]-1, was Naoki Sakai's second project for Olympus. It has clear references to the Art Deco Bakelite era of the box Brownies (see page 125) made by Kodak in the 1940s. The cream-coloured plastic, the fluted façade, the rectangular form of the camera, and the silver-coated operating buttons were full of references to objects from the past, but not a recreation of any one single model. In an unusually subtle and creative way, Sakai was inventing a past that had never actually existed. His approach revealed the way in which design can be used to manipulate our emotions, to make us feel nostalgic for a past that did not exist. It was manufactured in a limited edition of 20,000 units.

Kenox FX-4 camera

Date: 1994

Designer: FA Porsche

Manufacturer: Samsung, Seoul, Korea

Dimensions: 14.9 × 8.3 × 7.4cm
(5¾ × 3¼ × 3in)

After Japan had overtaken Europe's consumer electronics companies and camera manufacturers in the 1970s, it started to move production to factories in other parts of Asia, where it could lower costs, but found itself being challenged by South Korean companies. Initially, Samsung offered low-cost, generic products, but then began to move up the value chain by building up brand identity to overtake Sony. The Kenox FX-4 was a significant example of this process in action. Samsung, which had been founded in 1938 as a trading company, had no previous experience making cameras. However, just as the analogue-film era was about to go into decline, Samsung started its own brand, Kenox, and hired the design studio founded by the Porsche-car dynasty to give its flagship product, the FX-4, a distinctive look and feel.

Olympus IS 500 SLR camera

Date: 2002

Designer: Olympus

Manufacturer: Olympus, Tokyo, Japan.
Made in China.

Dimensions: 12.5 × 8.7 × 12.4cm (5 × 3½ × 5in)

Olympus has had a long history of exploring distinctive new formats for its products. The IS 500 was its attempt to make a camera that would do everything for the user – selecting a focus and lens aperture all by itself – while also producing images with at least some of the qualities of a camera that demanded serious creative decisions from the user. It was something that might be described as an early form of artificial intelligence. It was an ambition reflected in the bulky and aggressive-looking form that the camera took.

This was an object that clearly suggested more ambitious aims than simply taking snapshots, even if it asked little more of its user than to press a button. Olympus built in a whole series of features that could mimic the qualities a skilled user could achieve with a traditional single-lens reflex camera.

Bell & Howell Filmo 70A cine camera

Date: 1923

Designers: Albert Howell, Donald Bell

Manufacturer: Bell & Howell, Chicago, IL, US

Dimensions: 2.3 × 17 × 27.9cm (1 × 6½ × 11in)

Albert Howell, an inventor, and Donald Bell, who had worked as a cinema projectionist, started Bell & Howell before World War I to manufacture equipment for Hollywood filmmakers. Their products helped to popularize the 35mm format. In 1917, they designed a camera that could offer a cheaper alternative to 35mm film simply by splitting it in half and using 17.5mm film. But, when Kodak offered them the chance to work with its new 16mm film, they realized the advantages of a partnership with a company that had national reach, and redesigned their original product. The result was the Filmo range of cameras, which were aimed at the amateur market. The 70A was the first in a series that remained in production until the end of the 1960s. It had a spring drive and held 30m (100ft) of film, which at 16 frames per second could produce about four minutes of playback.

Eastman Kodak 16mm movie film

Date: 1923

Designer: Eastman Kodak

Manufacturer: Eastman Kodak, Rochester, NY, US

Dimensions: 7.6cm (3in) diameter

George Eastman always looked for ways to grow the market for the products that his factories made. Producing expensive 35mm film for commercial cinema studios was never going to be enough for him. He wanted moviemaking to be affordable enough for ordinary consumers. They might not have the resources or skill to make a feature-length film, but were interested in capturing the first steps taken by their grandchildren or the graduation ceremony of their daughters. They did not need images with particular sharpness and could only afford limited amounts of film. Kodak produced its first 16mm film aimed at this audience in 1923. The first 35mm films made for Hollywood used a highly flammable nitrate base, while Kodak used 16mm cellulose acetate that they called 'safety' film.

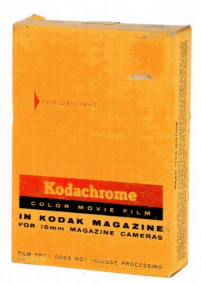

Cine Kodak Eight: 8mm movie film

Date: 1932

Designer: Eastman Kodak

Manufacturer: Eastman Kodak, Rochester, NY, US

Dimensions: 7.6cm (3in) diameter

Just as 16mm film was originally created as an affordable alternative to 35mm film to give amateurs the chance to make cine films, so in turn Kodak introduced the 8mm format, which was less expensive than its predecessor. Over time, 16mm equipment was refined to the point that it could be used by professional broadcasters, such as the BBC. Kodak initially introduced 8mm film by adapting existing 16mm film stock, punching extra holes along its edges. The resulting film was run through the camera twice, each time exposing only one edge. The exposed film was processed and then cut in half, allowing the two halves to be spliced together. A 7.6m (25ft) spool could make one continuous 15.2m (50ft) film, or a sequence four minutes long, when the camera was set to a speed of 16 frames per second.

Bolex H16 16mm cine camera

Date: 1935

Designer: Paillard-Bolex

Manufacturer: Paillard-Bolex, Geneva, Switzerland

Dimensions: Approx. 32 × 12 × 26cm (12½ × 4¾ × 10¼in)

Jacques Bogopolsky's name lives on in the first two letters of the Bolex brand, but he had already sold his patents to the Paillard company five years before the Bolex H16 had its debut in 1935. Paillard manufactured a wide range of products including Hermes typewriters and Thorens gramophones.

The H16 was the beginning of a long series of cine cameras that spanned the gap between professional and amateur use. The basic format and the lens quality remained, while the camera was made available with a selection of lenses and controls that could be used to feed in film at variable speeds. Over the years, the H16 was enhanced with the introduction of devices that helped the user achieve an accurate focus more easily.

Pathé Duplex Lido cine camera

Date: 1954

Designer: Roger Tallon

Manufacturer: SCI Pathé, Paris, France

Dimensions: 5.6 × 12.6 × 16cm (2¼ × 5 × 6¼in)

While most cine-camera manufacturers offered amateurs 8mm film, Pathé had been making 9.5mm film since the 1920s. Unlike 8mm film, which Kodak perforated on both edges to allow it to be mechanically driven in front of the lens, Pathé put holes only between each frame, which allowed for a much larger image area and better-quality results.

In an attempt to boost sales of the format, Pathé came up with the idea of running the film horizontally through the camera rather than vertically. It was wide enough to run

through the camera twice and, when it was returned from processing, the film was split in two, offering twice as much running time. The product offered better value for money and, with a stylish-looking case designed by the up-and-coming designer Roger Tallon, Pathé believed that they had a world beater. In fact, the machine was too complicated to have much success, and subsequent versions of the Lido were simplified.

Nizo Heliomatic 8 S2R 8mm cine camera

Date: 1954

Designers: Richard Fischer, Robert Oberheim, Dieter Rams

Manufacturer: Niezoldi & Kramer, Munich, West Germany

Dimensions: Approx. 60 × 125 × 165cm (23½ × 49¼ × 65in)

The long-established firm of Niezoldi & Kramer was one of the pioneers of Germany's cine-camera industry, technically innovative and noted for the quality of its manufacturing processes. It became well-known for its Nizo cine products. The Heliomatic 8 range, produced in the 1950s, had an aluminium body, a clockwork drive, and was equipped with a pistol grip and trigger mechanism. There was a handle on the top, and a leather carrying case.

Mamiya 8mm Super GL cine camera

Date: 1958

Designer: Mamiya

Manufacturer: Mamiya Optical Co. Ltd,
Tokyo, Japan

Dimensions: 19 × 12.7 × 6.3cm (7½ × 5 × 2½in)

Mamiya was a company that specialized in still cameras, but also produced a range of cine cameras in the late 1950s and 1960s. The first cine cameras used wind-up mechanisms to drive through the film, which came in 15.2m- (50ft-) long reels, and could typically offer no more than four minutes of playing time. This was not the way to produce a feature film, but offered a means of recording family moments in the snapshot-style that a smartphone does today. Unlike today, watching these films also required a projector and, most likely, a demountable screen. Mamiya had a battery-powered electric motor to drive the film, a built-in light meter and a sturdy metal body.

Kodak Brownie 8mm cine camera

Date: 1960

Designer: Eastman Kodak

Manufacturer: Eastman Kodak, Rochester, NY, US

Dimensions: 6.35 × 14 × 14cm (2½ × 5½ × 5½in)

As the use of the Brownie brand suggests, Kodak attempted to bring the same kind of low-cost simplicity to moviemaking with its 8mm camera that the original box Brownie had for still photography. The camera, which had a fixed-focus lens, originally sold for just £19.99 ($24.50). It was driven by a clockwork motor and had a capacity of just 7.6m (25ft) of 8mm movie film – about enough for roughly two minutes of projection time. The camera's case was formed out of moulded polystyrene, which housed a phenolic front panel that held both

the lens and shutter mechanism in place. There was an exposure control with a dial around the lens, which used symbols reflecting light conditions for those users unfamiliar with the f-stop numbers that they corresponded to. F-stop numbers represent the width of the lens aperture, which controls both the amount of light the film is exposed to and the depth of field that will be in sharp focus in the resulting image.

Yashica U-matic 8mm cine camera

Date: 1961

Designer: Yashica

Manufacturer: Yashica, Nagano, Japan

Dimensions: 25.4 × 6.3 × 16.7cm
(10 × 2½ × 6½in)

The Yashica company was born as a components supplier in 1949, and started out manufacturing electric clocks, before moving into making cameras. It branched out into cine cameras in the 1950s, and introduced a more modern range with the U-matic. The company grew rapidly and was acquired by Kyocera, another Japanese company, which closed the brand in 2005. Inspired perhaps by the Impossible Project's revival of Polaroid manufacturing, the new owners of the Yashica trademark launched a crowdfunding campaign in 2017 to bring Yashica and the qualities of analogue film back to the consumer.

Bell & Howell 414 PD 8mm cine camera

Date: 1961

Designer: Bell & Howell

Manufacturer: Bell & Howell, Chicago, IL, US

Dimensions: 14.5 × 7 × 17cm (5½ × 4¾ × 2in)

The 26 seconds of film taken by Abraham Zapruder in Dallas on a November day in 1963 using a Bell & Howell 414 PD cine camera were for many years the most scrutinized moving images in the history of the world. Using a piece of equipment aimed at the higher end of the amateur market – it cost £154 ($189) at the time, about the price of an Apple smartphone in today's money – Zapruder was horrified to find that he had captured the assassination of President John F. Kennedy. He sold his film to *Life* magazine, which printed them frame by frame. Those images subsequently became a central part of the investigations into the assassination, which included a forensic examination of the design and characteristics of the camera, and what they might mean for the interpretation of the images that it had made.

Minolta Zoom 8 cine camera

Date: 1962

Designer: Minolta Camera Co. Ltd

Manufacturer: Minolta Camera Co. Ltd, Osaka, Japan

Dimensions: 22.1 × 18.6 × 7cm (8¾ × 7¼ × 2¾in)

Cine-camera manufacturers needed to recruit first-time users to buy their products by drawing attention to their usability and affordability. Minolta's advertising campaigns featured ski slopes, suggesting the ability of this new gadget to capture the glamour of the activities that their users were able to pursue. It also underlined the technical capacity of the product, and the fact that it did not require expertise in use: 'Now shoot in any available light,' ran the campaign. 'You sight and shoot, and that's all,' ran the copy. Yet, potential users were also reassured that they were not missing out on image quality. The Minolta Zoom 8 might have a simple two-tone box shape, but it would be 'every bit as accurate as the hand-held light meters the professionals use', suggested the sales pitch. It could focus to as close as 1.5m (5ft), but it was cheap. 'Compare feature for feature and then compare the price,' urged Minolta's advertising.

Minolta Autopak-8 D4 cine camera

Date: 1970

Designer: Minolta Camera Co. Ltd

Manufacturer: Minolta Camera Co. Ltd, Osaka, Japan

Dimensions: 7 × 12.7 × 20cm (2¾ × 5 × 4in)

Minolta aimed its Autopak-8 D4 at a more sophisticated variety of user. The advertising promised 'a significant step forward for the 8mm creative revolution', and the Autopak claimed to offer 16mm-level quality thanks to its special features and accessories, such as an electromagnetic shutter release in place of a mechanical button. It also had what the company called an 'intervalometer', which was an automatic repeating mechanism that allowed for single-frame exposure at any of eight different time intervals.

Minolta suggested to users that these features might allow for nature studies of blooming flowers or billowing clouds. There was even a remote-control unit, to allow the user to include themselves in the frame, and the ability to couple the camera with a cassette player to add sound to the picture.

Braun Nizo 801 8mm cine camera

Date: 1975

Designers: Richard Fischer, Robert
Oberheim, Dieter Rams

Manufacturer: Braun AG, Frankfurt,
West Germany

Dimensions: 21 × 27 × 7cm (8¼ × 10¾ × 2¾in)

German camera manufacturer Niezoldi &
Kramer struggled financially in the 1950s,
and was acquired by Braun in 1962. Braun had
transformed itself in the years after World War
II from a manufacturer of dependable radios
into a company that was associated with the
essence of contemporary design.

Braun, itself, would subsequently become
the subsidiary of an American conglomerate,
but for the following 18 years, the combination
of the design rigour of Braun and the technical
excellence of Nizo produced a series of
remarkably refined industrial objects. The
Nizo 801, sculpted for the shape of the user's
hand, was one of the most impressive, and
transformed the identity of Nizo products
from the sturdy engineering look of its earlier
incarnation (see page 153).

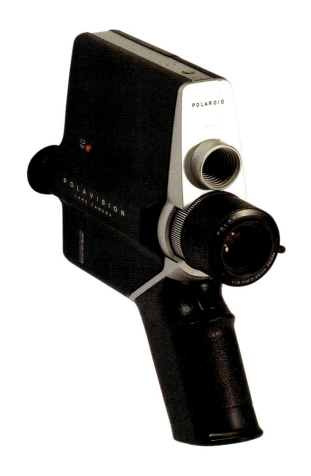

Polaroid Polavision cine camera

Date: 1977

Designer: Edwin Land

Manufacturer: Polaroid Corporation, Cambridge, MA, US

Dimensions: Viewer: 28.5 × 29.2 × 42.7cm (11¼ × 11½ × 16¾in); Camera: 21.6 × 6.4 × 18.4cm (8½ × 2½ × 7¼in)

The Polavision system was Edwin Land's final enormously ambitious project for Polaroid. It had three components – a camera, a film cassette and a television-size viewer. At a time when 8mm cine film had to be mailed to a laboratory for processing, Polavision was viewable in less than a minute, as the processing took place inside the viewer. It had a slot to insert the cassette, which was projected onto the screen, offering up to three-and-a-half minutes of moving colour pictures – adequate by the standards of the time, and undoubtedly ingenious. The problem was that Polavision could not record sound, and its colour rendering was much less impressive than what the SX 70 (see page 139) could offer. It was a disastrous, and costly, failure. Polaroid wrote off £55.5 ($68) million, and Land eventually left his own company.

The Impact of Television Broadcasting

The technology to make television broadcasting and viewing possible was one thing. Putting it to work to provide something worth watching was another. The more there was available to see on a television, the more incentive there was to purchase one. And the larger the potential audience, measured by the number of television screens, the more that broadcasters were ready to invest in offering content. From the beginning, television had two different models – a public broadcasting model that supported news and cultural programming, and a commercial version that funded content by selling advertising space on its programming.

In the seven years between the start of regular television broadcasts by the BBC and 1939, when World War II interrupted the service, no more than 20,000 sets had been sold in Britain. In 1950, just 4 per cent of British homes had a television, but by 1957, it was more than 50 per cent. By the 1960s, there was a television in three out of every four homes in the country, and eventually above 95 per cent of households had at least one television. The growth of television was even faster in the US. The number of television sets in use there rose from 6,000 in 1946, to 12 million by 1951. By 1955, half of all US homes had one.

By 2012, all of the British sets were technologically obsolete, as the BBC had completed its five-year plan to switch off its analogue broadcasts. Digital television is a different experience, and the proportion of viewers who tune in to traditional broadcast television each week is in steep decline, down to 79 per cent in 2022.

In the 1960s in the UK, with only two BBC channels, and a single commercial rival, broadcasting for limited hours, there were vast audiences for the most popular programmes, which the entire country watched at the same time. In the process, television transformed culture. The sets were large and expensive pieces of furniture that occupied a conspicuous place at the centre of the home. Television was a shared experience for entire families, before smaller, cheaper sets were distributed around the home.

Even more dramatic was the impact of televised news on political life, bringing the trauma of famine and war into living rooms. The effect wore off, but in the US the constant footage of Vietnam, often described as the first war to be televised, fuelled mass protests. Governments anxious about the impact on the electorate, tried to control political content with varying degrees of subtlety.

In both the US and Europe, the universal availability of television has also had a huge impact on the cinema industry, reducing cinema-going by one third almost immediately, threatening the viability of the old 1,000-seat picture houses, and transforming the output of the studios.

(1) Very few inventions are the result of a single technical insight, and television is no exception. Without the Nipkow disc, invented in 1884, the Scottish engineer John Logie Baird would not have been able to pioneer his model C30 line television, which he is pictured here demonstrating in 1934.

(2) The extent of the impact that television could have on political life became clear during the 1960 presidential campaign. Jack Kennedy and Richard Nixon's first televised debate was watched by over 70 million people.

(3) In the 1950s, the television set rapidly became an essential part of domestic equipment in the majority of households, thanks to credit and hire-purchase finance. Competing manufacturers sold their sets by advertising smart technology.

(4) The French manufacturer Grandin tried to suggest that their televisions were in the same league of precision and performance as a Mirage fighter jet.

2

3

4

Bush TV22 television

Date: 1950

Designer: Bush Radio Ltd

Manufacturer: Bush Radio Ltd,
Plymouth, England

Dimensions: 39 × 40 × 32cm
(15¼ × 15¾ × 12½in)

The Bush TV22 monochrome television
receiver brought television viewing into large
numbers of British homes for the first time.
It was the set around which the country
gathered to watch the coronation of Queen
Elizabeth II in June 1953. It was restricted to a
black-and-white picture and what today would
seem like a diminutive 22.9-cm (9-in) screen
that offered a far from sharply defined image.
It could, however, be tuned by the owner to
either of the two BBC transmitters in use in
1950. In 1955, when commercial television
was introduced in Britain, Bush manufactured
a Band III convertor that allowed its existing
sets to be adapted to pick up the new stations.

The Bush TV22 came in a walnut-effect
Bakelite case and had a curvaceous Art
Deco-style shape.

Panoramic 111 console stand television

Date: 1957

Designer: Philippe Charbonneaux

Manufacturer: Téléavia, Toulouse, France

Dimensions: 140 × 63 × 59cm
(55 × 25 × 23¼in)

Sud Aviation, the company that built France's first jetliner, the Caravelle, diversified into consumer electronics by setting up Téléavia, a company that was later absorbed by Thomson. One of its first products, the Panoramic, was an early example of a high-definition television set in commercial production. It mixed advanced technology with radical aesthetics. Some accounts attribute its design to Flaminio Bertoni, the Italian who spent most of his career in France, where he worked closely with André Citroën. But the Pompidou Centre, which holds an example in its collection, is confident that it is the work of another car designer, Philippe Charbonneaux.

The set is split into two parts that seem to have little connection visually or conceptually. The screen is contained in a two-tone organic shell form that can swivel above the lower element, a piece of angular walnut furniture, which contains the tuner, controls and loudspeaker. The whole sits on four legs equipped with castors.

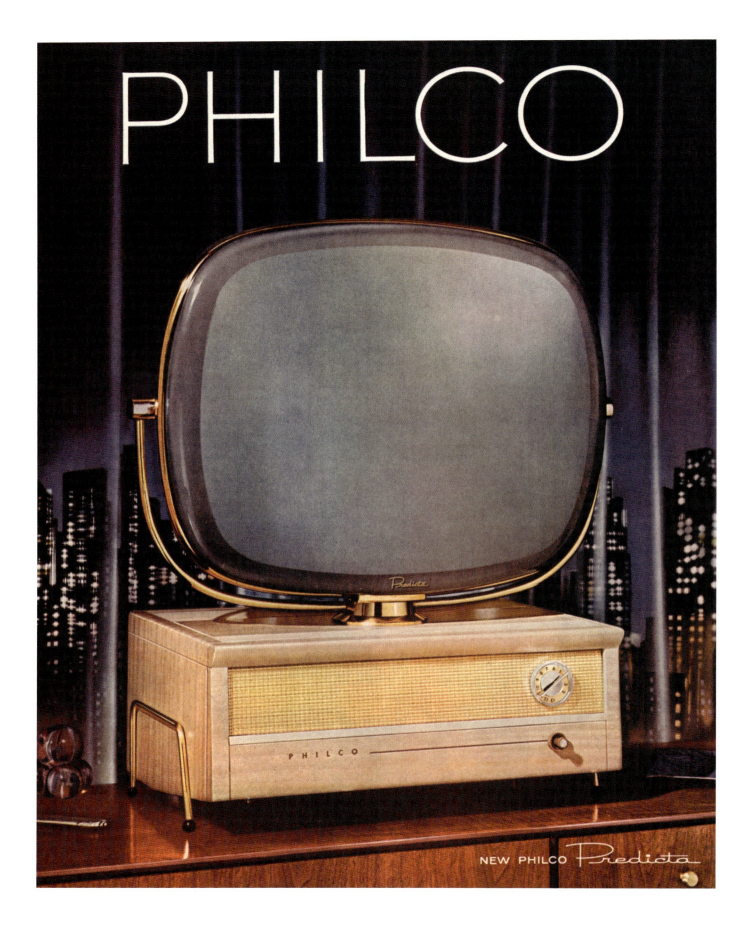

Philco Predicta Princess 3410 television

Date: 1959

Designers: Herbert Gosweiler, Catherine Speyer Winkler, Severin L. Jonassen, Richard J. Whipple

Manufacturer: Philco (Philadelphia Storage Battery Company), Philadelphia, PA, US

Dimensions: 62.2 × 62.5 × 27.3cm (24½ × 24¾ × 10¾in)

The Philco company achieved early success with its black-and-white television sets, but found itself overtaken by RCA in the US market. The Predicta Princess, with its radical design and claims to represent advanced technology, was an essential part of its fight back. The somewhat breathless advertising campaign claimed the Princess came from the world of tomorrow.

In fact, the French company Téléavia had already launched the P111 (see page 165), which, like the Predicta Princess, split the television screen and the speaker and controls into two distinct parts. Catherine Speyer Winkler, one of the few women involved with the industrial design of television, produced a more resolved look for the 3410, holding the screen in a brass-finished frame that allowed it to tilt and swivel. There was a range of bases, some designed to be mounted on a shelf or a table, others that were floor standing. Some base units were finished in timber, others in painted metal or brightly coloured plastic.

Sony TV8-301 television

Date: 1960

Designer: Shimada Satoshi

Manufacturer: Sony, Tokyo, Japan

Dimensions: Approx. 22 × 21 × 25cm
(8¾ × 8¼ × 9¾in)

Sony's first portable television originated from co-founder Masuro Ibuka's conviction at the end of the 1950s that, despite the company's success with tape recorders and transistor radios, its future would depend on entering the television market. The TV8-301 was advertised as 'an all-transistor personal, truly portable'. None of this was strictly true: it was heavy, weighing 6kg (13¼lbs), and the batteries added another 1.8kg (4lbs). The tubular form with a vizor shielding the screen was a new configuration for the television. It revealed the essential nature of a cathode ray, which was usually kept hidden within a large boxy container. It is true that it was mostly transistorized, but a couple of valves were still needed. Early transistors were also susceptible to temperature fluctuations, making the TV8-301 a less-than-reliable buy. Production lasted just two years.

Doney portable television

Date: 1962

Designers: Marco Zanuso, Richard Sapper

Manufacturer: Brionvega, Milan, Italy

Dimensions: 29.8 × 34.9 × 29.8cm
(11¾ × 13¾ × 11¾in)

The Doney was one of the first all-transistor television sets, allowing for a much smaller casing than a comparable screen-sized valve set. Zanuso, an architect, and Sapper, an industrial designer, worked together to reduce the case to the minimum, tailoring it precisely to the dimensions of the 35.6-cm (14-in) screen at the front, where they stripped away the picture-frame setting that characterized many televisions at the time. The moulded, gloss-plastic case was slightly tapered and perforated with deep grooves to dissipate the heat from the cathode-ray tube. The set was designed to sit on a tabletop or a shelf, with adjustable chromed-steel feet to put it on the floor. It had a retractable metal carrying handle inset into the case.

Sony TV5-303 portable television

Date: 1962

Designer: Sony

Manufacturer: Sony, Tokyo, Japan

Dimensions: 14 × 20 × 19cm (5½ × 7¾ × 7½in)

The TV5-303 learned the lessons of its predecessor, the TV8-301. It was tested to destruction to see how it stood up to vibration, humidity and temperature changes. It was smaller and lighter, and far more reliable. It went through an extraordinarily elaborate development process, which involved the production of a new kind of cathode-ray tube. This was kept a closely guarded secret to avoid giving Sony's competitors an insight into their new strategy. By the time the transistor that revolutionized the television went on sale in Sony's New York showroom, they could not keep pace with demand.

The 5-303 had a less provisional-looking form than Sony's earlier attempt at a portable television – a rectangular case with a control panel to the right-hand side of the screen.

Portavia P111 television

Date: 1963

Designer: Roger Tallon

Manufacturer: Téléavia, Toulouse, France

Dimensions: 39 × 52 × 30cm
(15¼ × 20½ × 11¾in)

Just six years after Charbonneaux's curious-looking television (see page 165), Roger Tallon's design for Téléavia, which carries the same designation, looks like an altogether more confident piece of modernism. Interestingly, Téléavia went to another designer with a strong record in transport. Philippe Charbonneaux had worked in the car industry, Tallon was responsible for the industrial design of the French high-speed trains, the TGV.

Téléavia's advertising made use of its aerospace heritage. One advertisement featured the white plastic television set against an image of Concorde, the supersonic airliner, then still at the design stage. In an unsubtle hint about its portability, one magazine advert showed an elegant female – in a Chanel suit and white gloves – carrying the television. According to Tallon, the P111 'was the first time the shape, the function, and the material absolutely intertwined'.

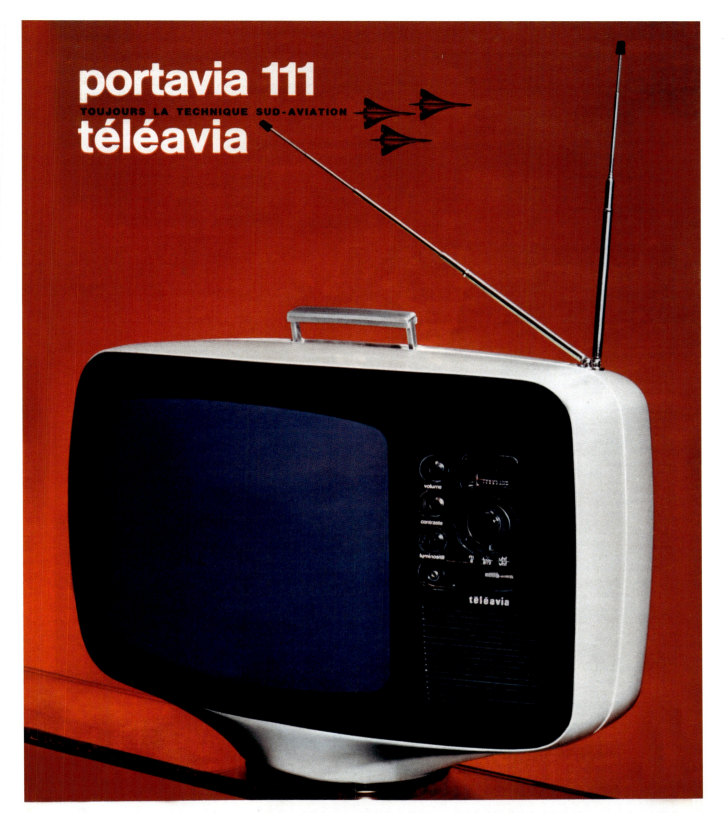

portavia 111
TOUJOURS LA TECHNIQUE SUD-AVIATION →
téléavia

l'élégance de ce prestigieux "portable" fera votre conquête

venez le voir chez l'un de nos 3.000 dépositaires (liste sur demande 48 Avenue Victor Hugo PARIS)

en voiture... en week-end... en caravane... d'une pièce à l'autre... en réunion   ECRAN 41 cm - FILTRAVIA - 2 CHAINES

Braun FS 80-1 television

Date: 1964

Designer: Dieter Rams

Manufacturer: Braun AG, Frankfurt, West Germany

Dimensions: 66 × 106.5 × 59cm
(26 × 42 × 23¼in) (including stand)

The FS 80 – with initials taken from the German word *fernseher* meaning television – was perhaps the most resolved of all the televisions produced by Braun, a series which began in 1955 with Hans Gugelot's FS-G. Dieter Rams was careful to consider the design of the back of the FS 80 with as much care as the front elevation. It was conceived as an unobtrusive, free-standing object mounted on a steel tube, with three feet that allowed it to rotate, reminiscent of Charles and Ray Eames' lounge chair. Rams allowed the curved glass screen of the cathode-ray tube to protrude just a fraction from the front surface of the box that contained it. Both box and screen have radiused corners, although the screen has a gentler curve. The rear surface has two rectangular grilles to dissipate heat, and is free of any clutter of wires.

Algol portable television

Date: 1964

Designers: Marco Zanuso, Richard Sapper

Manufacturer: Brionvega, Milan, Italy

Dimensions: 27.5 × 26.1 × 35.8cm
(10¾ × 10¼ × 14in)

Following on from the Doney (see page 169), Zanuso and Sapper's Algol was a more playful, and also more sophisticated, portable television – although both were limited to black-and-white reception. The Doney sits parallel to the floor, while the Algol tilts up at the screen end. Zanuso suggested that it was like a pet dog, looking up at its owner from the ground.

Like many of Brionvega's original products, the Algol has since been resurrected with modern electronics and is still in production today. Outwardly, it takes the same form, but is dependent on new technology to function.

WEGA Vision 2000 television

Date: 1964

Designer: WEGA

Manufacturer: WEGA (Wuerttembergische
Radio Gesellschaft), Stuttgart, West Germany

Dimensions: 64 × 60 × 42cm
(25¼ × 23½ × 16½in)

WEGA, the German radio, television and
record-player manufacturer, produced the
WEGA Vision 2000 in an attempt to create a
modern-looking television after a series of
conventional cabinet sets. While it was not
the only manufacturer to split the controls and
loudspeaker from the screen into two visually
distinct components, WEGA's was perhaps
the most convincing. It used teak for the
rectangular loudspeaker box, with a white
plastic inset for the control panel. The
cathode-ray-tube screen was accommodated

in plastic raised up from the teak box on a
rod that allowed it to swivel. It didn't stay in
production for long, but it set a precedent for
desktop computers in the 1980s. A prototype,
dated 1962 in the design collection of the
Neue Sammlung Pinakothek der Moderne
museum in Munich, was distinctive enough to
attract the attention of Hartmut Esslinger, who
would then go on to work for Apple computers.

Radiola RA 2870 television

Date: 1968

Designer: Radiola

Manufacturer: Radiola, Dreux, Paris, France

Dimensions: 37 × 38 × 37cm
(14½ × 15 × 14½in)

Radiola, which should not be confused with a Swedish manufacturer of radios and televisions with the same name, had been acquired by Philips from the Netherlands by the time it produced the RA 2870. The two-tone, spherical plastic case stood out from the rest of Radiola's product range, which was mostly made up of conventional-looking, rectangular timber-faced boxes. The sphere form, adopted at the time by many manufacturers of electronic equipment, suggested a bold, futuristic approach, influenced by the early satellites that had triggered the race to space. But, as far as technology was concerned, the Radiola had nothing to distinguish it from its competitors.

Sony KV 1310 Trinitron television

Date: 1968

Designers: Sony engineers, led by Masaru Ibuka and Susumu Yoshida

Manufacturer: Sony, Tokyo, Japan

Dimensions: 38.1 × 38.1 × 45cm
(15 × 15 × 17¾in)

By the time that Sony launched the first Trinitron, Japanese and American television stations had been broadcasting in colour for almost a decade. The problem was making affordable, high-quality receivers. In 1960, there were no more than 1,000 colour sets in the whole of Japan, and they cost the equivalent of £12,269 ($15,000) in today's prices. Early colour-television technology was based on three electron guns discharging on the inner face of the television tube. It was complicated to make, hard to mass produce, far from reliable, and did not produce sharp or bright colours. Sony developed the Trinitron system, which both simplified the manufacturing and produced a better picture. It brought the price down to £980 ($1,200), and Sony went on to sell 280 million sets.

Brionvega ST 201 Black Cube television

Date: 1969

Designers: Marco Zanuso, Richard Sapper

Manufacturer: Brionvega, Milan, Italy

Dimensions: 25 × 31.1 × 29.4cm
(9¾ × 12¼ × 11½in)

Designer Marco Zanuso said of the ST 201 that 'instead of a dialogue between spectator and object, a surreal tension would be created. When switched off, the object is an abstract thing that holds you at a distance, when on, it vanishes, and is replaced only by an image.' In fact, the acrylic cube was designed to conceal not just the screen, but the set's inner workings, too. It was originally supplied with an equally elegantly moulded plastic case that came in a contrasting snow-white colour.

Panasonic TR-001 miniature television

Date: 1970

Designer: Panasonic

Manufacturer: Matsushita Electric Industrial Co. Ltd, Osaka, Japan

Dimensions: 11 × 19 × 6cm (4¼ × 7½ × 2¼in)

Naturally, Panasonic advertised the TR-001 as the world's smallest television set; it was predominantly the point of making a screen so small. Measuring just 3.8cm (1½in) diagonally, it needed a magnifying lens to make sense of the images it showed. The lens came in the form of a detachable box-like fitting that covered the tiny screen. The TR-001 was powered by built-in rechargeable batteries.

In 1971, it won the German design prize, *Die Gute Industrieform* (Good Industrial Form), but the TR-001 is a curious-looking machine, with the control placed on the flat steel slab that forms its side and the screen placed at the narrow end, somehow suggesting that the set is always looking in the wrong direction.

Rigonda VL 100M television

Date: 1972

Designer: Mezon Works

Manufacturer: Mezon Works, Leningrad, Soviet Union

Dimensions: 53.3 × 38.1 × 58.4cm (21 × 15 × 23in)

The VL designation, supposedly in tribute to Vladimir Lenin, is a reflection of how different the assumptions behind product design in the Soviet Union were from those of the contemporary capitalist world. Consumer electronics in the Soviet Union were either manufactured for export to earn badly needed hard currency, or else made available very sparingly as privileges to favoured workers and Communist Party members at home. Any that were left were sold through waiting lists many months long in department stores that were mostly characterized by empty shelves. In either market there was little scope for designers to style their products. Soviet products sold in the West because they were the cheapest available by a considerable margin. At home, there was no alternative.

Rigonda's miniature television sets were not built to seduce, and they show their limitations. Yet, they have a certain kind of naïve charm.

Panasonic TR-005 Orbitel television

Date: 1973

Designer: Panasonic

Manufacturer: Matsushita Electric Industrial Co. Ltd, Osaka, Japan

Dimensions: 30.5 × 25.4 × 25.4cm (12 × 10 × 10in)

The advertising campaign for the Orbitel suggested that the set, clearly inspired by the aesthetics of Stanley Kubrick's film *2001: A Space Odyssey*, really was a visit from an alien civilization. 'Attention Earth People. I am called Orbitel. My number is TR-005. I am straight from the space age with technology to match. My advanced Elecro Tuner can take you from Very High Frequency to Ultra High Frequency programs without having to reach for a separate control. My 5-in (12.7-cm) black-and-white screen, measured diagonally, is so detailed, it will turn your head. But you won't have to, because I swivel a full 180 degrees on my beautiful tripod base.'

Beovision 3500 television

Date: 1974

Designers: David Lewis, Henning Moldenhawer

Manufacturer: Bang & Olufsen, Struer, Denmark

Dimensions: 61 × 41 × 42cm (24 × 16¼ × 16½in)

David Lewis was Jacob Jensen's successor as Bang & Olufsen's lead designer. He shared Jensen's preference for simplicity and pure geometry, but added his own distinctive take on design. It was this continuity, together with a reputation for technical innovation and acoustic quality, that allowed Bang & Olufsen to maintain its own independent identity, long after most of its European peers, such as Braun, WEGA and Brionvega, had given up. The Beovision 3500, with its svelte, white-plastic case, carefully designed control panels, and circular brushed-steel stand, was a new departure for the company, representing a move away from timber cabinets. It was intended to be seen as a free-standing object, with front, back and sides detailed with the same sensitivity to its context.

Euromatic 405 television

Date: 1976

Designer: Kauno Radijo Gamykla

Manufacturer: Kauno Radijo Gamykla, Vilnius, Lithuania, Soviet Union

Dimensions: 24.5 × 16.5 × 25.5cm
(9½ × 6½ × 10in)

After Lithuania was annexed to the Soviet Union during World War II, Stalin established the Kauno Radijo Gamykla, or KRG, as a state-owned factory. It made consumer electronics for the whole of the Soviet Union, as well as other satellite states. Initially, it produced radios, although did not offer shortwave frequencies, as these would have allowed listeners to pick up Western broadcasts. The product range expanded to include tape recorders and, after 1973, black-and-white television sets. These were luxuries in the domestic market, where they were known as the Silelis or the Elektronika. They were sold cheaply in Western Europe, where they were branded as the Euromatic, to raise hard currency.

Panasonic TR 535 television

Date: 1976

Designer: Panasonic

Maunfacturer: Matsushita Electric Industrial Co. Ltd, Osaka, Japan

Dimensions: 32.4 × 12.7 × 25.4cm
(12¾ × 5 × 10in)

The TR 535 was one of a range of battery-powered portable televisions manufactured by Panasonic. Unlike the smallest of the range – the TR 515, which had a tiny screen positioned at the front of the box – the TR 535 had a somewhat larger screen that popped up from the top of the box when in use, offering a better viewing angle. It could be pushed back in when being carried by the handle.

Sony KV 1375 portable television

Date: 1977

Designer: Sony

Manufacturer: Sony, Tokyo, Japan

Dimensions: 33.7 × 43.7 × 36.6cm
(13¼ × 17¼ × 14½in)

By the late 1970s, the market for colour televisions in Japan and America was nearing saturation. Sony's success with the Trinitron had been based on technical excellence and affordability. The KV 1375, known as the Citation model, had to seduce potential customers. The name refers to the new Citation business jet, closely associated with modernity, glamour and efficiency.

The set was marketed as a 'personal' television – an open invitation to customers to purchase more than one set for their homes. The KV 1375 was designed for the kitchen and the bedroom, or the student dorm room, as well as the living room. The set had a handle, which also incorporated an aerial, to justify its claim to portability, although at 5kg (11lbs), you would not want to carry it far.

WEGA 3050 television

Date: 1978

Designer: Hartmut Esslinger

Manufacturer: WEGA (Wuertermbergische Radio Gesellschaft), Stuttgart, West Germany

Dimensions: Approx. 64 × 67 × 48cm
(25¼ × 26½ × 19in)

When Hartmut Esslinger began working for WEGA, it was still a family-owned electronics business based in Stuttgart, where he was a student. WEGA was going through a generational shift, and was looking for a new design language for its products. Esslinger, who set up the Frog design consultancy shortly afterward, was happy to oblige. The collaboration was to result in some striking designs, but did not maintain WEGA's independence. In 1975, it was acquired by Sony. Esslinger's involvement with the WEGA brand survived the change of ownership, and the 3050 television set is from that period.

Sinclair Microvision TV1A pocket television

Date: 1978

Designer: John Pemberton

Manufacturer: Sinclair Radionics,
Cambridge, England

Dimensions: 17 × 10.4 × 4.4cm
(6¾ × 4 × 1¾in)

Clive Sinclair's ideas about miniaturizing
technology, and making it affordable, were
given a convincing visual identity by John
Pemberton, the industrial designer who
worked with him. The Microvision was an
important example. The rights to manufacture
Sinclair's first attempt at a miniature television
were later sold to Binatone, who made a
cheaper looking plastic case rather than the
stylish metal box that Pemberton designed for
the original. The later version used less power,
but still had the electronic components that
allowed it to be used anywhere in the world.

Sony Watchman FD-210 personal television

Date: 1982

Designer: Sony

Manufacturer: Sony, Tokyo, Japan

Dimensions: 8.7 × 19.8 × 3.3cm
(3½ × 7¾ × 1¼in)

The Watchman brand aimed to do for personal
television what the Walkman had done for
personal stereo. The first model had a
black-and-white, 5-cm (2-in) display, and
weighed around 650g (23oz). Liquid Crystal
Display (LCD) flat screens would soon make
high-quality miniature displays, but Sony were
working with cathode-ray tubes – which were
bulky. Sony's engineers managed to shrink
the volume by changing the geometry of the
relationship between the so-called electron
gun and the tube, placing them in parallel
inside the Watchman.

Sony produced a stream of Watchman
models in different styles and with different
capabilities. They moved from black-and-white
to colour screens, offered water-resistant
Sports models, and swelled in size.

Seiko LCD television wristwatch

Date: 1982

Designer: Seiko Epson Corporation

Manufacturer: Seiko Epson Corporation, Suwa, Nagano, Japan

Dimensions: Screen: 3.2 × 3.2cm (1¼ × 1¼in)

For Seiko, the idea of a television wristwatch was as much a marketing opportunity as a practical consumer product. It reached international markets a year after its launch in Japan, when Roger Moore, playing James Bond, used one in the film *Octopussy*. The LCD screen had a time display, but to use it as a television, it had to be hooked up to a separate tuner the size of a small transistor radio. In order to add sound you needed to plug in headphones, too. The Seiko operating manual suggested placing the tuner in an inside jacket pocket and trailing the wire connection to the steel watch through the jacket sleeve.

The television wristwatch was never more than a gadget, but nevertheless it pointed to the direction that technology would take. When Apple introduced successful wearable computing, it was with a device that took the familiar form of the wristwatch.

Sinclair Flatscreen TV80 television

Date: 1983

Designer: Rick Dickinson

Manufacturer: Sinclair Research Ltd,
Cambridge, England

Dimensions: 40 × 10 × 18cm (15¾ × 4 × 7in)

Sinclair Research Ltd described its TV80
as a flat-screen television but, in fact, it was
dependent on a specially made cathode-ray
tube placed behind a flat sheet of Perspex.
Cathode-ray tubes were already an obsolete
technology by this time, as liquid crystal
screens were being tested. The television was
certainly small – so small, in fact, that a Fresnel
magnifying lens was placed in front of the
5-cm (2-in) screen to make the tiny picture
seem larger than it really was.

The TV80's most technically advanced
feature was its capacity to be used anywhere,
enabled by switching between the four
different broadcasting systems in use around
the world. Sinclair was also an early user of
lithium batteries for the TV80, an innovation
that they shared with Polaroid cameras.

Epson ET-10 miniature television

Date: 1984

Designer: Seiko Epson Corporation

Manufacturer: Seiko Epson Corporation, Suwa, Nagano, Japan

Dimensions: 16 × 80 × 3.1cm (6¼ × 31½ × 1¼in)

Founded in 1942, the roots of the Seiko company were in watch manufacturing, where it was quick to develop new timekeeping technologies, and made quartz watches from 1969 onward. Seiko developed a pioneering liquid-crystal digital watch in 1973, which was the starting point for a continuing research programme aimed at a commercial active-matrix liquid-crystal visual display. This enabled Seiko to become a late entrant to the already crowded field of television manufacturing. The Epson ET-10 had a 5-cm (2-in) square screen set in a box that had a marked resemblance to a transistor radio. It was known as the Epson Elf in the US and the Televian in Japan.

Panasonic TR-1030P miniature television

Date: 1984

Designer: Panasonic

Manufacturer: Matsushita Electric Industrial Co. Ltd, Osaka, Japan

Dimensions: 15 × 8 × 4cm (6 × 3 × 1½in)

Packing so many intricate circuits into such a tiny space was a considerable achievement. But Panasonic's TR-1030P, also known as the Travelvision, did not produce an ideal viewing experience. As with most miniature televisions, it came with a magnifying lens that fitted over the black-and-white cathode-ray screen to produce a more acceptable picture. In order to achieve a workable viewing angle, the case had a fold-out foot, allowing the screen, flush with the front face of the set, to be tilted up toward the viewer.

Panasonic Alpha Tube TH28-DM03
television monitor

Date: 1985
Designer: Panasonic
Manufacturer: Matsushita Electric Industrial
Co. Ltd, Osaka, Japan
Dimensions: 69 × 64 × 59.2cm
(27¼ × 25¼ × 23¼in)

The Alpha Tube monitor was Panasonic's
response to Sony's development of the Profeel
range (see page 188), and its recognition that
the nature of viewing was shifting away from
exclusive broadcast television, toward the use
of video. Both Sony and Panasonic expected
video to develop in a similar way to consumer
audio and result in component systems.

In design terms, the Alpha Tube makes
the essential form of the cathode-ray tube
apparent. The monitor is no longer an attempt
to hide it inside a boxy cabinet of more or less

attractive shape. Rather, the set is the tube.
Panasonic suggested that the starting point for
the process was to place a naked cathode-ray
tube on the floor. With the screen tilted up at
10 degrees to enable it to be seen comfortably
by someone seated on the floor, the Alpha
Tube's form emulated the Japanese domestic
way of life that features tatami mats and futons
placed directly on the floor.

Sharp 3 LS 36 miniature television

Date: 1986

Designer: Sharp

Manufacturer: Sharp, Osaka, Japan

Dimensions: Approx. 15.2 × 25.4 × 17.8cm (6 × 10 × 7in)

Industrial design in the mid-1980s was dominated by a wave of post-modernism. Consumers could be reasonably confident that manufacturers were offering reliable products, and no longer needed the reassurance of functional, technocratic-looking televisions or music systems. Instead, they began to take on a playful, toy-like quality. Sharp was particularly associated with this tendency, exemplified by the 3 LS 36 miniature television. For no obvious reason, it is divided into two elements – a base and a screen connected by

a tilting mechanism, giving it some of the winsome quality of a domestic pet. But it was the shocking pink colour that attracted the most attention. Purists such as Dieter Rams, who believed in making domestic appliances as unobtrusive as possible, were offended.

Sony Profeel Pro KX-21HV1 television

Date: 1986

Designer: Haryuki Kato

Manufacturer: Sony, Tokyo, Japan

Dimensions: 40.5 × 30.4 × 50.6cm
(16 × 12 × 20in)

The Profeel took a radical new approach to television screens, both visually and conceptually. It was developed by Sony to take account of the multiplying sources of video input. The television screen was not necessarily going to be used to watch broadcast television, and the boundaries between professional and home use were being blurred.

The Profeel set out to provide high-quality images on a monitor screen as part of a system of components that offered the same potential for video that a high-fidelity system had for sound. The monitor would need to be used with either a tuner, a VCR or a personal computer.

Visually, the Profeel was different, too. Contained within an open cube, it became popular in exhibition displays, where it could be stacked up to create a video wall, displaying either multiple images or forming a single large image.

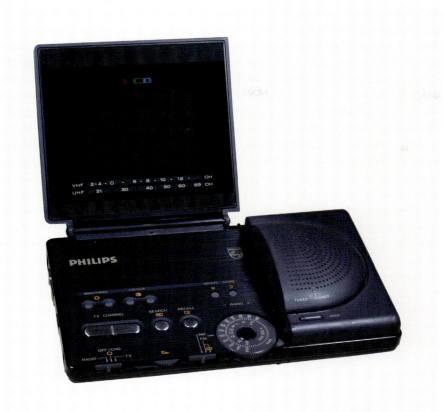

Philips LCD pocket colour television 3LC2050

Date: 1990

Designer: Philips

Manufacturer: Philips, Eindhoven, Netherlands. Made in Japan.

Dimensions: 16.3 × 3.7 × 11.5cm (6½ × 1½ × 4½in)

Like a laptop computer, the 3LC2050 television set has a hinged top, which opens when in use to reveal the screen, as well as the tuning and volume controls. The loudspeaker sits alongside the screen and can also be used to listen to radio broadcasts. Folding the screen flat protects it from damage, should you choose to actually carry it in your pocket.

Jim Nature portable television

Date: 1994

Designer: Philippe Starck

Manufacturer: Saba, Villingen, Germany, for Thomson Consumer Electronics, France

Dimensions: 37.1 × 40.2 × 38.1cm (14½ × 15¾ × 15in)

Starting out as a radio manufacturer, Saba made its first television in 1951. The brand was acquired by the French conglomerate Thomson, 30 years later, but the merged business struggled in the face of low-cost Asian competitors. Its last-ditch defence was to appoint Philippe Starck to design a range of radical new products. Jim Nature, with its moulded woodchip cabinet (a knowing reference to the wood cases of early television sets), was one of the most interesting. There was a fabric carrying handle, and a plastic control panel was inset into the case in a mildly unsettling contrast between rough and smooth. Flat-screen technology would soon make Jim Nature's cathode-ray technology obsolete, and Thomson did not survive as a television manufacturer.

Philippe Starck

Philippe Starck's prolific career as a furniture designer began with a commission from the French president François Mitterrand for his suite at the Élysée Palace. By the time the Thomson group recruited Starck as its creative director, he had already made his name designing nightclubs and fashion-conscious hotels and restaurants for Ian Schrager, the inventor of the boutique hotel. Starck was one of the figureheads of the 1980s as the designer decade, constantly being photographed for magazine covers and offering his tongue-in-cheek justifications for designing three-legged café chairs; one less leg for the waiters to risk tripping over, he claimed.

In a last-ditch attempt to give a radical new identity to Thomson, the struggling consumer electronics company that had been nationalized by the French government, Starck was brought in as much for his star quality as for his technical abilities. For a while, he transformed the role of the designer from a technician into a showman. Thomson looked for a touch of Starck stardust to differentiate its generic-looking products.

Starck pushed Thomson's product line in new directions. He had developed a playful, distinctive style – a kind of updated Art Deco with a touch of surrealism – and a fondness for giving his products unlikely names. He called one of his clock radios Coo Coo, and named another model the Moa Moa. Discarding the conventional box shape adopted by most radios, he designed a trumpet-shaped alternative which he called Lalala. The Moosk was an organic, freeform cloud, which could hang on the wall and be tuned to both AM and FM stations.

Starck also disrupted the conventions of television design, mixing wood and plastic. The Jim Nature portable television (see page 189) used chipboard, but he also played with glossy veneer – a reminder of those early television sets that tried to look more like polite drawing-room furniture than a technical machine. For one project, he even liberated the cathode-ray tube from its usual container, and set it free to rock from side to side on the floor.

Thomson manufactured televisions that Starck had designed for its Saba subsidiary, supplied Telefunken with boom boxes and radios, and Alessi with clocks. They represented a kind of baroque, last phase for a European electronics industry that had already been eclipsed by Asian manufacturers. In the end, Starck's stream of inventive designs from 1995 to 1997 was not enough to save Thomson from the twin threats that faced it: competition from low-cost manufacturers and the investment required to maintain a grip on rapid technological development.

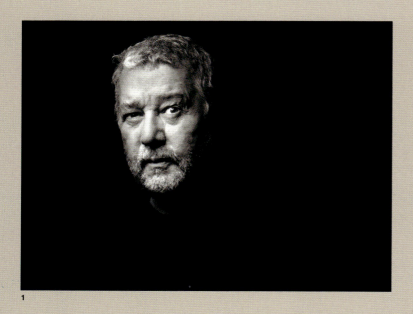

1

(1) Thanks in large part to Philippe Starck's indefatigable energy and constant stream of new products, the 1980s came to be known as the designer decade. He is pictured here in Paris, October 2022.

(2) The most original of Starck's many designs for the French electronics manufacturer Thomson was the television set that he named Jim Nature (see page 189). There was nothing else in the market quite like the moulded chipboard case and military-style webbing handle.

(3) Starck's Coo Coo, made by Thomson for Alessi, looked more like a clock than a radio, but in fact combined both functions in its coloured case.

(4) The Ola telephone handset, also made by Thomson, took on a molten liquid form that seemed suggestive of alien life.

2

3

4

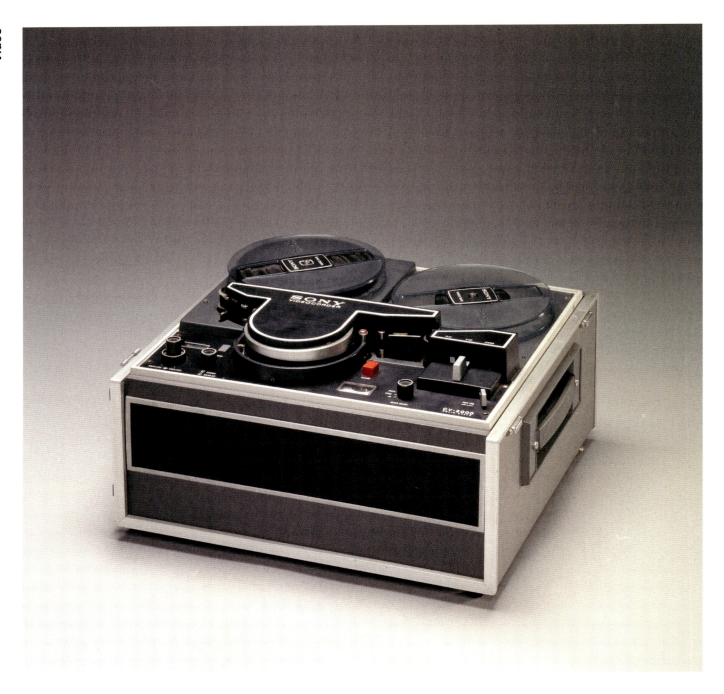

Sony CV-2000 VCR

Date: 1965

Designer: Nobutoshi Kihara

Manufacturer: Sony, Tokyo, Japan

Dimensions: 58 × 41 × 44cm
(22¾ × 16 × 17¼in)

The pioneering nature of Sony's launch of its first video-recording machines is evident in the advertising campaign that it devised for the new product; it needed to explain to potential customers exactly what they would use this remarkably expensive equipment to do. In fact, it wasn't just one object – the kit included a camera, a monitor screen, and an open reel-to-reel recording deck and playback machine, all packed into matching suitcases. Sony came up with more than one message. The CV-2000 VCR was both a 'television tape

recorder for the home', and also intended for 'business, education, and scientific use'. The advertising even had to spell out that 'You can electronically record anything you see or hear, and play it back instantly. You can erase the tape immediately, and reuse it, or keep it indefinitely.'

Ampex VR 5003 VCR

Date: 1965

Designer: Ampex

Manufacturer: Ampex, Redwood City, CA, US

Dimensions: Approx. 28 × 45 × 40cm
(11 × 17¾ × 15¾in)

Ampex had built up considerable experience in audio recording before moving to video recording. Its first products were aimed at professional markets. The US navy bought Ampex equipment to record take off and landings on its aircraft carriers, but from the outset it was looking to expand into the domestic market. It offered a £24,485 ($30,000) domestic video recorder through Nieman Marcus as early as 1963, which included a television, and was built into a 2.7m- (9ft-) long timber console. For that money, a team of Ampex engineers would arrive to install it. The VR 5003, which used 2.5-cm (1-in) open-reel video tape, was still a rarity in the home. Although it was described as portable, it took a fair amount of strength to lift it.

Philips LDL 1002 VCR

Date: 1969

Designer: Philips

Manufacturer: Philips, Vienna, Austria

Dimensions: 42 × 19.5 × 34cm
(16½ × 7¾ × 13½in)

In the days before the video cassette and Philips video recorder, the LDL 1002 used open-reel tape to record and play back video. The machine was designed to be used with the reels facing up, rather than placed on its narrow side with the reels facing outward. It came with a transparent Perspex cover, in a format much like the stereo record decks of the time. It was rapidly superseded and remained in production for only two years.

Sony SL-6300 Betamax VCR

Date: 1975

Designer: Sony

Manufacturer: Sony, Tokyo, Japan

Dimensions: 45 × 21 × 40cm

(17¾ × 8¼ × 15¾in)

Before its shift to producing content after buying a US film studio in 1989, Sony's success was based on continuous technical innovation, moving from transistor radios to television, and from television to video. It started selling bulky, and expensive, Umatic video-tape machines in 1971. Sony set itself the target to produce a video recorder that could work with a cassette no larger than the size of a paperback book. The result was the technically impressive Betamax. Sony's Betamax pre-dated the launch of the JVC rival VHS tape by a year. Although it was technically superior, Sony's video format was superseded by VHS, mainly because Sony priced its products too high, and for once failed to market them effectively. The SL-6300 VCR was sold in two forms, as a standalone and in a unit combined with a 45.7-cm (18-in) Trinitron colour-television set.

Sony HVC-F1 video camera

Date: 1981

Designer: Sony

Manufacturer: Sony, Tokyo Japan

Dimensions: Approx. 34 × 62 × 25cm
(13½ × 24½ × 9¾in)

The HVC-F1 video camera was designed to take moving images with a fixed F1.4 lens and 6x optical zoom. It was seen as a radical departure – termed by *The New York Times* as filmless photography – but Kodak vice president John R. Robertson was less impressed, telling the *Times* that electronic photography 'will be hard-pressed to approach the low cost and high quality of silver imaging, and it is not obvious that the mass market should or will turn in that direction'.

The HVC-F1 was large and unwieldy, and required connecting by cable to a separate video recorder. It used Sony's patent MF Trinicon imaging tube, a development of the cathode-ray tube, to capture video images.

The HVC-F1 was abandoned just two years later, when Sony launched the Betamax format, its first video camera with a built-in recorder.

JVC GR-C1 camcorder

Date: 1984

Designer: JVC

Manufacturer: JVC, Yokohama, Japan

Dimensions: 10.8 × 13.6 × 31.4cm
(4¼ × 5¼ × 12¼in)

JVC invented the VHS format, launched in 1976, in direct and ultimately successful competition with Sony's Betamax (see page 194). Initially, it required a collection of individual pieces of equipment connected by cables to function. The GR-C1, launched eight years later, was the first all-in-one machine that combined a camera and a recorder, using a special 30-minute VHS tape. With an adaptor, this could be played back in a standard video-cassette recorder. The GR-C1 could also play back through the viewfinder.

Sony CCD TR-V35E camcorder

Date: 1989

Designer: Sony Design Studio

Manufacturer: Sony, Tokyo, Japan

Dimensions: 10.7 × 10.7 × 20.9cm

(4¼ × 4¼ × 8¼in)

Sony called their camcorders (video cameras aimed at amateur users) Handycams – the point being to emphasize how small they were in comparison with their competitors' video cameras, which were so large and heavy they needed to be supported on the shoulder. With 8mm video tape, Sony could make much smaller cameras that could be carried in the palm, and used with one hand. Sony had called its first transistor 'pocket' size. It marketed the Handycam as 'passport size'.

Panasonic M50/M40 VHS camcorder

Date: 1996

Designer: Panasonic

Manufacturer: Matsushita Electric Industrial Co. Ltd, Osaka, Japan

Dimensions: 13 × 24.5 × 47.9cm (5 x 9½ x 18in)

Panasonic's M50 was a big machine and therefore not particularly convenient to carry. It was expensive and fragile, so it came in a protective suitcase that could save it from damage, as well as accommodate all the essential adaptors, chargers for the lithium batteries, cables and accessories.

However, the M50 did offer film students all the basic tools that they needed to make a professional-looking film. It also gave journalists the opportunity to make their own broadcast-quality reports without a team of technicians. Unfortunately, the quality of the images wasn't the same as film, and it would soon be overtaken by digital technology.

Communication

Of all the new analogue technologies developed in the nineteenth century, the capacity to use electric current to transmit messages along copper wire has turned out to have had the most far-reaching consequences. It has had the effect of transforming our relationship with time and distance, and the way that we communicate with each other.

The level of investment that was required to install the first telegraphic systems meant that the resources of the state, or well-funded corporations, were needed to realize them. They had military, governmental and commercial uses, and were regarded as pieces of strategic infrastructure. The wider public had only limited access, through postal systems.

Once the copper wires were in place, they could be used for analogue technologies more complex than laboriously transmitted morse-code messages. The more data that was being communicated, the more copper was needed. By the end of the nineteenth century, overhead telephone lines crowded New York's streets with a thick spider's web of multiple layers of copper wire.

Telephones offered voice calls. Telex machines came next, giving business users the capacity for the rapid exchange of large amounts of text. Facsimile machines transformed visual images into electric pulses that could also be transmitted on copper wires and printed by a remote machine.

(1) Telephone wires over New York, 1887. The simplest way to construct a telephone and telegraph network was to string copper wire from pole to pole following road and railway lines. In American cities, this produced an unsightly mess of wires before they were later buried underground.

(2) The first telephones used a hand crank to generate the electricity needed to ring the bell at the other end of the line.

1

2

1838 Samuel Morse, an accomplished painter as well as scientist, demonstrated his telegraph system, based on precedents in the UK.

1874 The first commercial typewriter, the Sholes and Glidden typewriter (see page 222), was sold in America. The price was set at £100 ($125).

1876 Alexander Graham Bell made the first telephone call to his assistant, Thomas Watson, to ask him to come to see him.

1926 The architect Gilbert Scott designed the cast-iron K2 telephone box, to accommodate public pay phones in Britain's streets.

(3) The first commercial typewriter was manufactured by the Remington company of Ilion, New York, in 1874. Remington's bold marketing campaign included this 1939 poster suggesting its products dominated the world.

(4) A travelling US salesman—in the Balochistan region of what is now Pakistan—in the 1910s. The camel carries boxes of Remington typewriters and an advertising sign. Though Remington was originally a gunmaker, it diversified into sewing machines and the name then became synonymous with typewriters once it was sold to its competitor, the Standard Typewriter Manufacturing Company.

4

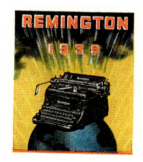

3

While the telegram was used to send urgent messages, it never became a domestic technology. Sending a telegram required the use of a specialist operator to dispatch and receive it, and in the case of Britain, a Post Office motorcycle dispatch rider to deliver the message. The owner of the copper wires charged by the word, which led to the development of 'Cablese' – a special language designed to pack maximum meaning into the minimum number of words, and a forerunner of the tweet and text message.

The first commercially made typewriters reached the market in the US in the 1870s, just before the development of the telephone. Their creation made the modern world of business and government bureaucracy possible. While manual typewriters have largely disappeared, their legacy survives. We still access computers through a keyboard with a layout – the so-called QWERTY after the top line sequence of letters – that was developed for the typewriter by Christopher Latham Sholes (see page 220).

1931 Norwegian artist Jean Heiberg designed the Ericsson DBH (see page 206), defining the modern form of the telephone.

1935 IBM began to sell its first electric typewriter, the Model 01.

1946 Motorola began marketing car phones based on radio technology.

1959 Xerox, initially known as Haloid Xerox, moved from 'wet' chemical copying to dry photocopying.

5

6

(5) AT&T launched its Picturephone (see page 209) service at the New York World's Fair in 1964, where a bank of video phones connected users with each other and a similar installation at Disneyland. Despite predictions that it would achieve one million users by 1980, and featuring in Stanley Kubrick's film *2001: A Space Odyssey*, it proved a commercial flop.

(6) A telephone booth at 42nd Street and Lexington Avenue, New York, date unknown. Made from aluminium, steel and glass, for most of the twentieth century telephone booths were the closest most people could get to making a call in the street. Britain's cast-iron equivalent were known as telephone boxes.

(7) Motorola's DynaTAC (see page 213), the first commercial mobile phone, was launched in 1973. Ten hours of charging time allowed for up to 30 minutes of conversation.

(8) Landlines, even with contemporary looking handsets like the Trimline from 1965 (see page 210), have been disappearing. Less than 25 per cent of Americans were using a landline telephone in 2023.

1959 Olivetti bought the largest US typewriter manufacturer, Underwood, with a plan to rival IBM.

1960 Telephone answering machines first became available in the US.

1964 Xerox started making telephone facsimile machines, beginning with the Long Distance Xerography (LDX) System, which could transmit up to eight pages per minute.

1973 The first mobile phone call was made by a Motorola executive, while standing in a Manhattan street.

Exactly who invented the telephone is contested. In 2002, it was the subject of a resolution passed by the US House of Representatives, acknowledging the nineteenth-century Italian-American inventor, Antonio Meucci. Canada's parliament passed a motion in response, reasserting the claim of the rather more famous Scots-born Canadian citizen, Alexander Graham Bell, who once shared a laboratory with Meucci. Yet, along with Samuel Morse's work on the telegraph, which made instant, long-distance communication possible for the first time, the telephone transformed the world.

The telephone, which allowed voice-to-voice communication over long distances, pre-dated the radio. It was seen as a vital service throughout most of the world, and so became subject to public ownership. Until the privatization wave of the late twentieth century, telephones were rented from the government or, in the case of the

US, a monopoly corporation, and so were not designed with a consumer market in mind, giving them the anonymous, utilitarian appearance of industrial equipment.

For most of the twentieth century, if people wanted to use a telephone outside the home or the office, their only realistic choice was a telephone box – an object on an architectural scale. The first truly portable phone, the Mobira Cityman 900 made by Nokia, took six hours to charge its nickel-cadmium battery and delivered no more than an hour of talk time. Most mobile phones were still safely tethered to a reassuringly heavy lead-and-acid car battery.

The end of the state's monopoly on the use of copper wires changed the nature of the telephone and the fax, and they became consumer items. The old suppliers found themselves competing with new entrants to the market, such as Swatch and Alessi – companies that were much more experienced in appealing to the consumer.

7

8

1984 Telephone services were privatized in the UK, ending a state monopoly and opening up the market for handsets.

1984 In the US, AT&T's monopoly on telephony was dismantled.

1989 The Swiss watch company Swatch made its first telephone, signalling that handsets had become fashion-conscious items.

2011 The last factory manufacturing manual typewriters in India – the Godrej and Boyce plant in Mumbai – closed.

Product Directory

Telephones

From its first incarnation to its final eclipse by the smartphone – when Apple launched the first iPhone in 2007 – the analogue telephone went through at least four incarnations. The first version, designed in 1880, put a handset on a box with a dial. It was followed in 1892 by the iconic candlestick format, which continued to appear in many variations, until it was overtaken by Jean Heiberg's classic 1932 model for Siemens, which reverted to a better-resolved version of the earlier handset and base configuration. The classic Heiberg model also went through a series of refinements, including the replacement of the dial with push buttons, before it was replaced by the brick-like mobile phone.

Typewriters

The typewriter kickstarted the world of bureaucracy, allowing for the creation of carbon copies, files and easily legible records at the end of the nineteenth century. It created a whole new industry for young women, who became typists, which lasted for almost a century. The keyboard of the typewriter has had a long-lasting afterlife as the interface for all our interactions with the digital world but, before that, the typewriter was adopted as a creative tool for writers.

Type Marker

The Dymo marker was a new product category used to print adhesive labels. The letters on the selection disc were organized alphabetically, unlike typewriters. A pistol grip embossed one letter at a time, creating a distinctive font.

Copiers

The designer Raymond Loewy's role in giving the Gestetner Duplicator 66 of 1929 an impressive new look created an early office status symbol. Yet, the longer-term significance of an affordable copier was political. In the Cold War era, repressive regimes felt threatened by any technology that might allow dissent and tried to control every means that could disseminate views that they considered dangerous. Typewriters and copiers were subject to strict registration.

Teleprinters and Facsimile Machines

The teleprinter never escaped from its original incarnation as a piece of office equipment. It was bulky, expensive, noisy, designed to be robust, and was always a little too complicated for domestic use. The facsimile machine was different. There was no need for keyboard inputting, so anyone who could make a telephone call could use it. This ease of use transformed it into a piece of consumer electronics, but its drawback was its lack of longevity, as fax printouts faded quickly.

Western Electric 20B Candlestick telephone

Date: 1904

Designer: Western Electric

Manufacturer: Western Electric, New York, NY, US

Dimensions: 16.5 × 29.5 × 25.1cm
(6½ × 11½ × 10in)

Western Electric, a subsidiary of American Telephone and Telegraph Company (AT&T), was not the only manufacturer of candlestick phones – a type which emerged in the late 1890s – but it was the first to secure a patent for the tube-shaft telephone. The phone had a microphone transmitter, or mouthpiece, which formed the top of the tube. The receiver, or earpiece, was supported on a hook projecting horizontally from the tube that also served as a switch. The handset was connected to a wall-mounted box, which contained the bell that rang to signal an incoming call, as well as the electrical circuits, and a connection to the copper wires that linked the set to the telephone exchange. Early models, made before automatic exchanges became common, came without a dial.

Ericsson DBH 1001 telephone

Date: 1931

Designers: Johan Christian Bjerknes, Jean Heiberg

Manufacturer: Norsk Elektrisk Bureau, Oslo, Norway

Dimensions: 13.7 × 22.5 × 17.5cm
(5½ × 9 × 7in)

Bjerknes and Heiberg gave the telephone a form that remained definitive for half a century, surviving even the transition from rotary to push-button dialling. Heiberg worked as both a painter and a sculptor, and his design for the telephone made the most of Bakelite – a material with the potential to be freely modelled. With Bjerknes's technical input, Heiberg gave the handset a different character from the dialling unit, which also contained the bell, and an ingenious integral tray for keeping telephone numbers and messages. The handset clearly suggests the different functions of the microphone mouthpiece and the earpiece receiver. The forms complement the pyramidal form of the dialling unit, with its sharply sculpted, curved sides.

Ericophon Cobra telephone

Date: 1954

Designers: Ralph Lysell, Hugo Blomberg

Manufacturer: LM Ericsson, Karlscrona, Sweden

Dimensions: 21.6 × 9.8 × 11.1 cm (8½ × 3¾ × 4½in)

The birth of the Ericophon was a long, drawn-out process that began as early as 1941 when Ralph Lysell, a designer newly returned to Sweden from a spell working in America, was commissioned by Hugo Blomberg, Ericsson's chief engineer, to explore the form that a one-piece telephone – combining dial, receiver and microphone in a single object – might take. Lysell's initial clay models had an Art Deco feel that clearly suggested the form of a snake rearing its head, as implied in the nickname. It was originally intended to be

moulded in Bakelite, and most likely in black, but by the time Ericsson finally decided to go ahead, a new thermoplastic, known as ABS, had become available, which allowed for a much wider range of colours. Lysell had time to modify the form of the Ericophon into a more abstract shape. After a prototype was evaluated in 1954, the Cobra went into full production in 1956, with more than two million subsequently sold around the world.

Ansafone KH-90CD answering machine

Date: 1960

Designer: Kuzuo Hashimoto

Manufacturer: Pioneer Electronic Corp, Tokyo, Japan, for Ansonics, Inc., El Segundo, CA, US

Dimensions: 22.8 × 20.3 × 35.5cm (9 × 8 × 14in)

The metal case in gun-metal grey, the chrome toggle switch and the Bakelite knob gave this machine the look of a piece of serious military equipment. Yet, this appearance was somewhat undermined by the flamboyant Ansafone logo rendered in three-dimensional gold-effect lettering – more like a juke box than the control panel for a guided missile. The first generation of answering machines were designed to work with standard desk telephones, which were placed on top of the Ansafone box. In out-of-office mode, an incoming call triggered a pair of metal arms to slide under the handset and lift it off the hook. The machine had two tapes: one to play a recorded message, inviting callers to leave a message, while warning that they only had 30 seconds to make it; a second tape recorded the message, ready for playback.

AT&T Picturephone

Date: 1964

Designer: Henry Dreyfuss & Associates

Manufacturer: Western Electric, for AT&T, New York, NY, US

Dimensions: Screen size: 13.34 × 12.7cm (5¼ × 5in)

First shown at the 1964 World's Fair in New York, the Picturephone had a commercial launch in two US cities (Pittsburgh and Chicago) in 1970. Forty years before the smartphone, the Picturephone offered two-way, black-and-white video communication, with hands-free audio on a speaker phone, using existing copper wire. AT&T offered the Picturephone through public booths. It advertised the service as a cross between the telephone and the television, and believed that it would be a huge financial success, predicting one million sets would be sold within the first few years. In fact, it was an instant commercial failure. AT&T concluded that people did not like seeing each other on the telephone, and abandoned the project within 12 months.

Motorola TLD 1100 radio telephone

Date: 1964

Designer: Motorola

Manufacturer: Motorola, Chicago, IL, US

Dimensions: Approx. 22.9 × 12.7 × 10.2cm
(9 × 5 × 4in)

Motorola began supplying radio receivers to Illinois police cars in 1930. This car-phone system was based on wireless technology that connected a moving user with an exchange. The first radio car-phone users in the 1940s pressed a button that connected them to an operator who would place the call for them. Each car phone was assigned a special five-digit number that the base station called. The low numbers were a reflection of the very limited capacity of the system. The Motorola TLD 1100 was much more sophisticated – it was assigned a seven-digit number, like landline users, and had a dial allowing users to place calls themselves. The TLD 1100 had two components: one was designed to be fitted to the car dashboard, and came with a rotary dial to make calls; the other had the circuit boards needed to locate available radio channels.

Trimline 220 telephone

Date: 1965

Designers: Henry Dreyfuss, Donald Genaro

Manufacturer: Western Electric, New York, NY, US

Dimensions: 8.9 × 21.6 × 7cm
(3½ × 8½ × 2¾in)

The Trimline 220 was the most radical reworking of the mass-produced telephone since Jean Heiberg's sculptural Bakelite model more than 30 years earlier. Dreyfuss's design consultancy worked with Bell Labs, the research arm of the US telephone monopoly, on a more compact and convenient telephone. The big shift was to shrink the size of the set and to reposition the dial from the base unit, incorporating it into the receiver, somewhat freeing the user during a call. Dreyfuss used injection-moulded ABS plastic for a sleek, sculptural form. The rearrangement of the dial meant that it was invisible when not in use, making the telephone a much less intrusive presence in the domestic context. The dial had a warning light that came on when the handset was picked up off the base.

Grillo telephone

Date: 1965

Designers: Marco Zanuso, Richard Sapper

Manufacturer: Società Italiana
Telecomunicazioni (SIT) Siemens, Milan, Italy

Dimensions: 7 × 16.5 × 8.3cm
(2¾ × 6½ × 3¼in)

Architect Marco Zanuso and industrial designer Richard Sapper brought the sculptural quality that marked their work on televisions and radios to the Grillo telephone. They carried out a radical reconfiguration of the conventional elements of the telephone, which had remained little changed since Jean Heiberg created the archetype for the Bakelite phone (see page 206). Instead of a dialling unit with a separate handset, Zanuso and Sapper combined these into a single object, with a folding mouthpiece that covered the dial when not in use. The Grillo came in a range of colours, and its shape anticipated the clamshell form that mobile phones would later adopt. The ringer was housed in the wall socket needed to connect the handset to a telephone landline. SIT-Siemens made much of the compactness of the Grillo, which they advertised as a palm-sized telephone, as well as the unusual chirping ring tone. The name Grillo is the Italian word for a cricket.

Western Electric 2500 telephone

Date: 1968

Designer: Western Electric

Manufacturer: Western Electric, New York, NY, US

Dimensions: 20.3 × 22.8 × 12.7cm (8 × 9 × 5in)

The Western Electric 2500 was America's first mass-produced touch-dial telephone, a development made possible by transistorized tone-generating circuits that took the place of rotary dials. It was a product of the days of America's telephone monopoly. For decades, the 2500 phone was so universal that it became almost invisible – it was the generic telephone. The words 'Property of the Bell System, not for sale' were stamped on the bottom of each model.

Western Electric had a long-term relationship with industrial designer Henry Dreyfuss and the consultancy that he started. In 1949 Dreyfuss worked on the Western Electric 500, the 2500's predecessor, which came with a rotary dial. The updated phone retained the basic form of the older model but reconfigured its front.

Iskra ETA 80 telephone

Date: 1978

Designer: Davorin Savnik

Manufacturer: Iskra, Kranj, Yugoslavia

Dimensions: 7.3 × 22.2 × 25.4cm (2¾ × 8¾ × 10in)

Iskra was founded as a state-owned telecommunications and electronics company in what was then Yugoslavia, now Slovenia. It was responsible for a number of innovative designs under the leadership of Davorin Savnik, who oversaw every aspect of the company's identity in the 1960s and 1970s. Savnik trained as an architect and a designer. Savnik's extremely refined silhouette for the Iskra telephone won several design prizes, and it was acquired for the permanent collection of the Museum of Modern Art (MoMA) in New York. In essence, it was an update of the typology that had been established by Jean Heiberg for Ericsson half a century earlier (see page 206). Later versions used push-button dialling rather than the original rotary dial. The ETA 80 was popular enough to persuade other manufacturers to copy the design.

DynaTAC 8000X mobile phone

Date: 1984

Designers: Martin Cooper, Rudy Krolopp

Manufacturer: Motorola, Chicago, IL, US

Dimensions: 33 × 4.4 × 8.9cm
(13 × 1.75 × 3.5in)

Scientist Martin Cooper built on Motorola's achievements in radio telephony and car phones to produce the first commercial mobile phone. He worked with Rudy Krolopp, Motorola's head of industrial design, to shape the 8000X. The DynaTAC name was an acronym that stood for 'dynamic adaptive total area coverage'.

This was not the kind of phone that you could slip into a pocket or lose in a cab. In order to accommodate its relatively primitive battery, it was big enough to justify its nickname of 'the brick'. It took ten hours to fully charge the phone and offered just 30 minutes talk time, with a retail price of £3,260 ($4,000) (more than £8,970 ($11,000) in today's currency). The DynaTAC was the portable phone that defined the 'greed is good' era, as dramatized in the 1987 film *Wall Street*. Michael Douglas's character, Gordon Gekko, is shown using the 8000X to call Charlie Sheen from the beach in the Hamptons, waking him up with the 'money never sleeps' line.

Ettore Sottsass

Ettore Sottsass never treated the machines that he worked on simply as utilitarian pieces of equipment. He understood them as playing an important part in the rituals of everyday life, and accordingly tried to give them a character and a personality. The Tekne 3 typewriter, for example, looked like a modestly scaled domestic shrine, with its architectural form and its sculpted tapering keys.

Sottsass looked for ways to give objects an emotional resonance. He saw the Valentine typewriter as much more than a piece of office equipment. It was, as he once suggested, a machine designed – among other things – to keep poets company on lonely country afternoons. Sottsass used colour and pattern as an essential part of his approach to design for mechanical calculators, fax machines, telex machines, typewriters and telephones. Throughout his career, Sottsass was able simultaneously to pursue projects that involved mass-produced industrial machines, while also creating one-offs that could be understood as works of art. He was what is sometimes described as a radical designer, which is to say that he understood design as being about more than making desirable objects to encourage consumers to buy them.

A close friend of Allen Ginsberg – the Beat poet from California, who also introduced him to Bob Dylan – Sottsass was born in Innsbruck in 1917, the son of an Italian-speaking citizen of the Austro-Hungarian empire. As an architecture student at Turin's Polytechnic, he spent much of his time learning from the modernist painter, Luigi Spazzapan. After fighting in Mussolini's war in Yugoslavia, Sottsass opened his own studio in Milan. His breakthrough came in 1959 when, even though he had little industrial experience beyond designing simple domestic objects, Adriano Olivetti and his son Roberto recruited him to join the team they assembled to build the company's first mainframe computer, the Elea 9003. Sottsass asked himself, what should a computer look like? Not like a washing machine, he wrote in his notebook.

Sottsass worked as a consultant for Olivetti for the next 20 years, on a sequence of business machines and typewriters. The colourful Valentine portable was one, but there was a string of other machines, too, including telex machines and mechanical calculators. At an age that many would be considering retirement, Sottsass established the Memphis Group, an international collective of designers. In 1981, they produced the first of five annual collections – including pieces of furniture, clocks, lamps and a television – which were a manifesto for his approach. Some critics described it as post-modernism, and it certainly represented a more flamboyant and subversive approach than the conventional idea of modern good taste.

1

(1) Ettore Sottsass (1917–2007) during the 'Fiera del Mobile' trade show, Milan, Italy, 1982, seated on a couch he designed for the Memphis collection.

(2) and (3) Sottsass wanted the Valentine typewriter (see page 229) and Enorme telephone (see page 217) to give their users a sense of emotional engagement.

(4) As a consultant for Olivetti, Sottsass was responsible for bringing a playful aspect to office equipment, such as the Summa 19 calculator of 1970, pictured.

2

3

4

BeoCom 2000 telephone

Date: 1986

Designers: Lone Lindinger-Loewy,
Gideon Lindinger-Loewy

Manufacturer: Bang & Olufsen,
Struer, Denmark

Dimensions: 7.8 × 21 × 21.3cm (3 × 8¼ × 8½in)

The BeoCom 2000 was a new departure for
Bang & Olufsen – its first telephone handset.
It was a response to the new market opened
up by a wave of privatizations in European
state-owned telecommunications companies.
Until the 1980s, domestic telephones in many
countries had remained government property,
and were only rented by the consumer. In such
circumstances, there was minimal choice
in style or colour. Privatization ended that
monopoly, and opened the market to a much
wider variety of handsets.

The BeoCom 2000 was designed to reflect
the identity established by the company's
audio products, and took a radically different
approach to the form of the telephone. Lone
and Gideon Lindinger-Loewy gave a wedge-
shaped form to the dialling unit and used
press-button dialling. It was analogue
telephony, but the system software allowed for
up to 20 numbers to be stored in its memory.

Enorme telephone

Date: 1986

Designer: Ettore Sottsass, David Kelley

Manufacturer: Enorme Corporation, US

Dimensions: 5.7 × 19.4 × 10.2cm
(2¼ × 7½ × 4in)

Ettore Sottsass made his reputation working for Italian manufacturer Olivetti, designing its first mainframe computer, as well as a series of typewriters and a range of office furniture. In 1980, he launched the post-modern Memphis Group with a colourful collection of playful-looking furniture and domestic objects that set out to subvert conventional ideas about functional design.

After he left Memphis, Sottsass worked with art collector and investor Jean Pigozzi, and David Kelley, founder of the IDEO design consultancy to set up the Enorme Corporation, with the intention of manufacturing a range of consumer electronics. Kelley's firm was working on Apple computers at the time. Sottsass designed his home in California and an apartment for Pigozzi in London. The striking telephone, which Sottsass designed in his signature colours and pure geometric forms, turned out to be the company's only product.

Nokia Cityman 1320 mobile phone

Date: 1987

Designer: Nokia Corporation

Manufacturer: Nokia Corporation,
Espoo, Finland

Dimensions: 4 × 18.5 × 8cm (1½ × 7¼ × 3in)

Motorola was working on the DynaTAC portable phone (see page 213) even before Nokia had taken the decision to set up its Mobira subsidiary and move beyond car phones to producing mobile phones. Yet, it was Nokia that got the credit for making the first credible commercial mobile phones and, for a decade or more, they were the dominant manufacturer of mobile phones. The Cityman 1320 suffered from being bulky, expensive, and having limited battery life, but it made an impact on a market that, at that time, was limited to affluent business users. In the UK, for example, there were no more than 200,000 mobile phone users in 1987. Nokia benefitted from a skilful publicity campaign that involved Mikhail Gorbachev, then the president of the Soviet Union, making a call to the Kremlin using a Cityman 1320.

Sony CM R111 mobile phone

Date: 1993

Designer: Sony Corporation

Manufacturer: Sony Corporation,
Tokyo, Japan

Dimensions: 5 × 18 × 7cm (2 × 7 × 2¾in)

Since it made its first transistor, miniaturization has been a Sony speciality. Its mobile phones were no exception. In the pursuit of making the CM R111 as small as possible, Sony's engineers devised an external microphone in the form of a spring-loaded stick. At the touch of a button it clicked into position, supposedly at a comfortable distance from the earpiece.

The evolution of the analogue mobile phone, from the first brick-like Motorola DynaTAC (see page 213) to Sony's tiny CM R111, saw each succeeding model become smaller and smaller, until it reached the point that it became less convenient to use. After digitalization made the smartphone possible, the process went into reverse, and the mobile phone has evolved into an object dominated by a screen rather than a keypad.

Nokia 232 mobile phone

Date: 1994

Designer: Frank Nuovo

Manufacturer: Nokia Corporation,
Espoo, Finland

Dimensions: 5.3 × 14.7 × 2.3cm (2 × 5¾ × 1in)

Nokia's bestselling 232 model was central to Alicia Silverstone's character, Cher Horowitz, in the 1995 film *Clueless*, a witty portrayal of high-school teen life in Beverly Hills, and mobile phones were about to become a central part of that way of life.

Frank Nuovo, Nokia's American vice president in charge of design, treated the 232 as a consumer item, rather than a piece of business equipment, offering a large range of colours and finishes. Technically, it had a 16-hour battery stand-by life. Despite its screen, and its 98-number memory store, this was still an analogue phone and it belonged to a period in which each new generation of mobile phone was smaller than its predecessor – a design phenomenon that was abruptly reversed in the digital smartphone era.

The QWERTY Keyboard

Although it was devised to be used with the very first mechanical typewriter, a black tin box manufactured by Remington in 1874, and decorated with colourful and realistic representations of roses, the so-called QWERTY keyboard – named for the sequence of six letters on the top row – is still the primary means of interacting with the modern digital world for those cultures that use the Latin alphabet.

Christopher Latham Sholes, who patented the design for the typewriter and licensed it to Remington, had originally planned to arrange the keys in seemingly logical alphabetical order. He changed his mind at the last moment, after finding that operating letters spaced next to each other on the keyboard caused the mechanism to jam, and came up with QWERTY instead, placing those letters that are used in sequence most commonly as far apart as possible. After a slow start, Remington made a commercial success of the machine, and its competitors adopted the same format.

Since QWERTY became the dominant layout, it has proved impossible to dislodge, even if it is neither logical nor necessarily the most efficient arrangement. The QWERTY arrangement might avoid some clashes, but is no help avoiding potential jams when the letter 'r' is typed after 'e', for example.

Researchers at Kyoto University recently suggested that it was telegraph operators using early typewriters to transcribe morse-code messages who preferred QWERTY to an alphabetical order, which they found confusing and slow. Since they made up a large section of the first market for typewriters, the manufacturers complied.

Over the years, there have been a number of attempts to dethrone QWERTY. In 1936, American educational psychologist, August Dvorak, patented a keyboard layout with the top line 'aoeuid', supposedly allowing for faster, more accurate typing. He calculated that a majority of words could be typed using letters only from the top row. It might be a more logical arrangement, but with millions of typists trained to use a QWERTY keyboard, it failed to achieve widespread acceptance.

The growing incidence of repetitive strain injury in the 1980s provoked other attempts to find a more comfortable, ergonomically appropriate keyboard. Lillian Malt came up with the Maltron keyboard, which sits on a base designed to reduce wrist strain and groups keys in five distinct clusters, with a letter layout that allows the most commonly used words to be typed only by keys on the top row.

(1) The 1874 Sholes and Glidden typewriter (see page 222). Christopher Latham Sholes came up with the idea of the typewriter in an attempt to make a machine that would allow its users to put words on paper much faster than they could working by hand with a pen.

1

2

(2) The typewriter was originally envisaged as a transcription machine, with a keyboard that the user would search to find the right letter, typically a telegraph operator. Touch typing and the birth of the modern office workspace came later.

(3) Remington adapted their first model, adding lowercase letters to the typewriter and introducing a shift key to allow the keyboard to keep its existing layout.

3

Remington No. 1 typewriter

Date: 1874

Designer: Christopher Latham Sholes

Manufacturer: E. Remington and Sons, Ilion, NY, US

Dimensions: 35.6 × 43.2 × 30.5cm (14 × 17 × 12in)

Christopher Latham Sholes, Samuel Soule and Carlos Glidden began work on what came to be known as a typewriter as early as 1867. They made a number of prototypes and attempted to put them into production, but ended up selling a stake in the project, in 1873, to the Remington company.

Sholes and Glidden borrowed elements from existing technologies – the keys are like those used for telegraph systems and the type bars are derived from piano mechanisms. Remington brought its expertise, not just in

making small arms, but also from the manufacture of sewing machines. The Remington No. 1 used a foot-operated sewing machine treadle to move the carriage return. Sholes and Glidden initially designed a keyboard with the characters placed alphabetically, but when the Remington No. 1 went on sale the layout of the keys had been changed to the QWERTY keyboard, which is still used on almost every digital device today.

Underwood 6 typewriter

Date: 1930

Designer: Underwood Elliott Fisher

Manufacturer: Underwood Elliott Fisher, Hartford, CT, US

Dimensions: 25.4 × 45.7 × 33cm (10 × 18 × 13in)

John Underwood first became involved with typewriters as a supplier of typewriter ribbon to the Remington company, before deciding to go into manufacturing in 1900, when he acquired Franz Wagner's design for what became the first Underwood typewriter. The Underwood was easier to use and to make than Remington's machines and, within ten years, it had become the dominant brand, producing more typewriters from its Hartford, Connecticut, factory than all its competitors put together. Underwood initially made what were called standards; large, heavy machines for desk use. These models were followed by portables, used by both Ernest Hemingway and William Faulkner, among many other professional writers.

The Underwood 6 had an open-frame design that put its mechanical parts on display, and developed a wide range of features for professional typists, including a selector to allow the use of different coloured ribbons and margin releases.

Lettera 22 portable typewriter

Date: 1950

Designer: Marcello Nizzoli

Manufacturer: Olivetti, Ivrea, Italy

Dimensions: Approx. 8.3 × 29.8 × 32.4cm
(3¼ × 11¾ × 12¾in)

Marcello Nizzoli played a key part in establishing the reputation of Italian firm Olivetti as an internationally successful manufacturer with a commitment to design excellence in every field. He worked as an artist, designer and architect before meeting Adriano Olivetti, son of the company founder, Camillo, just before World War II. Nizzoli embarked on a series of projects for the company that included sophisticated mechanical adding machines, as well as one of the most charismatic typewriters ever made.

Nizzoli gave it a much more compact form than its pre-war predecessors, emphasizing its lightweight portability. Gunter Grass, Joan Didion and William Burroughs were all users.

Now that typewriter manufacturing has all but ended, it is hard to remember the intimate relationship that so many writers had with the machines with which they spent so much time.

olivetti

Lettera 22

Selectric electric typewriter

Date: 1961

Designer: Eliot Noyes

Manufacturer: IBM, Lexington, KY, US

Dimensions: Approx. 16.5 × 47.5 × 38cm
(6½ × 18½ × 15in)

Electric typewriters were part of the IBM range from the mid-1930s, and took much of the physical labour out of typing, but they depended on a powered version of the traditional mechanical typewriter keys. The Selectric did away with the mechanical striking system and replaced it with a typeball, commonly described as a 'golf ball'. The letters of the alphabet, numbers and symbols were cast into its surface. Pressing a key caused the ball to rotate the correct letter into position for it to strike the ribbon and leave an impression. The typeball could be quickly replaced, as required, to offer a wide variety of different typefaces. Chairman and CEO of IBM, Thomas Watson Jr called it 'the most totally distinct invention we have ever made as a company'.

The sculptural form of the Selectric, in a range of colours from office grey to black and red, was the work of Eliot Noyes, an architect who began his career at MoMA in New York, where he had attracted the attention of Watson Jr. After seeing the striking Olivetti showroom in New York, designed by Ernesto Rogers, Watson recruited Noyes to implement a coherent design strategy for IBM. This was a project that ranged from graphic design (for which he recruited Paul Rand), the architecture of IBM's factories, and its products, of which the Selectric was one of the most impressive. It remained in production for a decade before being replaced by the Selectric II.

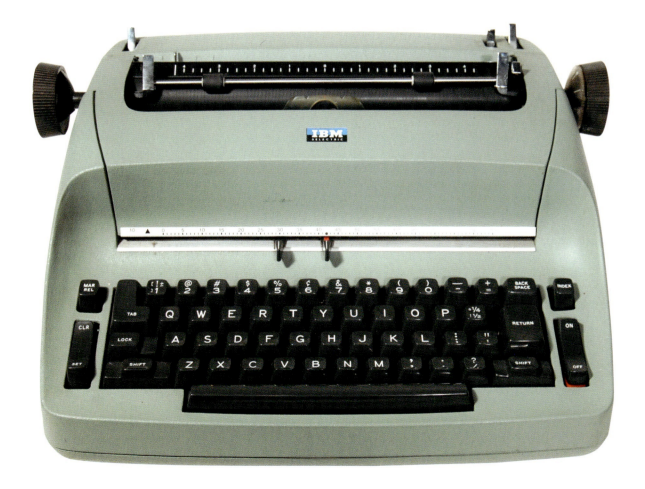

Praxis 48 typewriter

Date: 1964

Designer: Ettore Sottsass, Hans von Klier

Manufacturer: Olivetti, Ivrea, Italy

Dimensions: 16 × 46 × 34cm
(6¼ × 18 × 13¼in)

The Praxis 48 was sold in the American market as an Underwood model, the company that Adriano Olivetti bought shortly before his death aged just 60. At the time, it was the largest foreign takeover of an American industrial company. The acquisition financially overstretched Olivetti, placing the future of the business in doubt. Adriano Olivetti believed that acquiring Underwood would bring access to American know-how and markets, but despite Underwood's long history, it was Olivetti that had the superior technology.

Sottsass had been working for Olivetti since he shaped Italy's first mainframe all-transistor computer, the Elea 9003 in 1959. He went on to develop a team for the company that worked on a series of typewriters. The Praxis 48 was an electric machine that looked handsome, with its architectural form, its tactile casing, the sharp use of the colour green for the keys and other controls, and sculpted keyboard. However, it could not match the sophistication of IBM's Selectric, launched three years earlier.

Bright red
Dark red
Sultry red
Super red

valentine

olivetti

Valentine typewriter

Date: 1969

Designer: Ettore Sottsass, Perry King

Manufacturer: Olivetti, Ivrea, Italy

Dimensions: 35 × 34 × 12cm
(13¾ × 13¼ × 4¾in)

The Valentine typewriter's vivid colour was a signal from designer Ettore Sottsass that it was not to be seen as a piece of office equipment that chained us to the workplace. Instead, the bright-red plastic of the most famous version, accentuated by the impact of bright-orange spools, immediately suggested a more playful machine. Other colours were used, too, such as blue and ivory – a characteristic that influenced Steve Jobs and Jony Ive when they came up with the citrus-fruit colour palette for the iMac 30 years later.

Sottsass wanted to make a machine that did not feel too precious, one that could be manufactured as cheaply as possible to make it affordable and accessible, rather than an elitist status symbol. In order to simplify the mechanism, Sottsass had planned to eliminate lowercase letters, and he wanted to use the cheapest, most basic form of plastic for the body. Yet, both ideas were vetoed by Olivetti's marketing department. They did, however, adopt a radical marketing campaign, which presented the Valentine as a natural outcome of the revolutionary radicalism of the 1960s. Sottsass suggested that it was a machine 'designed to keep lonely poets company on weekends in the country'. As much care went into the case – a kind of plastic bucket that, at a pinch, you could sit on to type – as the manufacturing of the machine itself.

Olivetti Lettera 35 typewriter

Date: 1974

Designer: Mario Bellini

Manufacturer: Olivetti, Ivrea, Italy.
Made in Spain.

Dimensions: Approx. 27 × 37 × 8cm
(10¾ × 14½ × 3¼in)

During the 1970s, Olivetti had two industrial design teams, one led by Ettore Sottsass and the other by Mario Bellini. The two developed their own, very distinct languages. Sottsass, who was close to the Beat poet Allen Ginsberg and went on to set up the Memphis Group, was the most nuanced in his questioning of the role of the designer in the commercial world. Bellini, on the other hand, had a skill for making seductive objects to encourage consumers to buy them.

The aesthetic qualities of typewriters in the early days had been limited by the parameters of casting or folding metal sheets. Bellini was able to design a sequence of typewriters for Olivetti, both electric and manual, that used moulded plastic to achieve freer shapes. He was equally adept with sharp, wedge-shaped forms, or, as with the Lettera 35, a more curvaceous form.

Olivetti Lexikon 82 electric typewriter

Date: 1976

Designers: Mario Bellini, with A. Macchi
Cassia, G. Pasini, S. Pasqui

Manufacturer: Olivetti Spa, Ivrea, Italy.
Made in Glasgow, Scotland.

Dimensions: Approx. 11.5 × 38.7 × 38cm
(4½ × 15¼ × 15in)

Olivetti proudly launched the Lexikon 82 as the
world's first portable electric typewriter. Like
Ettore Sottsass's Valentine (see page 229), a
manual portable, the Lexikon 82 was part of
Olivetti's strategy of making products that were
no longer tied to the office environment or the
connotations of work. Bellini's design certainly
made it look like the latest thing when it was
launched, with a choice of a black or two-tone
moulded-plastic body. Its changeable typeballs
also allowed users a choice of font.

However, at almost 9kg (20lb), not counting
the carrying case, it was too heavy for anybody
to want to carry it far. Additionally, while the
electric motor took a lot of the labour out of
pounding mechanical keys to type, Olivetti's
quality control in its Glasgow factory was not
up to the task of assembling the machine with
enough precision to enable the Lexikon 82 to
type in perfectly straight lines.

Olivetti

Three generations of the Olivetti family built a company with a unique combination of engineering brilliance, social obligation and entrepreneurial ambition, that has now all but vanished. In 1970, the company employed almost 75,000 people in factories from Sao Paolo, Brazil, to Glasgow, Scotland. In 2022, this figure was fewer than 300.

Founder Camillo Olivetti returned home from Stanford University in California to establish Italy's first typewriter factory in 1908, in the town of Ivrea, near Turin. His son, Adriano, took over leadership during the Fascist era and, in the years after World War II, expanded the company by taking over the Underwood Typewriter Company in the US.

Olivetti's engineers produced sophisticated four-function mechanical calculators, built one of the first all-transistor mainframe computers, and have a plausible claim to be credited with the earliest desktop computer. Each new model built on what had gone before. Olivetti's most elaborate mechanical calculator, for example, was the product of 50 years of continuous development that began with the original Olivetti typewriter. These were remarkable machines that commanded premium prices – and which remained in production for a long time. As a result, they were highly profitable. To build products such as the Divisumma 24 (see page 283), demanded skills that the world has now lost, an entire factory, and such pre-existing units as the printing mechanism, based on typewriter components. Olivetti set a path for culturally sophisticated brand building and the manufacture of charismatic products that was followed at a respectful distance by its competitors, first IBM, then much later by Apple.

Adriano Olivetti appointed his son-in-law, Giorgio Soavi, a writer and a close friend of Alberto Giacometti, as the company's corporate design director. He and Renzo Zorzi, who edited Primo Levi's first book, led the selection of architects, artists and designers who worked for Olivetti: Louis Kahn built Olivetti's factory in Pennsylvania; James Stirling designed its training centre in Britain; Carlo Scarpa, Gae Aulenti and Ernesto Rogers produced its showrooms; and Milton Glaser and Herbert Bayer designed its posters. The company's first American showroom on Fifth Avenue was designed by Ernesto Rogers in the 1950s, where Marcello Nizzoli's typewriters impaled on marble stalagmites attracted the enthusiastic attention of IBM's leader, Thomas Watson Jr. He was impressed enough to hire Eliot Noyes to lead IBM's own corporate-design strategy, alongside Paul Rand, and Charles and Ray Eames.

The network of Olivetti factories and technical offices, in and around Ivrea in 1970, was the personification of an industrial system that seemed like the height of modernity at the time, but which is now extinct. There were machine shops and presses, assembly lines, maintenance shops and warehouses. There was an office that worked on nothing but typefaces for all Olivetti's typewriters. At its height, Olivetti employed 12,000 workers in Ivrea – skilled tool makers, draftsmen and technicians, but also physicists and engineers, nursery school teachers and marketeers. There was a functioning foundry, working with hand-carved wooden moulds that were used to sand-cast aluminium parts for Marcello Nizzoli's Lettera typewriters – techniques that are now mostly only used by artists such as Jeff Koons, rather than in factories. The components would be hand finished and then enamel painted in an oven.

In their nature, creative designers are not naturally drawn to the idea of becoming corporate employees, based in out-of-the-way company towns like Olivetti's headquarters in Ivrea. The Olivetti strategy, from the time of Adriano's leadership, was to embed designers within the company, but at the same time to give them the independence they needed to bring other experiences to its products. It simultaneously supported Ettore Sottsass and Mario Bellini in their own studios – with their own teams, technical draftsmen and studios – in Milan, 100km (60 miles) from the factories and management offices in Ivrea, and it maintained a liaison office in Ivrea. It was an arrangement that allowed designers immersion within the organization, but also the independence to cross-pollinate Olivetti with their experiences with other clients.

1

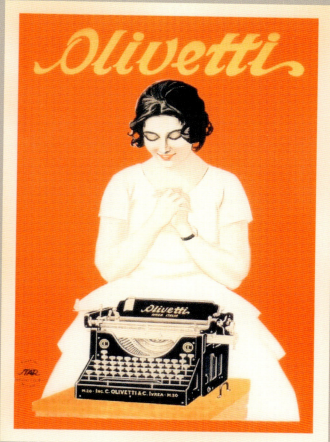

2

(1) and (2) Olivetti worked
with a wide range of artists
to create posters advertising
its products, moving from
classical themes to the more
contemporary approach
of Marcello Dudovich,
responsible for the image of
a young woman apparently
overwhelmed by the new
M20 typewriter of 1930.

(3) Olivetti Lettera 22
portable typewriter, 1950
(see page 224).

3

ETP 55 portable typewriter

Date: 1986

Designer: Mario Bellini

Manufacturer: Olivetti, Ivrea, Italy.
Made in Singapore.

Dimensions: 12.4 × 41 × 33cm
(4¾ × 16 × 13in)

The electric typewriter market was dominated by IBM and its Selectric (see page 226), a model that it had been making since the 1960s. Olivetti's first electric portable, the Lexikon 82 (see page 231), used a golfball system rather than conventional keys. The Lexikon 82 was a beautiful machine, but too heavy to be truly portable, and its combination of a golf ball and a traditional moving carriage taken from manual typewriters made for uneven typing.

It was replaced by the lightweight ETP 55, also designed by Mario Bellini, which placed letters around the edges of a flat disc. The ETP 55 was lighter and, in contrast to the rounded forms of the Lexikon 82, had a sharp wedge form, like the one that Bellini used in his design for a cassette-tape deck for Yamaha (see page 93). The ETP 55 had a pale blue-and-cream colour scheme that was very much a reflection of the post-modern wave of the period.

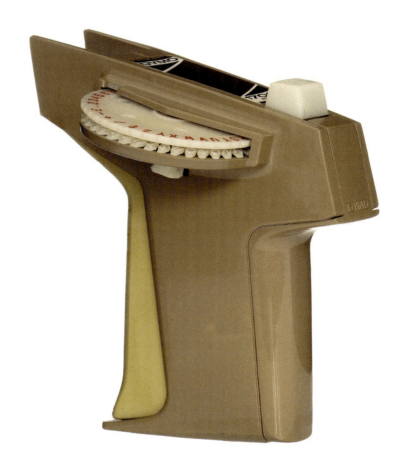

Dymo 1700 tape printer

Date: 1961

Designer: David Souza

Manufacturer: Dymo Corporation, Berkeley, CA, US

Dimensions: 14 × 12.7 × 1.3cm (5½ × 5 × ½in)

Rudolph Hurwich established the Dymo Corporation in 1958. Its first successful product was a handheld, personal labelling device, designed by David Souza, who assigned his patent to Hurwich. The tape printer relied on an adhesive plastic film and a disc containing raised letters. The machine embossed the tape, one letter at a time, and then spooled it out, ready to be sliced off when it was complete. The backing tape was removed and the tape placed in position. It was really a form of stationery, much like headed notepaper and business cards, but by coupling it with such a distinctive object, it became a part of the language of graphic design – the Dymo font can still be found on album covers and posters.

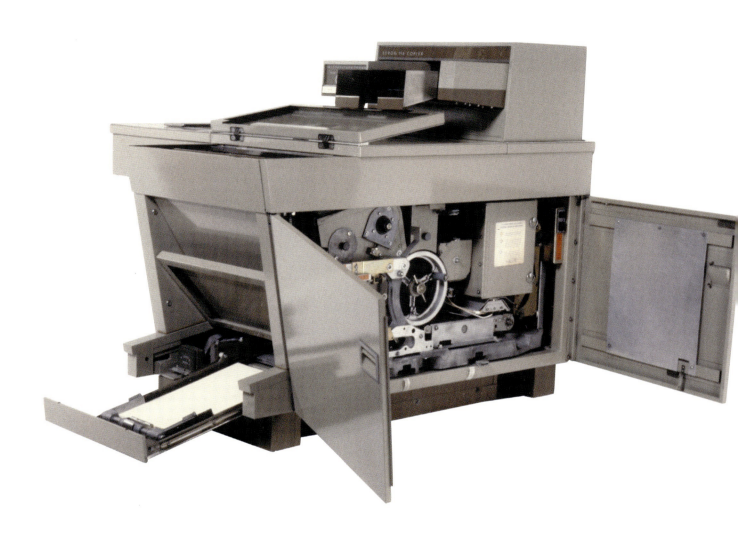

Xerox 914 copier

Date: 1959

Designers: Chester Carlson, James Balmer, Don Shepardson, John Rutkus, Hal Bogdenoff

Manufacturer: Haloid Xerox, Rochester, NY, US

Dimensions: 107 × 117 × 114cm (42 × 46 × 45in)

Analogue photocopiers were a breakthrough technology that made duplicators redundant. But, unlike digital photocopiers, which scan a single image of the original and use it to make an infinite number of copies or transmit it like a facsimile machine, an analogue copier needs to scan the original each time it makes a copy. Haloid was a company that started out making chemical copying paper, but acquired the patents needed to make plain paper copies using the xerography method invented by Chester Carlson. The 914 was named for its

maximum copy size of 22.9 × 35.5cm (9 × 14in), and could produce seven copies a minute.

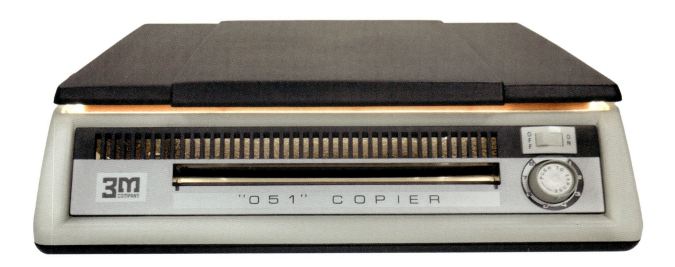

3M 051 dry copier

Date: 1971

Designer: 3M

Manufacturer 3M, St Paul, MN, USA

Dimensions: Approx. 22.9 × 38.1 × 7.6cm
(9 × 15 × 3in)

The 3M Company offered a low-cost
alternative to photocopying for personal users
that did not require large numbers of copies.
It depended on heat-sensitive paper that was
positioned under the document to be copied.
This was exposed to infrared light inside the
copier that caused a copy of the original image
to appear on the paper. The 3M 051 was
designed to copy paper up to 21 × 35.6cm
(8¼ × 14in).

Copy-Jack Plus, handheld photo copier

Date: 1986

Designer: Plus Corporation

Manufacturer: Plus Corporation, Tokyo, Japan

Dimensions: 5 × 14 × 12cm (2 × 5½ × 4¾in)

The Plus Corporation specialized in office equipment and stationery supplies before it moved into electronics. The Copy-Jack Plus was made during a period when Japan was flooded with gadgets designed to look as cute as possible to appeal to consumers, even if they were of questionable utility. The Copy-Jack's matt-black plastic form looked much like an Olympus camera of the same period. It offered instant copies of documents and receipts, printed on a narrow strip of paper – a role that is now taken by smartphone cameras. The Copy-Jack Plus was passed over the document to be copied, and the resulting images were transferred to the roll of paper contained within the machine.

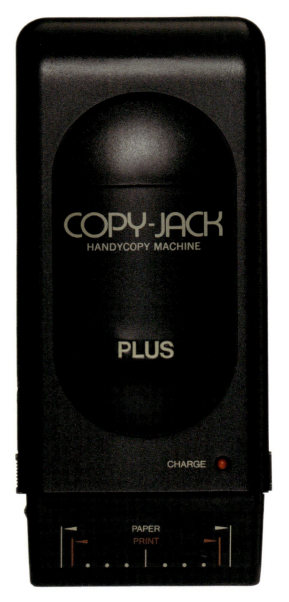

Creed Model 7 teleprinter

Date: 1931

Designer: Creed & Company

Manufacturer: Creed & Company,
Croydon, UK

Dimensions: 49.5 × 59.7 × 26.7cm
(19½ × 23½ × 10½in)

Communicating through the early telegraph systems of the nineteenth century was slow and required an operator skilled in the use of morse code. The teleprinter was developed to address the problem: a keyboard connected to telegraph or telephone wires could be used to remotely trigger a keyboard stroke at the receiving teleprinter, speeding up the process and doing away with Morse code.

Post-office monopolies used teleprinters to send telegrams. It was a process that involved the customer dictating a message, for which they were charged by the word, giving rise to a specially condensed form of language. The post-office telex operator typed the message, and the receiving machine recorded a printout, which was pasted onto a telegraph form, then delivered to the final recipient – often by a motorcycle despatch rider. Commercial users, such as banks and newspapers, had their own teleprinter machines, which could be used to communicate in a way that could be seen as a forerunner to email.

ASR 32 teleprinter

Date: 1964

Designer: Teletype Corporation

Manufacturer: Teletype Corporation,
Chicago, IL, US

Dimensions: 55.8 × 46.9 × 21.5cm
(22 × 18½ × 8½in)

Teleprinters began as a method to speed up telegraphy. The first teleprinters replaced operators trained in Morse code with an electro-mechanical method of transmitting messages. Before the widespread availability of computer systems, teleprinters were used as a means of instantly sharing large quantities of information in written form. They depended on a large and costly machine connected to the copper wires of the telephone system, and so were restricted to commercial users such as newspapers, banks, hotels and transport companies. Because they could be programmed to run punched-tape codes, teleprinters were also used as interfaces with computer systems, allowing them to input programmes and output their results. The Teletype Corporation was one of a number of manufacturers, and its ASR (automatic send and receive) 32 was one of its most successful models. Such machines had an afterlife in the 1970s, when secondhand models were connected to telephones for use by the deaf.

Canon Fax 110 facsimile machine

Date: 1987

Designer: Canon Inc.

Manufacturer: Canon Inc., Tokyo, Japan

Dimensions: 28 × 25 × 9cm (11 × 9¾ × 3½in)

The technology used by fax machines dates back to the nineteenth century and the invention of the electric printing telegraph. Optical scanning arrived in 1902, which allowed photographs to be transmitted in the same way. Yet, it was only in 1966 that Xerox produced the first modern fax machine, paving the way for the technology to be used in what became a domestic consumer object.

Japanese manufacturers, such as Canon, produced their own models and found a ready market for them. The Japanese language lends itself to the medium – a handwritten note can be transmitted quickly and easily, and it was an effective means of communicating an address in Japan's idiosyncratic street-numbering system. When Canon started manufacturing fax machines, they were still competing with the postal system but, as a communications system, they gave way to email within 20 years.

OFX 325 facsimile machine

Date: 1990

Designer: George Sowden

Manufacturer: Olivetti, Ivrea, Italy

Dimensions: 30 × 32.5 × 7cm
(11¾ × 12¾ × 2¾in)

Olivetti came late to the manufacture of fax machines and looked for a Japanese joint-venture partner ready to share its expertise, eventually signing an agreement with Sanyo.

Designer George Sowden had worked on mechanisms to feed printers with paper, but the first fax machines depended on heat-sensitive paper supplied from a roll. Sending a fax involved feeding sheets in at one end, while incoming messages spilled out at the other. But the technology was changing fast; plain paper copying was a much more convenient option and, in Japan, manufacturers were already working with it. Sanyo were unwilling or unable to help, so Olivetti found another partner, Canon, to build a second generation of fax machines.

Information

Until the end of the twentieth century, analogue methods were used to represent physical phenomena including size, time, sound, temperature, electric current and light levels, as well as to measure, record, remember and store information of all kinds. Writing, paper and printing were all developed to this end. Dials and gauges followed. These are the tools that have been used for everything from predicting the weather to dealing with illness.

Maps have been used as analogue representations of the world for thousands of years. Analogue compasses have roots in the Han dynasty of China, when a spoon-shaped magnetite-ore lodestone on a bronze plate was used first for the purposes of geomancy and then as an aid to navigation. Rulers have been used as a measure, or a yardstick, throughout the ages. The clock, which is at least 600 years old, is still an effective way of representing time. The sundial is far older than that, and represents another means of analogue timekeeping. Scientists have been proposing various methods of measuring

relative humidity, which is to say air moisture, since the fourteenth century. These have included weighing salt and sponges, and measuring hair. The slide rule, which was a simple analogue calculator, dates back to 1622, while the mercury thermometer dates from 1714.

While these analogue instruments had utilitarian origins, their cultural significance was celebrated by the elaboration and craftsmanship that went into their making and embellishment.

If information storage in the digital sense is a file in the cloud, the analogue version was a book on a shelf in a physical library. The analogue equivalent of a search engine was an index and a card catalogue. Yet, automated storage and retrieval systems developed for warehousing have taken over from the traditional Dewey Decimal system of bibliographers and cataloguers.

Technically speaking, analogue as a category is not completely dead, even if there are now effective ways of replicating much of what it had to offer using digital means, and in more affordable ways. There are many examples of

(1) From 1662 until the 1970s, the slide rule was the cheapest and simplest form of mechanical calculator; an analogue 'computer' that could perform complex multiplication and division based on logarithmic principles (see page 283).

(2) The combination of a pocket sundial with a compass was the product of several centuries of evolution.

2

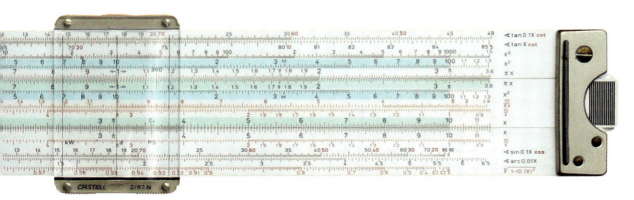

1

253 CE The Greeks and Romans imported Egyptian obelisks and sundials used to measure time and learned from them.

1620 Working with the logarithmic tables invented by the mathematician John Napier, William Oughtred was responsible for manufacturing the first slide-rule calculator.

1680 Robert Hooke's anchor escapement refined the earlier work of Christiaan Huygens work, resulting in the Longcase grandfather clock.

1714 The invention of the mercury thermometer by Daniel Fahrenheit (see page 250). A pocket-sized version of the foot-long device was developed in the nineteenth century.

3

4

(3) Solari di Udine's long history as a clock-making company found a new form in its monumental split-flap departure board, designed to match the architecture of Eero Sarinen's terminal for TWA at Kennedy airport in New York.

(4) The mechanism for Terraillon's kitchen scale (see page 254) works on the same principle as the spring balance. The ample container included in Richard Sapper's design makes it a useful cooking utensil.

1770 Richard Salter, using the research of the physicist Robert Hooke, devised a method of accurately measuring weight using a spring, without the need for a counter balance.

1791 The French Academy of Sciences defined a new standard measurement, the metre, as one ten-millionth of the distance from the equator to the north pole.

1795 The unit of mass, the gram, was defined as the absolute weight of a volume of pure water equal to the cube of the hundredth part of the metre, and at the temperature of melting ice.

1843 Lucien Vidi designed the aneroid barometer, using a measurement of the expansion or contraction of a sealed metal chamber to predict weather in response to atmospheric pressure.

5

(5) Originally devised in 1890, the Arithmometer (see page 282), a mechanical computer, was still being manufactured in large numbers in the Soviet Union until the 1970s.

(6) Junghan combined Swiss watchmaking skills with the visual logic of the Bauhaus-trained artist and architect, Max Bill, who designed their watch faces.

devices that use both analogue and digital technologies, such as modern cameras equipped with analogue image sensors that are then converted into digital signals. There are also certain everyday objects, such as the wristwatch, that, while logically should by now have been extinguished by far cheaper, more reliable and more accurate digital replacements, have, in fact, survived. Expensive watches were kept on life support by investment from Swiss watchmakers in advertising and marketing long enough to enjoy a second incarnation. Apple's successful choice to make its wearable computing device in the

form of a wristwatch – rather than Google's failed attempt to make smart eyeglasses – has contributed to the continuing longevity of the watch, albeit with digital rather than analogue technology driving it.

Thanks to the continuing appetite to mark out our lives by the possessions that we own, and our continuing preference for passing them on to our descendants, the watch has taken on the character of jewellery. So many analogue technologies came to the premature end of an evolutionary road, but watch mechanisms have adopted evermore baroque complications.

6

1879 Anxious about staff theft, James Ritty devised the Ritty Incorruptible Cashier (see page 251) to keep an accurate record of the takings in his saloon.

1890 Mechanical calculators, such as Thomas de Colmar's Arithmometer, were the forerunners of modern computing.

1893 The Austrian inventor Josef Pallweber was the first to patent and manufacture a flip clock.

1904 Louis Cartier made a more elegant version of the timepieces worn by British soldiers (see page 274).

7

(7) The Volkswagen speedometer (see page 253) was designed to be cheap to manufacture and easy to install, in keeping with the original idea of an affordable 'people's car'.

(8) George Nelson suggested that since most people tell the time by looking at the position of the hands on a clock, numerals are superfluous, so he left them off his Ball clock (see page 256).

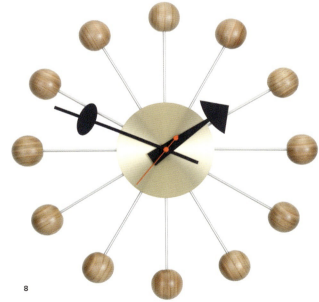

8

1916 Swiss watchmaker Edouard Heuer devised the Mikrograph stopwatch (see page 273), capable of accurately recording intervals of time to within a hundredth of a second.

1940 Camillo Olivetti added four-function calculating machines to his range with the Summa MC4 (see page 282).

1960 The Accutron Spaceview watch (see page 275) was the first to use a battery-powered oscillating tuning fork, miniaturized for a wristwatch.

1983 Release of the Swatch (see page 276), a remarkably successful response to the challenge of cheap and reliable quartz watches.

Product Directory

Measurement

Analogue devices that measure natural phenomena, such as weight or air moisture, depend on two distinct elements. One is a device capable of taking a reading, and the other is the means to display the result. Thermometers combine both of these in a single form. Mercury in a glass tube, calibrated in degrees Centigrade and Fahrenheit, expands in response to heat. In contrast, the dials and gauges on a car dashboard work by relaying information about speed and engine performance from remote sensors in an instantly understandable form.

Clocks

Time was once under the control of the church, or the state, embedded in the architectural form of clocks in town halls and church towers as civic landmarks. Mass-produced clock mechanisms democratized time in the twentieth century and the domestic clock lost its portentous quality. It was no longer a costly and imposing gift, given to mark a major life event, such as marriage or retirement, and became either modestly functional, in the manner of Braun's clocks, or frankly decorative like George Nelson's inventive range of mid-century modern designs that more or less abandoned numerals and the delineation of minutes.

Clock Radios

The major reason for combining a clock and radio was to use a pre-tuned radio station as a less violent wake-up call than an alarm. This was the main driver in their design: the controls needed to be legible and simple enough to make sense late at night in semi-darkness. In the 1980s, one or two manufacturers who had been making pre-programmable tea and coffee makers, added radios to the mix, in a level of complexity that proved a step too far.

Timers

Some categories of object are designed to do less rather than more. You could use a clock to tell you that you had soft boiled your breakfast egg for precisely three minutes, as well as the time of day. A kitchen timer can only do one of those things, but does it more effectively. A stopwatch doesn't tell the time of day. It has an inappropriate degree of precision for the kitchen, but not to judge a record-breaking race.

Wristwatches

It took several centuries for the clock to shrink to the scale of the pocket watch. Yet, the wristwatch, largely the product of the twentieth century, triggered a rapid and explosive burst of innovation. An early driver was the advent of mechanized warfare in which synchronized operations were vital. The wristwatch was more practical than a pocket watch. From this utilitarian beginning the wristwatch evolved into the most widespread form of male jewellery.

Calculators

After the abacus, and before the electronic calculator, the world relied on two basic methods of making rapid and accurate complex calculations. There were mechanical calculators of various kinds that relied on elaborate systems of cogs and wheels, which were set in motion by pressing buttons, or adjusting the position of cog wheels. And there was the slide rule – much less costly, but which demanded a certain amount of expertise to read the results.

Pocket compass

Date: Eleventh century

Designer: Unknown

Manufacturer: Various

Dimensions: Approx. 7.5 × 5.2 × 1.2cm
(3 × 2 × ½in)

An analogue compass uses the earth's magnetic field to identify magnetic (rather than true) north in order to provide a directional guide. The first culture to make use of magnetism for navigational purposes was the Chinese Han dynasty (206 BCE–220 CE), which found that lodestone – naturally occurring magnets – could be used for directional purposes well before the Christian era. In more modern times, the compass used a magnetized needle on a pivot or a bearing that allowed it to align with magnetic north. This was initially developed in China during the eleventh century, from where it was rapidly communicated to Western Europe.

Mercury thermometer

Date: 1714

Designer: Daniel Gabriel Fahrenheit

Manufacturer: Daniel Gabriel Fahrenheit

Dimensions: Approx. 30cm (12in) in length

Daniel Fahrenheit spent his working life as a physicist, but was both a scientist and a craftsman. He had the skill to blow glass, which allowed him to make a range of scientific instruments that he designed himself. His first attempt at a thermometer used alcohol, which he later replaced with the more toxic, but also accurate, mercury. He conceived of the Fahrenheit scale as being based on three fundamentals: zero was the reading that his mercury-filled glass tube recorded when immersed in iced water; the reading of 30 degrees was assigned to the result of immersing the tube in water that was on the point of turning to ice; and the reading of 90 degrees was assigned to the result of placing the mercury tube under the tongue.

National Cash Register

Date: 1885

Designer: James Jacob Ritty

Manufacturer: National Cash Register
Company, Dayton, OH, US

Dimensions: 38 × 43 × 33cm (15 × 17 × 13in)

The mechanical cash register has its roots in the lack of trust that many shop keepers felt for their employees. It was designed to provide a permanent record of every sales transaction and cash receipt. The Ritty Incorruptible Cashier was patented in 1883. It included a bell that rang every time a cash transaction took place, ensuring that the shop manager would be aware of it. Ritty sold his patent to what became the National Cash Register Company. The early machines were elaborate and ornate, made of cast brass, suggesting their significance visually. They were designed to draw attention to themselves to ensure that cash transactions did not take place without people knowing.

Bugatti type 54 dashboard

Date: 1932

Designer: Ettore Bugatti

Manufacturer: Bugatti, Molsheim, France

Dimensions: Approx. 121.9 × 15.2cm
(48 × 6in)

A car dashboard, with its steering wheel, gear lever and brake pedals, along with all the dials and gauges to tell you what the engine is doing, how fast you are driving, and how much fuel there is in the tank, could itself be described as an analogue system. Before power steering – and the Bugatti Type 54 was certainly made before this – the steering wheel turned the car to the left or the right to a degree that was directly related to the amount of physical effort that you put into the movement.

Ettore Bugatti was famously a perfectionist about the cars that he built in modest number, and which carried his name. While the car itself was finished in Bugatti blue, the dashboard had a bare-metal engineering finish, with a constellation of smaller dials placed symmetrically around the larger speedometer. Where possible, Bugatti branded the dials with his own name, but he was prepared to work with Jaeger-LeCoultre, the watchmaker that had added instruments for cars and aircraft to its catalogues.

Odometer

Date: 1938

Designer: VDO Tachometer Werke

Manufacturer: VDO Tachometer Werke, Frankfurt, Germany

Dimensions: 11.2cm (4½in) diameter

As the Greek origins of the name Odometer suggest, the concept of a mechanical device to measure the distance travelled by a vehicle goes back to early classical civilizations. VDO (Vereinigte Deta–OTA), a company established in 1928, began by manufacturing tachometers, – otherwise known as speedometers – with a device that counts the revolutions that the vehicle's axles make per minute. The Odometer played a vital part in providing a permanent record of the car's history, registering miles on the clock.

The VDO brand name was applied to the instrument panel of the Volkswagen Beetle from the time of its first incarnation as the KdF-wagen, part of Hitler's attempt to build the so-called 'people's car'. It remained the component supplier throughout the Beetle's 65-year production history.

Citroën DS 19 dashboard

Date: 1955

Designers: Flaminio Bertoni, André Lefèbvre

Manufacturer: Citroën, Paris, France

Dimensions: 149.9 × 20.3cm (59 × 8in)

The Citroën DS 19 represented 20 years of research by the company, and was designed to demonstrate that France was capable of producing a car as technologically advanced as anything that America could make. The car had an advanced suspension hydraulic system and power steering as standard.

Bertoni, who was responsible for the styling, gave the interior a remarkable single-spoke steering wheel, and an instrument panel set in a sweeping set of complex, curved and smooth surfaces. Author Roland Barthes said of the dashboard that 'the slim panes of matt metal, the small levers topped by a white ball, the very simple dials, all this signifies a kind of control exercised over motion, rather than performance. One is obviously turning from an alchemy of speed to a relish in driving.'

Terraillon 4000 kitchen scales

Date: 1969

Designers: Marco Zanuso, Richard Sapper

Manufacturer: Terraillon, Annemasse, France

Dimensions: 18 × 13 × 12.3cm (7 × 5 × 4¾in)

Terraillon is now Chinese-owned and its domestic appliances, for the most part based on digital technology, are manufactured in factories in Shenzhen, sometimes dubbed China's Silicon Valley. But its roots are French, and it was founded by Lucien Terraillon in 1908 as a clockmaking business in Annemasse, a small town near the Swiss border, close to Geneva. In 1948, Paul Terraillon branched out into mechanical scales for kitchens and bathrooms, which he designed himself. As the company grew, Terraillon started to work with

Marco Zanuso and Richard Sapper to give a more sophisticated look to its products, and it moved some of its production to Italy. Starting in 1969, Zanuso and Sapper worked on a series of scales, made from injection-moulded ABS plastic. They featured a transparent plastic cover, which also forms the container, and came in a range of sizes; the 4000 had a larger capacity than the 2000.

Hygrometer

Date: 1978

Designer: Henning Koppel

Manufacturer: Georg Jensen, Copenhagen, Denmark

Dimensions: 10cm (4in) diameter, 4.4cm (1½in) depth

Georg Jensen established his studio in 1904 on an international reputation for virtuoso craftsmanship. After his death in 1935, the company continued to make the Arts-and-Crafts-inspired pieces that he had designed, and found others to work with. In 1945, artist Henning Koppel joined the company.

Koppel's work for Georg Jensen gave the company a new energy and extended to highly refined cutlery, sculptural holloware and jewellery, as well as more utilitarian products, such as the hygrometer. Made from stainless steel, it was designed as part of the weather-station set, that in addition to measuring relative humidity also offered a thermometer and barometric pressure. They shared a simple but elegant format.

Ball clock

Date: 1949

Designer: George Nelson

Manufacturer: Howard Miller Clock Company, Zealand, Michigan, US, now Vitra, Weil am Rhein, Germany

Dimensions: 33 × 5.7cm (13 × 2¼in)

George Nelson was the design director for the office-furniture manufacturer, Herman Miller, when he was commissioned to design a range for the company's clock subsidiary (originally called Herman Miller Clock Company, later renamed for the founder's son, Howard).

Nelson, who was also responsible for introducing Charles and Ray Eames to the furniture company, worked on a series of 14 clocks that were introduced to the market in 1949, and as strikingly different from the traditional clocks the company had been

making previously as the Eames lounge chair was from Herman Miller's pre-war products.

Nelson's analysis of the way people use clocks suggested numerals were not necessary – people tell the time from the position of the hands. Nelson's clocks were witty, decorative and sculptural objects. Vitra, which had been making Eames furniture in Europe since the 1950s, acquired Nelson's archive, and began re-editioning his clocks from 1999.

Junghans kitchen clock

Date: 1956
Designer: Max Bill
Manufacturer: Gebrüder Junghans AG,
Schramberg, West Germany
Dimensions: 25.2 × 18 × 5.6cm (10 × 7 × 2¼in)

Junghans was a German manufacturer of watches and clocks that worked with the Bauhaus-trained Swiss architect and artist, Max Bill, over many years. After World War II, Bill became the director of the Hochschule für Gestaltung school of design in Ulm, often described as the successor to the Bauhaus. It was the school that inspired Dieter Rams' approach to design for Braun, and Bill's work for Junghans followed a similar rationalist direction. His first design for the company was the so-called kitchen clock, designed to be attached to a wall, and which came with a timekeeper positioned beneath the main clockface. Bill followed it with a succession of other clock and wristwatch designs for the company.

Static clock

Date: 1959

Designer: Richard Sapper

Manufacturer: Lorenz, Milan, Italy

Dimensions: 9.5 × 6.5 × 6.5cm
(3¾ × 2½ × 2½in)

Tullio Bolletta, founder of the Milanese watchmaking company Lorenz, commissioned Richard Sapper to design a clock that would use an existing electro-mechanical movement, originally devised for use as a timing device for torpedo fuses. The resulting Static is a slightly mysterious sculptural object, formed from a milled solid block of stainless steel, hollowed out to contain the mechanism. The rounded form has a circular flat area at the base, on which it can rest, while a counterweight inside serves to stabilize the clock.

Sapper described the Static clock as difficult to make. 'It has this flat spot, which is cut into the volume for the clock to rest on the table,' he added. 'When you tip the clock over, it would roll on the table until it found the flat part, and then it would stand upright again. So, that was "the game" of that clock.' From 2019, Lorenz started making the clock using a new Quartz mechanism.

Secticon T2 clock

Date: 1960
Designer: Angelo Mangiarotti
Manufacturer: Portescap, La Chaux-de-Fonds, Switzerland
Dimensions: 15.2 × 13cm (6 × 5in)

Angelo Mangiarotti was a leading Italian architect and designer. His design for the Secticon had its origins in the Maritime, a clock made for a yacht that Mangiarotti fitted out in 1956. The Secticon range of clocks were first produced in 1960 by the Swiss manufacturer, Portescap, and the range included table and wall versions, made using brass and plastic. Alongside his architectural work, Mangiarotti was a talented artist, influenced by such figures as the sculptors Hans Arp and Constantin Brâncusi, and that sensibility is visible in the sculptural quality of the Secticon clocks. More recently, a German manufacturer, Klein & More, has produced a licensed version, with a body made from porcelain rather than plastic.

Braun

Although it is now part of the Proctor & Gamble conglomerate, and best-known for inelegant electric toothbrushes, Braun was originally started in Frankfurt, in 1921, by the German engineer Max Braun to build domestic radio sets. It added radiograms to the range in the 1930s and, after World War II, Braun expanded into household appliances, manufacturing electric food mixers and electric shavers.

After their father's death in 1951, Artur and Erwin Braun took over the firm. They set out to build a modern business that took its social responsibilities to its employees seriously. At the same time, they created a new brand identity and a novel approach to product design for Braun, which came to symbolize modern, democratic Germany. They established close links with the newly opened Ulm School of Design (which saw itself as the successor to the Bauhaus), and built up Braun's own design team, led after 1955 by Dieter Rams – perhaps the most influential German designer of the post-war era. Under Rams' leadership Braun manufactured toasters, clocks, watches, radios, hi-fi systems, television sets and cine cameras. As Rams once put it, he aspired to make them the equivalent of a supremely efficient English butler: they were invisible when not in use, and performed effortlessly well when needed.

The artist Richard Hamilton made Braun products the subject matter of a long series of his works, and wrote that they had the same place in his artistic imagination that Mont Sainte-Victoire had in Paul Cézanne's. The cool logic that Rams applied to everything that he did created a model that also inspired Jonathan Ive, the British industrial designer who worked closely with Steve Jobs for Apple. Rams tried to move away from short-term fashion, built-in obsolescence and conspicuous consumption. 'Less is more' was a catchphrase of the architect Mies van der Rohe, but Rams certainly believed in it, and added his own gloss, suggesting that good design meant less but better design. His designs, mostly monochrome, with just a few accents of colour to signal the key controls, and using as few materials as possible, haven't dated. But the technology on which his analogue products were based certainly has. Braun's parent company has stopped manufacturing the objects that Rams designed, but they have a continuing appeal for a certain kind of consumer. Proctor & Gamble has licensed production of replica versions of the original Braun clocks and watches, and examples of the real thing have become sought-after collector's pieces.

(1) Max Braun's two sons, Erwin and Artur, took over the radio business their father had started.

(2) The Braun RT 20 radio (see page 54) was designed for the company by Dieter Rams in 1963.

(3) The Braun wristwatch (see page 278) was originally conceived as a promotional gift for the firm's customers.

(4) Given that it is usually set late at night and switched off early in the morning, the controls of an alarm clock need to offer instant clarity.

1

2

3

4

Twemco QT-30 clock

Date: 1968

Designer: Twemco Industries Ltd

Manufacturer: Twemco Industries Ltd,
Hong Kong, China

Dimensions: 19.5 × 10.3 × 7.5cm (7½ × 4 × 3in)

Twemco was first established in 1968 and
now markets itself as offering 'retro' modern
flip clocks. Its products may have different
mechanisms to those designed by Gino Valle
for Solari of Udine (see page 245), but they
clearly owe a strong visual debt to its Italian
predecessor. It is a tribute to the legacy of that
moment in Italian design and technology that
Valle's design still seems relevant.

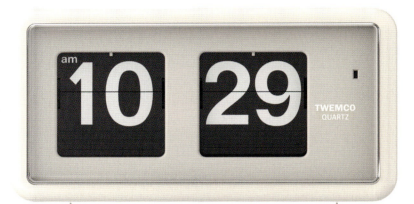

Sandwich alarm clock

Date: 1971

Designer: Richard Sapper

Manufacturer: Ritz-Italora, Milan, Italy

Dimensions: 8 × 6 × 3.5cm (3 × 2¼ × 1½in)

Industrial designer Richard Sapper suggested the name of this clock because, in order to stop the alarm from ringing, you had to squeeze the two halves of the 'sandwich' together.

The Sandwich – available in black, silver, white and red – was designed by Sapper for Ritz-Italora, a component supply company keen to reach consumers directly with a new range of products. It was a natural extension of their technical capacity to make timekeeping equipment for the consumer market.

Phase 2 Braun alarm clock

Date: 1972

Designers: Dieter Rams, Dietrich Lubs

Manufacturer: Braun AG, Frankfurt,
West Germany

Dimensions: 14 × 8 × 5cm (5½ × 3¼ × 2in)

The Phase 2 was Braun's take on the Solari split-flap numeral clock from the 1950s (see page 245). Designers Dieter Rams and Dietrich Lubs created a rigorously detailed case that put the display at the front of the clock and tilted up to show the time when it was placed on a table top. The Phase 2 was Braun's first and only flip-clock mechanism release.

Braun AB 20 alarm clock

Date: 1975

Designer: Dieter Rams, Dietrich Lubs

Manufacturer: Braun AG, Frankfurt,
West Germany

Dimensions: 8.6 × 6.3 × 4.3cm
(3¼ × 2½ × 1¾in)

Braun presented the AB 20 as a travel clock – an essential item to pack on any trip, along with the electric razor that the company also offered. It was designed to be as simple to use as possible, given that it was likely that the controls would only be used late at night or first thing in the morning, when users might not be at their most clearheaded. There are just two switches on the clock front, connected in a single unit. For the avoidance of doubt, one of them is marked 'on' and the other 'off'. The only other control is on the back, which allows for the adjustment of the clock hands, and for setting an alarm time. There were other, slightly more elaborate versions that came with a folding flap to protect the face, inscribed with world time zones.

Metropole clock

Date: 1982
Designer: George Sowden
Manufacturer: Memphis Milano, Milan, Italy
Dimensions: 24 × 24 × 81cm (9½ × 9½ × 32in)

Ettore Sottsass set up the Memphis Group of architects and designers at the start of the 1980s, with the aim of bringing about a fundamental reassessment of the form that everyday objects could take. Having worked with Sottsass at Olivetti, where he designed a series of products including fax equipment and calculating machines, George Sowden became a key member of the group.

As Memphis saw it, electronics had made the traditional design concept of using functional requirements to determine the shape of things redundant. A printed circuit did away with most moving parts, and so objects could be shaped not by how they worked, but by the message that the designer wanted them to send. Sowden's Metropole clock is vaguely suggestive of a domestic shrine or a household totem. It demonstrates Sowden's lifelong fascination with surface pattern and colour.

Richard Sapper

Richard Sapper followed an unusual route to becoming a designer: he took a business degree in Munich, where he was born in 1932, before studying engineering and then joining Mercedes-Benz in Stuttgart. His first job there was designing the wing mirrors for the Mercedes 300 SL sports car, but he grew tired of the constraints of working in the auto industry. After moving to Milan in 1958, Sapper spent most of his career in Italy, where he died in 2015.

Sapper developed a sophisticated design language, based on simplicity, pure geometric shapes, strong tactile qualities and a restricted colour palette. He worked briefly in Italian architect Gio Ponti's studio, then divided his time between the Rinascente department store's inhouse design office and the architect Marco Zanuso's studio. He left Rinascente to form a partnership with Zanuso that lasted until the 1970s, during the course of which they created some of the most memorable analogue television sets and radios ever designed, including the Doney, Algol and Black models for Brionvega, as well as the Grillo telephone handset. The Black was a mirror-smooth, black-glass cube that seems to disappear when not in use.

Working on his own, Sapper produced designs for clocks and watches for Lorenz and Heuer, among other companies, winning Italy's Compasso d'Oro design award for the first time in 1960, for the Static table clock, which made ingenious use of an army-surplus timing mechanism manufactured for use in torpedoes. Sapper housed the mechanism in a smooth metal case and gave it a bold, graphic face.

He is perhaps best known for the Tizio adjustable desk lamp and his kettle for Alessi. Both products reflect the mixture of his meticulous approach with practical detail. The Tizio has a minimal footprint, to leave the desk surface clear, and uses the structure to carry electric current, rather than unsightly cables. The kettle has a two-tone whistle, tuned to sound like an American train locomotive.

Sapper's first project as IBM's chief industrial-design consultant was a prototype for an electric typewriter that would have replaced Eliot Noyes' famous Selectric. His studied a space-saving vertical format, but IBM was already on the verge of launching its first personal computer, which would make the typewriter redundant. Sapper was, however, responsible for IBM's first laptop computer, the Think Pad, which was successful enough for the Chinese manufacturer Lenovo to acquire the rights to produce it once IBM had decided to abandon the hardware.

(1) Richard Sapper spanned the divide between analogue and digital design, working on televisions and radios, as well as IBM's first laptop computer, during the course of his career.

2

3

4

(2), (3) and (4) Working with his studio partner, Marco Zanuso, on the Grillo (see page 211), Sapper gave the traditional domestic phone a bold new look.

(5) Sapper's 1971 alarm clock for Ritz-Italora was known for obvious reasons as the Sandwich (see page 264).

(6) The Static clock (see page 258), the first of many designed by Sapper, was based on the reuse of a military surplus-timing mechanism, embellished with bold typography.

(7) Sapper designed a playful kitchen timer, the Escargot (see page 273), for Terraillon.

5

6

7

Braun ABW 21 wall clock

Date: 1987

Designer: Dietrich Lubs

Manufacturer: Braun AG, Frankfurt, West Germany

Dimensions: 20 × 4cm (7¾ × 1½in)

Dietrich Lubs' wall clock for Braun was in some ways an uncharacteristic design for a company that was celebrated for its restraint. The black outer rim contains two further circular elements, one of them white inscribed with concentric brass-coloured circles, the other cream coloured. In addition, there are brass-coloured markers at the four quarter-hour points, along with two different-sized numbers – one to indicate the hours, the other indicating minutes, in jarring profusion. The contrast with the 4833 Domo – the first, much more resolved wall clock that Lubs designed for Braun – is marked.

Alessi cuckoo clock

Date: 1988

Designers: Robert Venturi, Denise Scott Brown

Manufacturer: Alessi, Crusinallo, Italy. Made in Switzerland.

Dimensions: 40.6 × 40.6 × 12.2cm (16 × 16 × 4¾in)

In the 1980s, Alessi's catalogue of new household objects, from kitchenware to timepieces, was closely identified with the post-modern revolution that was transforming the landscape of design. Alberto Alessi had retained Alessandro Mendini as his creative consultant, and Mendini was interested in exploring the work of the dissenting voices in design who were questioning modernism and functionalism. Alessi worked with Charles Jencks, the critic who had written a polemic against modernism entitled *Language of*

Post-Modern Architecture, as well as Michael Graves, the most conspicuous of America's architects, who wanted a return to ornament and history.

Robert Venturi and Denise Scott Brown were also natural additions to the Alessi brand. They expressed their belief in popular culture as a valid inspiration for high culture with their fully functional, lurid yellow-and-green cuckoo clock – a convincing celebration of the power of kitsch.

Sony digimatic BFC 100E clock radio

Date: 1972

Designer: Sony

Manufacturer: Sony, Tokyo, Japan

Dimensions: 22.5 × 12 × 13cm (8¾ × 4¾ × 5in)

Sony made a variety of clock radios using split-flap numerals. Some had a vertical orientation, others took the form of a cube. The BFC 100E was one of the earlier models and had a horizonal format. The body of the clock radio had a sloped front and sat on a short, circular stalk. Controls on one side adjust the clock, while the other side is used to tune the radio. It offers the possibility of being woken by an alarm or the radio.

Panasonic RC 6500 clock radio

Date: 1973

Designer: Panasonic

Manufacturer: Matsushita Electrical Co. Ltd, Osaka, Japan

Dimensions: Approx. 17.8 × 7.6 × 12.7cm (7 × 3 × 5in)

Panasonic's clock-radio combination looked like nothing else that was available on the market. The controls, speaker and circuits were contained in a wood-veneer cabinet. The clock and the tuner dial were contained in two illuminated, transparent circles set into a second element placed at right angles to the wooden base. The dials on the clock were idiosyncratically shaped, in vivid green and yellow, while the alarm time was indicated by a bright red dot.

GE 7-4550A clock radio

Date: 1981

Designer: General Electric

Manufacturer: General Electric, Syracuse, NY, US. Made in Malaysia.

Dimensions: 16.5 × 16.5 × 26cm (6½ × 6½ × 10¼in)

Perhaps with a view to the more conservative tastes of the American market, General Electric's clock radio was housed in a box made of polystyrene, faced in a walnut-grain laminate. The analogue clockface and tuning dial were recessed behind a transparent screen, suggestive of a small television. Clearly, General Electric felt their customers needed help to understand the controls. On the side of the box, the word 'tuning' is moulded into the plastic case next to the ridged knob, and the switch allowing users to choose a radio station at the time selected is labelled 'Wake to Music'.

Mikrograph stopwatch

Date: 1916

Designers: Jules-Edouard Heuer,
Charles-Auguste Heuer

Manufacturer: Edouard Heuer,
Bienne, Switzerland

Dimensions: 5.7cm (2¼in) diameter

The Heuer company, an established Swiss manufacturer of pocket watches, produced its first stopwatch in 1916, setting a new standard for accuracy in time measurement. It was capable of accurately recording intervals of time to within a hundredth of a second, and was designed to be used in racing. It was a capacity that saw Heuer stopwatches used as the official timekeepers in the three Olympic games held after the end of World War I.

Escargot kitchen timer

Date: 1980

Designer: Richard Sapper

Manufacturer: Ritz-Italora, Milan, Italy
for Terraillon, France

Dimensions: Approx. 2.2 × 6.7cm (¾ × 2¾in)

The Escargot was the more playful of the two kitchen timers that Sapper designed for Terraillon. The name suggests the snail-like form of the timer, with a fin emerging from its shell. It could be set to time anything up to 90 minutes and came in a variety of colours. Sapper, himself, professed to prefer the elegant prototype that he made with no numerals on the face, just minimal graphic dots. However, the production version had bold-faced numbers to make things easier for customers.

Santos wristwatch

Date: 1904

Designer: Louis Cartier

Manufacturer: Cartier, Paris, France

Dimensions: 3.4 × 2.5cm (1¼ × 1in)

Louis Cartier's grandfather, Louis-Francois, established the family jewellery business in 1847 and it quickly gained a following with the French elite. The younger Cartier expanded the business internationally and broadened the product range to include elaborately decorated so-called 'mystery' clocks.

The Santos watch was born when Brazilian aviator Alberto Santos-Dumont, who became famous for circumnavigating the Eiffel Tower in a hot-air balloon, talked to Cartier about his need for a practical timekeeping device while he was in the air, without having to fumble for his pocket watch. The Santos, which went into volume production in 1911, may not have been the first wristwatch – there were earlier versions made for women – but the association with a star as adventurous as Santos-Dumont certainly established its appeal as a masculine timepiece.

Oyster Perpetual Datejust wristwatch

Date: 1945

Designer: Rolex

Manufacturer: Rolex, Geneva, Switzerland

Dimensions: 3.6cm (1½in) diameter

Hans Wilsdorf began his career importing watch mechanisms to Britain from Switzerland in 1905. He was convinced that once they were reliable enough, wristwatches would entirely supplant the pocket watch. Wilsdorf started manufacturing Rolex wristwatches that could reliably keep time. His next step was to make them waterproof. He launched the first waterproof version, with a hermetically sealed case, called the Oyster, in 1927, with the endorsement of a cross-Channel swimmer, Mercedes Gleitze. In 1931, Wilsdorf came up with the concept of a self-winding watch, the Perpetual. The next step was to add a calendar, with the date shown in a window on the dial.

Accutron Spaceview wristwatch

Date: 1960

Designer: Max Hetzel

Manufacturer: Bulova, New York, NY, US

Dimensions: 3.4cm (1¼in) diameter

Swiss engineer, Max Hetzel, took inspiration from a tuning fork to maintain the accuracy of a timepiece that had been used in clocks since the nineteenth century. He successfully miniaturized it for Bulova, to produce the Accutron Spaceview wristwatch in 1960. The Spaceview did not require winding, but rather was powered by a battery that kept the tuning fork vibrating. With no need for a hairspring or balance wheel (essential parts of conventional watch mechanisms that require extreme precision in manufacture to maintain accuracy), the Accutron could claim to guarantee 99.9977 per cent accuracy in its advertisements.

To demonstrate how the Accutron worked to potential customers, Bulova made a number of demonstration models with a transparent face that dissected its workings. This turned out to be so engaging that it was launched as a model in its own right.

LIP Mach 2000 Dark Master wristwatch

Date: 1973

Designer: Roger Tallon

Manufacturer: LIP, Besançon, France

Dimensions: 4cm (1½in) diameter

LIP grew into France's largest and most industrially advanced watchmaker, before collapsing in 1976 after a series of strikes and sit-ins that culminated in a period of workers' self management. LIP's most interesting watches came just before the company's collapse when Roger Tallon designed the Mach 2000 range, which looked like nothing else on the market. The asymmetric chronometer – with a movement bought in from Switzerland, dropped into an asymmetric, anodized, black metal case, and with a black rubber strap – was the most striking. Tallon used the Bauhaus's three primary colours for the spherical crowns used to adjust and wind the watch. Appealing though it undoubtedly was, Tallon's work was not enough to save the company from bankruptcy. The LIP trademark and Tallon's designs have been reproduced recently under licence.

Jellyfish GK 100 wristwatch

Date: 1983

Designer: Swatch AG

Manufacturer: Swatch AG, Bienne, Switzerland

Dimensions: 0.8 × 3.5 × 22.5cm (¼ × 1½ × 8¾in)

The traditional mass-market Swiss watchmaking industry came close to being wiped out in the 1970s by cheap Japanese wristwatches. The Swatch project was a successful response, aimed at making an affordable product that would appeal to a new generation of consumers. These watches were cheap enough to be considered disposable, making extensive use of plastics, thereby deliberately differentiated from the costly luxury end of Swiss watchmaking.

The first Swatch collection was launched in 1983 and hit sales of over 2 million in just two years. The Jellyfish, one of the early models, is in the collection of the Museum of Modern Art (MoMA) in New York.

Momento wristwatch

Date: 1987

Designer: Aldo Rossi

Manufacturer: Alessi, Crusinallo, Italy

Dimensions: 0.8 × 1.9 × 17.7cm (¼ × ¾ × 7in)

Faced with imports from Asia with which it could not compete on price, in the early 1980s, the Alessi company began to transform anonymous domestic objects by working with high-profile designers. In partnership with Swatch, the Swiss watchmaker, Alessi began producing watches, beginning with the Momento, designed by the Italian post-modernist architect, Aldo Rossi.

The idea of architects working at every scale, 'from the spoon to the city' as Ernesto Rogers once put it, was not new. Alessi turned their ideas into mass-market products. The Momento, like one of Rossi's buildings, ingeniously managed to play with memories of the past. The perfect circle face could be slipped out of the wrist strap and used as a nineteenth-century pocket watch.

LE RECTO
DONNE
L'HEURE

LE
VERSO
NOUS
RACONTE
L'HISTOIRE

swatch✚
SISTEM51

SWATCH MÉGASTORE – 104 Avenue des Champs-Elysées – Tél.: 01 56 69 17 00
Votre boutique en ligne: shop.swatch.fr

Braun AW 10 wristwatch

Date: 1989
Designers: Dietrich Lubs, Dieter Rams
Manufacturer: Braun AG, Frankfurt,
West Germany
Dimensions: 3.3cm (1¼in) diameter

While clocks were an essential part of Braun's product range, wristwatches were not a core product. Braun started offering branded watches to its larger customers as a sales incentive in 1977. The first had a digital read-out in a rectangular panel, somewhat awkwardly incorporated in a circular case. In contrast, the AW 10, largely the work of Dietrich Lubs, looked like a purer interpretation of the Braun design language. The AW designation stands for Analogue Watch, but Braun never made mechanical watches – its watches always had quartz movement.

In 1985, Braun became a subsidiary of Gillette, and then Procter & Gamble. From 2005, the Braun name has been licensed to various companies. Wristwatches branded as Braun products are now made in China.

Halo wristwatch

Date: 1994
Designers: Massimo and Leila Vignelli
Manufacturer: Pierre Junod, Bienne,
Switzerland
Dimensions: 3.4cm (1¼in) diameter

Pierre Junod manufactured watches for other brands such as Alessi and Georg Jensen before launching his own range. He had a long relationship with Massimo and Leila Vignelli, two Italian-born designers who moved to New York in the 1960s.

They said of the Halo watch, 'our basic idea was to transform the watch into a transparent weightless object [...] we designed a frame that covers the case and expands the glass of the face into a subtly colored expendable halo'. The watch is essentially a system, with a choice of different coloured aluminium rings forming the halo effect.

Girard-Perregaux Escapement LM wristwatch

Date: 2013

Designer: Nicolas Déhon

Manufacturer: Girard-Perregaux La-Chaux-des-Fonds, Switzerland

Dimensions: 4.8cm (2in) diameter

Over the years, Girard-Perregaux has produced a succession of handcrafted, beautifully made timepieces of increasing elaboration. Its chronometers were built to achieve extreme levels of accuracy and reliability. But as quartz and digital technology turned the Swiss watch industry upside down in the 1970s, Girard-Perregaux realized that its future lay with the collectors and enthusiasts prepared to pay six-figure prices for luxury watches. For the Escapement LM, engineer Nicolas Déhon used a silicon blade to ensure

that, as the energy stored in the watch each time it was wound up ran out, it still maintained a constant force on the mechanism, and so ensured that it did not lose accuracy.

The Wristwatch

As a typology, the wristwatch can be said to be a product of the twentieth century, and so essentially an expression of the modern world. The search for simplicity has exercised designers ever since the first wristwatches were created, as has the paradox of an artefact that has its roots as much in the traditions of scientific instruments as it does in the principles of jewellery.

Ever since Cartier made a wristwatch for Santos Dumont (see page 274), the challenge for all watch designers has been to work with the basic repertoire of face, hands and mechanism, while avoiding any awkward visual collision between timepiece and strap. There have been two distinct approaches: simplicity and complication. 'Simple' has come to be associated with modernity. It is the aesthetic of Steve Jobs and Apple. 'Simple' might be seen as the opposite of 'complication', which in watchmaking terms represents anything that goes beyond the watch's supposed role in timekeeping, such as phases of the moon, multiple time zones, or jumping hours. Yet, if a simple watch is about telling the time, does simplicity, which has come to mean minimalism, make it easier or more difficult to tell the time in the way that Santos Dumont wanted?

This is a question that touches on graphics. Roman numerals are likely no easier to read than Arabic, and neither is better at telling us the time. The truth is that we are so familiar with the conventions of a wristwatch that we work on the basis of the relative positions of the hands. Is having a second or a third hand simpler or less simple than a read-out? They may be simpler, but do they make it less or more easy to tell the time?

The longer wristwatches have existed, the more designers have been able to strip away the conventional markers. Nathan George Horwitt, a Russian-born American industrial designer, left the New York advertising world to patent a design for a watch in 1947 that had no numbers at all, and just a single circular dot where 12 o'clock usually sits. When it was picked up by the Museum of Modern Art (MoMA) in 1960, Horwitt hadn't got very far with it – just a handful of watches had been produced. MoMA's sniffy description calls it 'a watch face applied to conventional wristwatch'. That did not stop an aggressive marketing campaign by Movado, a watch company that named their version the 'Museum Watch', advertising it as having been selected to be part of the museum's permanent collection, much to the irritation of MoMA's curators.

The mainstream interpretation of modern simplicity for a watch design was Max Bill's work with the German watch- and clockmaker, Junghans. Bill was a Swiss artist, designer and architect, who trained at the Bauhaus in Germany under Walter Gropius. He went on to lead the post-war Ulm School of Design, which became closely associated with the monochrome restraint of Braun's consumer electronics. Bill designed a number of clocks for Junghans in the late 1950s and launched a range of wristwatches in 1962. The company continues to apply his name to products that he was likely not directly involved with.

'The basis of any aesthetics should, above all, be function,' Bill once said. 'An exemplary object should serve its purpose under all circumstances.' For Bill, that meant doing as little as possible. He used the conventional typology of timekeeping – two hands and clear numbering – but with an elegant logic, he moved the hours well clear of the seconds on the outer rim of the dial. For some designers, that was already too complicated. Two Danish architects, Claus Bonderup and Torsten Thorup, designed watches for Georg Jensen that stripped away numerals. They did not go as far as Horwitt, however, and used twelve dots rather than just one.

In the age of Swatch, the infinite variations of a legible watch face have been taken to their logical conclusion and beyond – every conceivable decorative scheme has been used, from artist designed Swatches using Keith Haring drawings to political messages to convey a positive approach to diversity, and even reworkings of classic watches from the 1940s.

(1) The realization of Nathan George Horwitt's idea for a wristwatch so minimal as to omit all numerals and replace the markings with a single dot.

(2) Junghans worked with Bauhaus-trained Max Bill, who was also the director of the Ulm School of Design, on a number of watches.

(3) Aldo Rossi's wristwatch for Alessi (see page 276) can be detached from its strap and reconfigured as a pocket watch.

(4) Swatch redefined the image of low-cost Swiss watches, using design innovations to make them competitive with cheap digital competitors.

Odhner Arithmometer

Date: 1890

Designer: Willgodt Odhner

Manufacturer: WT Odhner, St Petersburg, Russia

Dimensions: 29 × 11.7 × 14.8cm (11½ × 4½ × 5¾in)

Willgodt Odhner patented his design for a portable mechanical calculator, which relied on pinwheels marked with numbers, cranked with a handle and adjusted by wingnuts. It could carry out addition, multiplication and subtraction. Odhner opened his own factory in Russia and a second in Germany. After the revolution of 1917, the Russian factory was nationalized, and Odhner's sons Alexander and Georg Odhner started again in Sweden.

Under Soviet control, production of the Arithmometer moved from St Petersburg and it was renamed the Felix. In Sweden, the Odhners called their calculator the Original-Odhner, but struggled to compete with copies and clones being produced around the world. By the time production ceased in the 1970s, several million had been made.

Olivetti Elettrosumma 14 calculator

Date: 1946

Designers: Natale Capellaro, Marcello Nizzoli

Manufacturer: Olivetti, Ivrea, Italy

Dimensions: 20 × 41.5 × 17cm (8 × 16¼× 6¾in)

Olivetti started manufacturing mechanical calculators before Italy entered World War II, using the experience the company had built up making typewriters. Its post-war models began with the Elettrosumma 14, which had an electric motor to power the push-button keys used to input calculations and drive the mechanism that produced the result. It was limited to addition and subtraction, but was followed in quick succession by the Multisumma 14, which could perform multiplication, and then the Divisumma 14 full four-function machine, which allowed for adding, subtraction, division and multiplication, along with a printer to keep a running record of its calculations.

Divisumma 24 mechanical calculator

Date: 1956

Designer: Marcello Nizzolo

Manufacturer: Olivetti, Ivrea, Italy

Dimensions: 25.9 × 24 × 42.5cm
(10¼ × 9½ × 16¾in)

The Divisumma depended on an intricate mechanism to push, pull and click the cogs and levers into place, before providing the numerical answer to the series of mathematical questions that the sequence in which its buttons were pressed represents. Inside the aluminium skull is an intricate, beautifully engineered, metal brain. To build it demanded skills that the world has now lost – an entire factory, and such pre-existing units as the printing mechanism, based on typewriter components. The problem in the long-term was weaning Olivetti off its dependence on mechanical engineering. A mechanism as complex as the Divisumma 24 required a high level of maintenance, and the cost of this over two years was higher than buying an electronic calculator outright from one of Olivetti's Japanese competitors.

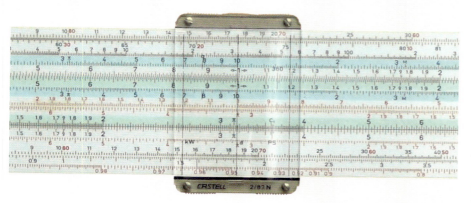

Faber Castell 2/83 N slide rule

Date: 1974

Designer: Faber Castell

Manufacturer: Faber Castell, Stein, West Germany

Dimensions: 38 × 5.7 × 0.5cm (15 × 2¼ × ¼in)

The slide rule was an essential working tool for engineers and mathematicians until well into the second half of the twentieth century, designed to quickly carry out multiplication and long division to a high level of accuracy, as well as to work on trigonometry and the calculation of square roots.

Founded in 1761, Faber Castell began as a pencil manufacturer, and started making slide rules out of mahogany in the 1890s. The 2/83 was the end of a long line of precision slide rules that offered multiple log scales for complex calculations. It was produced just at the point that it could no longer compete with increasingly affordable handheld computers, but for the best part of a hundred years, a slide rule in the top pocket of the jacket was the mark of a professional engineer.

Resources & Further Information

Designer Directory

Sound

Otl Aicher
(1922–91)

German graphic designer and typographer, who designed a signage system for the 1972 Munich Olympic Games (and, more playfully, the Munich dachshund, the first official Olympic mascot). Aicher's pictograms have since become standard signage, recognized the world over, which direct people to bathrooms, through subways and around airports. Aicher's other notable designs include German airline Lufthansa's corporate identity created in 1969. He also co-founded the Ulm School of Design in Germany.

Franco Albini
(1905–77)

Italian Rationalist architect, urban planner and furniture designer. Albini graduated with a degree in architecture from the Polytechnic of Milan in 1929, and soon after found work with architect, industrial and furniture designer, Gio Ponti. He set up his own studio in Milan in 1931. By the 1940s, Albini was designing chairs for Italian furniture manufacturer Cassina.

Peter Bang and Svend Olufsen
(1900–57), (1897–1949)

Danish electrical engineers, Bang and Olufsen, developed their first radio in the attic of Olufsen's parents' house in Jutland, Denmark. Shortly afterwards, in November 1925, they founded the electronics company, Bang & Olufsen, which continues to trade today. Their groundbreaking B&O Eliminator, which allowed a radio to be connected directly to mains electricity, was created in 1927, and became the company's first commercially viable product.

Trevor Baylis
(1937–2018)

English inventor of the wind-up radio. Among Baylis' early inventions were over 200 devices intended to help people with disabilities in their everyday lives, which Baylis named Orange Aids. These included one-handed bottle openers and foot-operated scissors. In the mid-1990s, Baylis developed the wind-up BayGen Freeplay radio. He was committed to sustainable product design, creating many products that didn't require polluting batteries and could be easily repaired, if broken.

Mario Bellini
(b. 1935)

Italian architect and designer, who spent two decades consulting for Olivetti. Bellini's career spanned both the digital and analogue eras, with product designs including the Totem RR130 music system, electrical typewriters and mechanical calculators. Bellini has been awarded the Compasso d'Oro for industrial design eight times.

Artur Braun
(1925–2013)

German businessman and electrical engineer. Son of the founder of electronics company Braun, who, with his brother, Erwin, took over management of the company after their father's death in 1951. Artur Braun's own designs include the Braun SK1 radio, which he created with Fritz Eichler in 1955, and the Braun electric razor.

Robert Davol Budlong
(1902–55)

American industrial designer, who designed many of Zenith's pre-war portable radios and most of Zenith's 'Trans-Oceanic' line. He also designed products for electrical home appliances company Sunbeam, including a toaster, an electrical shaver and a coffee maker.

Achille Castiglioni and Pier Giacomo Castiglioni
(1918–2002), (1913–68)

Italian architects and industrial designers. Achille Castiglioni joined Studio Castiglioni, the design practice founded in 1938 by his two older brothers, Livio and Pier Giacomo, in 1944. Livio left the company in 1953, but Achille and Pier Giacomo continued to work together. The 1950s and 1960s saw a flourishing of creativity in the world of Italian modernist design and the Castiglioni brothers were at the forefront of this movement, particularly with their lighting designs, including the Arco floor lamp.

Wells Coates
(1895–1958)

Born in Japan to Canadian parents, Coates was a Modernist architect and designer. Inspired by Le Corbusier's theory that houses should be 'machines for living in', Coates developed many progressive housing projects in London in the 1930s, most notably the Isokon apartment building in Hampstead. Alongside his architectural career, Coates was responsible for the classic circular Bakelite ECKO AD-65 wireless radio.

Andy Davey
(b. 1962)

British industrial designer and founder of the design firms Davey Agency/TKO and Actual. With TKO, Davey has worked with companies around the world on products as diverse as musical instruments, cars and furniture. Davey's designs for Actual are 'inspired by the harmony of science and nature' and celebrate lightness, science and space.

Gordon Edge, Peter Lee and Roy Gray

Audio engineers and designers at Cambridge Audio. Established by a group of Cambridge University graduates in 1968, Cambridge Audio was born from a desire to create a market-leading amplifier. The company's first product, the P 40 amplifier, was created by a team that included Peter Lee and Gordon Edge, with a case designed by Roy Gray.

Kajiwara Daisuke

Japanese product designer and creator of the model R-72 National Panasonic radio and Toot-a-Loop R-72S.

Fritz Eichler
(1911–91)

Prior to joining German electronics company, Braun, Eichler had worked as an art historian and theatre director, a creative background that served him well in overseeing design and branding at the company. Eichler initially joined Braun in 1953 as Director for Commercials, but was appointed Commissioner for Overall Design in 1955, a role which involved product and packaging design, as well as the creation of print adverts and advertising films.

Hans Gugelot
(1920–65)

Dutch engineer and industrial designer, who created modernist consumer products, including furniture, slide projectors and radios. Gugelot taught at the Ulm School of Design and designed many products with students and employees there, particularly for the German electrical-products company, Braun. Gugelot had a rational approach to design, which eschewed unnecessary decoration in favour of practicality.

Mark Hanau
(b. 1948)

Photographer and designer, who created most of Transatlantic Records' album art. At Hanau's instigation, British band Curved Air's debut record, *Airconditioning,* became the first rock album to be released in picture-disc format. This picture-disc process was refined and became known as the Han-O-Disc in honour of its creator.

Jacob Jensen
(1926–2015)

Danish industrial designer, who had a three-decades-long collaboration with Bang & Olufsen, and was a key player in the 'Danish Modern' design movement of the 1950s onward. Jensen established Jacob Jensen Design in 1958, which continues to be known today for its minimalist, innovative and intuitive design aesthetic.

Stefan Kudelski
(1929–2013)

Polish audio engineer, who created the Nagra series of portable audio recorders. The first professional-quality tape recorders, they transformed both Hollywood filmmaking and sound recording for radio. Kudelski's family fled their native Poland following the Nazi occupation of 1939, eventually settling in Switzerland. Kudelski built his first tape recorder while still a student at the Swiss Federal Institute of Technology in Lausanne, and invented the more sophisticated Nagra device in 1951, refining the design through to 1958.

Bill Lear and Richard Krauss

The Learjet stereo 8 and audio cartridge was designed by Krauss in 1964, while working under Bill Lear at the Lear Corporation, and it remained popular until the early 1980s when it was overshadowed by the compact cassette.

Ross Lovegrove
(b. 1958)

Welsh artist and industrial designer, who has designed products for companies such as Sony and Apple. Many of his pieces can be found in the permanent collections of museums around the world. Lovegrove has applied his organic style to everything from computers and speakers to chairs and lighting, creating an experimental design aesthetic.

Edmund Mortimer
(d. 1985)

Chief Engineer and Technical Sales Manager at British record manufacturer, Garrard, who designed the Garrard 301 Transcription record deck, the company's market-leading flagship product, in 1954. Mortimer assembled the very first Garrard in 1919 and continued to work at the company until his retirement in 1970.

Niro Nakamichi

Brother of Etsuro Nakamichi, who established the Nakamichi Corporation in 1948, after his wartime service in the Japanese navy working with sonar systems. Niro designed the Dragon cassette deck, launched in 1982, shortly after Etsuro's death.

Shuichi Obata
(b. 1932)

Japanese industrial designer and engineer, who created the Technics turntable models for Japanese electronics company, Matsushita (now Panasonic). Obata created the first electronic direct-drive turntable, the SP10, in 1969, and the SL-1200, in 1972. The SL-1200 would become the turntable of choice for decades to come, remaining popular with consumers even after the advent of CDs and music streaming.

Kozo Ohsone

(b. 1933)

Manager of Sony's Tape Recorder Business Division. When asked to develop a portable audio player that would revitalize Sony's flagging Tape Recorder division, Ohsone and his team modified an existing device, the 1977 Pressman, to create the Walkman. They also designed headphones for their device that weighed significantly less than any others on the market.

David Painter, James Teague, Victor Petertil

(1913–2003), (1919–96), (1903–95)

American industrial designers, who created the world's first transistor radio, the Regency TR-1. All graduates of the School of the Art Institute in Chicago, Painter, Petertil and Teague worked together at Barnes & Reinecke, Chicago's largest design and engineering office. In 1950, they formed Painter, Teague & Petertil. The TR-1 was developed here in 1954, and brought the trio wide renown. Their firm continued to design technical communication products for Regency until 1960, when Painter established his solo firm.

Dieter Rams

(b. 1932)

German designer, who worked with electrical products company Braun (1955–97) and furniture company Vitsœ (1959–present). By the late 1970s, Rams had established a series of influential principles for 'good design', which required products to be innovative, useful, unobtrusive, long-lasting, environmentally friendly and aesthetic.

Richard Sapper

(1932–2015)

German industrial designer, who was based in Milan, Italy, for much of his career. Sapper designed many products for companies such as IBM, Alessi and Mercedes-Benz, with his design aesthetic being one of minimalism and practical functionality. He opened his own design studio in Milan in 1959.

William Savory

(1916–2004)

American musician and audio engineer employed by Columbia Records, who was involved with their market launch of the 33⅓ rpm long-playing record in 1948. Savory had an extensive private collection of jazz recordings, created in the 1930s, when he used his audio-engineering experience to record jazz artists directly from the radio.

Clive Sinclair

(1940–2021)

English entrepreneur and inventor, who was instrumental in bringing the first mass-market home computer to UK consumers. Sinclair launched his electronics company, Sinclair Radionics, in 1961, with products including amplifiers, such as the Sinclair Micro-Amplifier and the X-10, as well as radios, like the Sinclair Slimline and Micromatic, marketed as 'the world's smallest radio'. Sinclair's first hi-fi, the Stereo 25, was released in 1966. His first electronic calculator followed in 1972, with computers following in the 1980s.

Jack Tiefenbrun

(1921–86)

Founder of the Textile Engineering company, which worked with a diverse portfolio of customers (including most notably the Singer Sewing Machine Company) to provide tools and fixtures for textile machinery. Tiefenbrun was born in Poland in 1921 and moved to Austria aged five. At the age of 17, he moved to Glasgow and took on his first job maintaining knitting looms and machinery. Tiefenbrun founded the Glasgow-based Textile Engineering in 1951, which now trades as Castle Precision Engineering.

Daniel Weil

(b. 1953)

British-Argentinian architect and industrial designer. After graduating in architecture from the University of Buenos Aires in 1977, Weil moved to London to study industrial design. Between 1982 and 1990, he designed and manufactured products for his own firm, Parenthesis, including the Memphis Collection of 1982 and the bag radio. In 1992, he joined design consultancy firm, Pentagram, as a partner. Weil defines his design aesthetic as technical, intellectual and stylistic.

James Pratt Winston

(b. 1933)

American designer with a space-age design aesthetic. Beginning his career at Womack Electronics, Winston left the company in 1968 to start the Weltron Company with his former boss, Charles A. Womack. Among their earliest products was the Weltron 2001, a brightly coloured spherical radio that went into mass-production in 1970, and is said to have been inspired by the visuals of sci-fi films including *2001: A Space Odyssey* and *War of the Worlds*.

Kozo Yamamoto

(b. 1972)

Japanese architect, employed at Tokyo-based architectural design firm PANDA. Yamamoto designed the NN House, a single-storey minimalist home in Tokyo, Japan. Yamamoto was commissioned by the owners to design a space that was light and airy, yet also private in the extremely densely populated city, and which provided a space for 'outdoor living'.

Marco Zanuso

(1916–2001)

Italian architect, designer and academic. Graduating with a degree in architecture in 1939, Zanuso became Professor of Architecture, Design and Town Planning at the Polytechnic of Milan from 1945 to 1986. He also established his own design studio in 1945, and formed a creative partnership with Richard Sapper in 1957, with whom he produced a range of products from chairs to telephones over the following two decades.

Vision

Oskar Barnack
(1879–1936)

German inventor and photographer. Barnack was head of development at the optical company Leica (Leitz Camera) in Wetzlar, Germany, and it was here, in 1913, that he developed what would later become the first commercially successful 35mm still camera, the Ur-Leica. Though the war delayed serial production of the Leica until 1925, Barnack used his camera extensively from 1914, taking numerous photographic series documenting the relationships between people and the environment, including, most famously, the 1920 Wetzlar floods.

Philippe Charbonneaux
(1917–98)

French industrial designer. Charbonneaux first began designing automobiles in the 1940s. He moved to the US in 1949 to join the General Motors Style Center team, where he produced sketches for car bodies that would be used for the 1953 Chevrolet Corvette. Returning to France in 1940, Charbonneaux became involved with designing the Delahaye 235 model. From the 1960s, he also began designing cars for Renault, Ford, Bugatti and Citroën. Throughout his career he also designed refrigerators, televisions, motorboats, lamps and alarm clocks.

Luigi Colani
(1928–2019)

German industrial designer and a leading figure in BioDesign – the human interpretation of shapes created by nature. Colani studied aeronautic engineering at the Sorbonne in Paris, beginning his design career in the 1950s when he designed cars for leading manufacturers, including Fiat, BMW, Volkswagen and Alfa Romeo. Among his consumer product designs are cameras and optics, furniture, glassware, lamps, hi-fi equipment, televisions, and watches and clocks.

Rick Dickinson
(1956–2018)

British industrial designer. His pioneering home-computer designs in the 1980s for Sinclair included the ZX81 computer, case and touch-sensitive keyboard, the ZX Spectrum home computer and its rubber keyboard, and the QL computer. He also designed the Flatscreen TV80 television.

William Kennedy Dickson
(1860–1935)

French-born British inventor, who played a key role in the practical development of cinematography. Dickson is credited with the idea that motion-picture film should be 35mm wide and with developing the emulsion process used in the film. He also played a key role (with Edison) in developing the phonograph. Dickson left Edison's employ in 1895 and, along with three partners, founded the American Mutoscope and Biograph Company in 1896, generally thought of as the first major American motion-picture studio.

Thomas Edison
(1847–1931)

American inventor and businessman. Holding a record-breaking 1,093 patents, Edison is one of history's most prolific inventors. At the age of ten, he set up a laboratory in his father's basement, the forerunner to his establishment of the world's first industrial-research laboratory in Menlo Park, New Jersey. His inventions in this lab include the carbon-button transmitter (1877) – still used in telephone speakers and microphones today – the phonograph (1877) and the incandescent lightbulb (1879).

Hartmut Esslinger
(b. 1944)

German–American industrial designer and founder of the Frog design consultancy. Esslinger first came to international attention after his designs for Sony caught the eye of Apple's Steve Jobs. Esslinger moved to California in 1983 to take up a contract between Apple and Frog. Adhering to the 'form follows emotion' design philosophy, Esslinger has also designed products for companies such as Logitech, Microsoft, IBM and Lufthansa.

Richard Fischer
(1935–2010)

A member of Braun's design team between 1960 and 1968, during which time he worked on the Nizo FA3 and Minox 35 compact camera.

Victor Hasselblad
(1906–78)

Swedish inventor and photographer. Born into a family that had been involved in the photographic industry since the 1880s, Victor Hasselblad left Sweden at the age of 18 to become an apprentice in the camera industry, first in Germany, then in France and the US. This experience culminated in 1926, when he was taken on as George Eastman's apprentice at Kodak. Returning to Sweden in 1937, Hasselblad opened his own shop, complete with a photo lab. The first of his camera designs, the HK-7, was developed in 1941.

Albert Howell and Donald Bell
(1879–1951), (1869–1934)

Albert Howell, a film-projector inventor and camera repairer, and Donald Bell, an engineer and film projectionist, established their company Bell & Howell in Chicago, in 1907, to design and manufacture equipment for the motion-picture industry. Among their products were 35mm film perforators (which helped to establish 35mm film as an industry standard), cameras, printers and projectors.

Masaru Ibuka
(1908–97)

Co-founder of the Sony Corporation. After graduating in 1933 from Waseda University's School of Science and Engineering, Ibuka was employed at motion picture film-processing company Photo-Chemical Laboratory. Together with Akio Morita, Ibuka founded the Tokyo Telecommunications Engineering Corporation (which in 1958 became known as the Sony Corporation) in 1946.

Nobutoshi Kihara
(1926–2011)

Japanese mechanical engineer known as 'the wizard of Sony' for his ingenious product development at the company, particularly the development of video-tape recording technology. After graduating from the Faculty of Mechanical Engineering at Tokyo's Waseda University, Kihara joined Sony in 1947, and worked on a variety of projects. He started working on video-tape recorders in the late 1950s, beginning a process which culminated in 1975 with Sony's production of Betamax technology.

Edwin Land
(1909–91)

American physicist, who invented instant photography and co-founded the Polaroid Corporation. Land became interested in polarized light while studying at Harvard University, successfully creating a polarizer in 1932. By 1936, he was using Polaroid material in sunglasses and, in the late 1940s, extended its use to camera filters. His Polaroid 95 Land camera of 1948 was able to produce a finished print within 60 seconds, and a colour process was developed in subsequent years.

David Lewis
(1939–2011)

British industrial designer. After graduating from London's Central School of Art in 1960, Lewis moved to Denmark to work as a freelancer for Bang & Olufsen. Among Lewis' early products were the Beovision 400 television set and the Beolab 5000 system. Lewis opened his own design studio in 1982, but continued to design for B&O.

Yoshihisa Maitani
(1933–2009)

Japanese designer, scouted by Olympus in 1954 (while still an engineering student at Tokyo's Waseda University), after his early patent for a camera was discovered by one of Olympus' designers. Maitani spent two years on the production line before being offered the design assignment that resulted in the creation of the highly successful Olympus Pen, a half-frame viewfinder camera. Other models, including the OM-1 and the cult-classic XA, followed over the next few decades.

Henning Moldenhawer
(1914–83)

Designer at Bang & Olufsen. Smaller, lighter and more modern-looking than previous radios, his Beomaster 900 set a new design trend among consumers, simultaneously shaping B&O's design aesthetic into what it is today. Alongside electronics, Moldenhawer also designed lighting and lamps for Danish manufacturer, Louis Poulsen, during the 1950s.

Hubert Nerwin
(1906–83)

Chief designer at German camera manufacturer, Zeiss Ikon, during the 1930s, Nerwin developed numerous cameras including the Contax II and Contax III, Contraflex twin-lens reflex, and Ikoflex models. Nerwin moved to the US after World War II, and went on to develop the revolutionary Instamatic cartridge for Kodak. Selling 7.5 million units in its first two years on the market and 50 million during the 1960s, the Kodak Instamatic is one of the world's most successful photographic consumer products.

Robert Oberheim
(b. 1938)

German camera designer, who designed Nizo camera models for German electronics company Braun while part of their design team (1960–94). He designed the Nizo 801 8mm cine camera under the supervision of Braun's lead designer, Dieter Rams.

Donald Paterson
(1913–1975)

British photographer and designer. Paterson founded his company Paterson Photographic in the 1940s, which manufactured home-darkroom equipment for amateur photographers, including film-development tanks, measuring graduates, film- and print- washing equipment, and photographic enlargers. Along with Eric Taylor, Paterson created the enlarger for 35mm and 126mm films, which won the Design Centre Award in 1973.

John Pemberton
(b. 1948)

Industrial designer at Sinclair Radionics. Pemberton designed the Sinclair TV1A Microvision pocket television in 1978 and the Sinclair Sovereign Pocket LED Calculator in 1976, so named because its release coincided with the Silver Jubilee of Queen Elizabeth II.

Naoki Sakai
(b. 1947)

Japanese car designer and creator of Nissan's *pike car* series, most notably the Be-1 in the late 1980s and Nissan Figaro in 1990. He has also designed cars and motorbikes for other leading manufacturers, including Suzuki and Toyota. Among his consumer product designs are the O-Product camera for Olympus, sofas for Cassina, and mobile phones for KDDI. Sakai also manages his own design company, Waterdesign, and has taught at Keio University in Fujisawa, Japan.

Philippe Starck
(b. 1949)

French industrial designer and architect, whose wide-ranging designs included furniture, interior design and household objects. Starck set up his first company in 1968, producing inflatable objects. In the 1980s, he refurbished the French president's private apartments in the Élysée Palace in Paris, and went on to design interiors around the world. Starck's industrial designs include water bottles for Glacier, kitchen appliances for Alessi, and watches for Fossil.

Roger Tallon
(1929–2011)

French industrial designer, who designed the French TGV high-speed train and is known for establishing the profession of industrial design in post-war France. Tallon designed for numerous companies and agencies during his 50-year design career, including Technès, Design Programmes, A.D.S.A, Kodak, Peugeot and General Motors. Tallon believed that the aim of design should be societal advancement; most of his work was technical and product driven as a result.

Walter Dorwin Teague
(1883–1960)

American industrial designer, architect and illustrator. Teague began his career working in advertising, establishing an industrial design consultancy in 1926 to advise his clients on product design, interior design and graphics. In 1927, he worked closely with engineers at the Eastman Kodak Company to restyle two of their cameras. In the 1930s, he became known for his railway and automobile designs but, by the 1950s, Teague was designing furnishings and interiors for the Air Force Academy at Colorado Springs, Colorado.

Nobuyuki Yoshida and Ryohei Suzuki

Japanese designers, who created Japan's first 35mm SLR camera, the Asahiflex 1, for the Asahi Optical Company (later known as Pentax). An experienced lens designer, Suzuki was employed in 1949 by Saburo Matsumoto, Asahi's president, as Chief Lens Designer. As Suzuki lacked experience designing cameras, Matsumoto also brought his former colleague, Nobuyuki Yoshida, on board as Chief Camera Designer.

Susumu Yoshida
(b. 1923)

Japanese engineer at Sony, who was part of the team that created the Emmy-winning Sony Trinitron television in 1968. Yoshida is credited with the idea of replacing the three in-line electron guns used in television tubes with a single gun with three cathodes. This innovation revolutionized colour television and, in both TV and computer-monitor form, the Trinitron would sell over 280 million units.

Frank Zagara

Industrial designer, who created the Kodak Instamatic 100 in 1963, the first Instamatic camera to be released in the US.

Walter Zapp
(1905–2003)

Latvian-born inventor. Zapp moved from Latvia to Germany in 1941, and established Minox GmbH, where he continued to manufacture improved versions of his Minox Riga subminiature camera, created in 1936. During World War II, secret services in several countries purchased the camera. Commercially, nearly one million subminiature cameras were sold during Zapp's lifetime.

Communication

Johan Christian Bjerknes
(1889–1983)

Norwegian engineer employed at Oslo's Elektrisk Bureau, a subsidiary of Swedish electronics company, Ericsson, who was tasked with creating a telephone device that would appeal to everyone. Artist Jean Heiberg created the shape in Bakelite plastic, designed to be easy to mass-produce, and Bjerknes used his electrical engineering experience to bring the design to life. The result was the Ericsson DBH 1001 model, first designed in 1931 and put on the market in 1932.

Martin Cooper
(b. 1928)

Motorola executive and 'father of the cell phone', credited with inventing the handheld mobile telephone. Cooper made the first call on a mobile telephone (in April 1973) using an early model of Motorola's DynaTAC phone. It was a heavy 'brick' phone with just 20 minutes of battery life that he used provocatively to call his rival at Bell Labs, Joel Engel. After commercializing the DynaTAC, Cooper left Motorola and moved to Silicon Valley.

Henry Dreyfuss
(1904–72)

American industrial design pioneer. Dreyfuss opened his first design office in 1929 and, in 1930, began designing telephones for Bell Laboratories. The most notable of these was the Princess phone, designed to fit in the hand of a teenage girl. He would go on to design other popular products, including refrigerators, alarm clocks, vacuum cleaners, cameras, and the Honeywell round thermostat.

Kazuo Hashimoto
(d. 1995)

Japanese inventor, who registered over 1,000 worldwide patents, including for the Caller-ID system. Hashimoto invented the Ansafone, the first telephone-answering machine, in 1954, and the first digital telephone-answering device in 1983. Self-educated, Hashimoto was awarded an honorary Doctor of Science degree by New Jersey Institute of Technology in 1994, in recognition of his outstanding contribution to the field of telephony.

Jean Heiberg
(1884–1976)

Norwegian painter (and a student of Matisse, in Paris), credited with designing the first modern telephone, informally known as the Bakelite, together with electrical engineer Johan Christian Bjerknes. The Ericsson DBH 1001 model was designed by Heiberg and first built by Bjerknes in 1930. It set a precedent for many subsequent telephone designs.

David Kelley
(b. 1951)

American engineer, designer, entrepreneur and educator. After graduating in electrical engineering, Kelley worked as an engineer at both Boeing and NCR before embarking on a master's degree in Engineering and Product Design at Stanford University in 1975. Kelley co-founded global design firm IDEO (in 1978) and founded Stanford University's Hasso Plattner Institute of Design. From 1978, he taught Stanford's Product Design programme, promoting the influential project-based methodology known as Design Thinking.

Perry King
(1938–2020)

British industrial and graphic designer. After moving to Italy in 1964, King started designing office equipment for Olivetti, including their Sistema 45 typewriter and, alongside Ettore Sottsass, the Valentine typewriter in 1969. From 1972, he was the design coordinator for Olivetti's corporate identity programme. King also designed products for other companies, including Arteluce, Flos, and Black and Decker. In 1976, he co-founded Milan-based design firm King Miranda Associates, with fellow designer Santiago Miranda.

Hans von Klier
(1934–2000)

Czechoslovakian artist and designer. Von Klier studied at the Ulm School of Design, graduating in 1959, and moving to Milan to work at Olivetti, initially in Ettore Sottsass' studio and later in the corporate identity team. In 1990, he founded his own design firm, Von Klier Associates.

Rudy Krolopp
(1930–2023)

Industrial design director at electronics company Motorola and lead designer on the project that resulted in the creation of the first mobile phone, the DynaTAC. This phone was invented and built in just six weeks from December 1972. Krolopp and his team refined and redeveloped the DynaTAC over the next decade, with the DynaTAC 8000X being approved for sale in the US in 1983.

Lone and Gideon Lindinger-Loewy

Danish designers, who created colourful corded telephone designs for Bang & Olufsen in the 1980s and early 1990s. The eye-catching BeoCom 1000 model came in black, blue, green and red, and was known for its high-quality sound.

Raymond Loewy
(1893–1986)

French-born American industrial designer. Loewy designed the logos and branding for Shell, Exxon, and the Greyhound Scenicruiser bus, as well as Lucky Strike packaging and the Air Force One livery, among many others. In recognition of his design impact across numerous industries, he was featured on the cover of *Time* magazine on 31 October, 1949. Among his industrial designs were products for equipment manufacturer, International Harvester, and railway designs and colour schemes, as well as consumer products such as electric shavers, toothbrushes, radios and office equipment.

Marcello Nizzoli
(1887–1969)

Italian artist, architect and designer. After an earlier career as an artist and graphic designer, Nizzoli worked as a consultant for Olivetti. His most notable creation was the Lettera 22 portable typewriter (1950), but he also undertook graphic design work, establishing the company's advertising division in 1932. As an architect, he designed living quarters for Olivetti employees from 1948 and the Olivetti office buildings during the 1960s.

Eliot Noyes
(1910–77)

American architect and industrial designer. With an academic and professional background in architecture and design, Noyes was a student of Walter Gropius and Marcel Breuer at Harvard. After working briefly for them, he was appointed Director of the Department of Industrial Design at MoMA in New York, from 1939 to 1946. In 1947, he founded his own architectural design practice, Eliot Noyes & Associates, designing private homes and public buildings. Much of his industrial design was undertaken for IBM – Noyes met Thomas Watson Jr (who took over leadership of IBM from his father) while working as a glider pilot during World War II.

Davorin Savnik
(1929–2014)

Industrial designer and architect. Savnik designed audiovisual equipment and telephones for Slovenian electronics company, Iskra.

Ettore Sottsass
(1917–2007)

Austrian-born, Italian architect, whose focus shifted from architecture to design in the mid-1950s when he became Art Director for design company Poltronova. In 1958, he began a long collaboration with Olivetti, where he began producing his first designs for typewriters. He also founded the 1980s design collective the Memphis Group, where he produced experimental pieces recognizable by their bold colours and graphic patterns.

George Sowden
(b. 1942)

After graduating in architecture from Gloucester College of Art in 1968, Sowden moved to Italy, settling in Milan in 1970. He joined Ettore Sottsass' team at Olivetti as a product designer, and was a member of the Memphis Group. He produced furniture and homewares, including the D'Antibes cabinet, Pierre table and Oberoi chair in 1981, and the 1982 Metropole casement clock. After Memphis, Sowden set up his own design studio, working on, among other things, a range of public telephones.

Information

Flaminio Bertoni
(1903–64)

Italian automobile designer. Bertoni emigrated from Italy to Paris in 1931, and worked as an artist and sculptor. He utilized these talents in his car designs for Citroën by creating sketches and scale models that he would then 'sculpt' in physical form. Together with engineer André Lefèbvre, Bertoni designed several Citroën models, including the Traction Avant (1934) and the 2CV (1948).

Max Bill
(1908–94)

Swiss architect, artist, industrial designer and graphic designer. Bill studied at the Bauhaus in Dessau from 1927 to 1929, and went on to become the director of the influential Ulm School of Design in 1953. He created some of the first watch and clock designs for Junghans, many of which are still made today, characterized by their rigour.

Ettore Bugatti
(1881–1947)

Italian-born, French automobile designer and manufacturer. After producing car designs for several companies from as early as 1899, Bugatti founded his own eponymous automobile company in 1909, and began designing and manufacturing a wide variety of cars, engines, tools and other industrial designs.

Daniel Gabriel Fahrenheit
(1686–1736)

Polish-born, Dutch physicist, inventor and scientific-instrument maker, who invented the mercury thermometer in 1714 and the Fahrenheit temperature scale in 1724. He is also credited with the discovery of the supercooling of water and establishing that boiling-point temperatures vary according to atmospheric pressure. Born to a wealthy merchant family, Fahrenheit spent most of his working life in Amsterdam and died in poverty, despite his scientific achievements.

Max Hetzel
(1921–2004)

Swiss engineer and inventor. Hetzel graduated in 1946 in electrical engineering from the Swiss Federal Institute of Technology in Zurich. He joined the Bulova Watch Company in 1948, and became the first person to use an electrical transistor in his wristwatch designs, establishing a new level of accuracy and technology in timekeeping that had never been seen before.

Henning Koppel
(1918–81)

Danish artist and designer, who designed furniture and homewares for the Georg Jensen firm, which epitomized the sleek, minimalist Scandinavian design aesthetic. Initially beginning his career as a sculptor and jeweller, Koppel began producing silver holloware for Georg Jensen in the late 1940s, and later expanded into porcelain and glassware. He also designed furniture for several other companies, including Kastrup and Orrefors and Kvetny & Sonner.

André Lefèbvre
(1894–1964)

Lefèbvre began his career as an aviation engineer in 1916, transitioning into the automobile industry in the interwar years, first at Renault in 1931 and then at Citroën from 1933. Together with fellow designers Flaminio Bertoni and Paul Magès, Lefèbvre helped create four of Citroën's most memorable twentieth-century models, the Traction Avant, 2CV, DS and HY.

Dietrich Lubs
(b. 1938)

German industrial designer. Lubs joined Dieter Rams' design team at the consumer electronics company, Braun, in 1962, where he worked on many of Braun's classic watch and clock designs. His typography was used on a wide range of products, including travel alarms, watches and clock radios. Together with Dieter Rams, Lubs designed Braun's first pocket calculator in 1975.

Angelo Mangiarotti
(1921–2012)

Italian architect and industrial designer. In 1964, Mangiarotti began designing for leading manufacturers alongside his building projects, including for Cassina, Artemide, Knoll and Poltronova. Mangiarotti also became art director of Colle crystalware factory in 1986, a collaboration which resulted in the creation of the 'Ice Stopper' glass.

George Nelson
(1908–86)

American architect and industrial designer. Nelson joined Herman Miller furniture company as Design Director in the mid-1940s and remained there until 1972, recruiting Charles Eames to produce some of its most innovative seating ranges. Nelson oversaw production of the Action Office, Herman Miller's pioneering range of office furniture, and designed a playful collection of clocks, now manufactured by Vitra.

Willgodt Odhner
(1845–1905)

Swedish engineer and entrepreneur. Odhner left Sweden for Russia in 1868 and, arriving in St Petersburg, found work in the machine factory of Ludvig Nobel. He developed prototypes for his Arithmometer in his spare time and opened his own workshop in 1887, with production of Arithmometers beginning in 1890.

Aldo Rossi
(1931–97)

Italian architect, urban designer, artist and product designer. After graduating from the Polytechnic of Milan in 1959 with a degree in architecture, Rossi opened his own architectural office in Milan. He first achieved fame through his architectural writings and teaching at universities, such as Yale and Cornell, and went on to design the Momento wristwatch.

Remigio Solari
(1890–1957)

Self-taught Italian designer and engineer. Solari's family's clockmaking business, Fratelli Solari, had been founded in 1725. Yet, it was brothers Remigio and Fermo Solari, who transformed the company into an internationally recognized brand in the mid-twentieth century through the invention of the flap system that would revolutionize the display of time and information around the world, beginning with the flip clock.

Gino Valle
(1923–2003)

Italian architect and designer. Valle created the Cifra 5 clock for Solari, which won the Golden Compass design award in 1956, and the Cifra 3 clock, the smallest clock with a direct readout still in production today. He also designed the Alphanumeric Teleindicators for airports and railway stations, including the one built at the TWA Terminal at the J. F. Kennedy Airport in New York in 1962.

Robert Venturi and Denise Scott Brown
(1925–2018), (b. 1931)

Husband-and-wife architectural team and founders of the American architectural studio Venturi Scott Brown (VSB). The couple met in 1960 at the University of Pennsylvania, where Scott Brown was studying for a masters and Venturi was teaching architecture. Among their most notable architectural designs of the 1970s and 1980s were the University of Michigan Campus Plan, the Seattle Art Museum, and the Sainsbury's Wing for the National Gallery in London. Later projects by VSB included the Museum of Contemporary Art in San Diego, California (1996) and the Provincial Capitol Building in Toulouse, France (1999).

Massimo and Lella Vignelli
(1931–2014), (1934–2016)

Italian husband-and-wife design team, whose designs span products, prints, interior design and architecture. Both architectural graduates, Massimo began his career designing lighting for Murano glassmaker Venini, while Lella worked as a junior designer for Skidmore, Owings & Merrill. They married in 1957, and established the Milan-based Lella and Massimo Vignelli Office of Design and Architecture in 1960, producing office accessories, homewares and furniture. Following a move to the US in 1965, their graphic-design works included the logo for American Airlines, the New York City Subway map, and the Bloomingdale's brown paper bag.

Hans Wilsdorf
(1881–1960)

German businessman and founder of watch manufacturers Rolex and Tudor. Wilsdorf is credited with creating the first waterproof wristwatch, the Rolex Oyster, in 1926. His watchmaking career began at a small Swiss watchmaking company in 1905. Soon after, he moved to London and set up the company that in 1908 would become known as Rolex. In 1919, headquarters were set up in Geneva and full-scale production began.

Louis Cartier
(1875–1942)

French jeweller, businessman and heir to the Cartier jewellery house. Cartier's father, Alfred, managed the family business from 1874 and impressed upon his son a desire to win international renown for Cartier. This was first achieved in 1902, when King Edward VII ordered 27 tiaras from Cartier for his coronation. That same year, Louis Cartier opened a large store in London, which he left in the care of his younger brother, Pierre. From 1909, Louis and Pierre were based primarily in New York City, where they opened a second store. In 1917, they acquired the Cartier Building, which became Cartier's North American headquarters.

Index

Image Credits

Every effort has been made to trace all copyright owners, but if any have been inadvertently overlooked the publishers would be pleased to make the necessary arrangements at the first opportunity.

Key: top = t; bottom = b; left = l; right = r; m = middle

UK Cover Credit: Marc Tielemans / Alamy Stock Photo.

US Cover Credit: Digital image, The Museum of Modern Art, New York / Scala, Florence.

2 INTERFOTO / Alamy Stock Photo. **7** Hasselblad Catalog. **9** Courtesy of Richard Sapper Archives (https://richardsapperdesign.com). **10** Commissioned photography. **11** George Rose / Getty Images. **13** Digital image, The Museum of Modern Art, New York / Scala, Florence. **15** Janette Beckman / Getty Images. **16mr** Lynden Pioneer Museum / Alamy Stock Photo. **16bm** Science & Society Picture Library / Getty Images. **17t** Piccia Neri / Alamy Stock Photo. **17mr** Rob Lavers Photography / Alamy Stock Photo. **17br** Christoph Sebastian / Ruhr Museum, Essen, Germany (https://ruhrmuseum.de). **18t** © QUITTENBAUM Kunstauktionen GmbH, 2023 München. (www.quittenbaum.de). **18ml** Cooper-Hewitt, Smithsonian Design Museum / Art Resource, NY / Scala, Florence. **18br** Records / Alamy Stock Photo. **19ml** Courtesy of Richard Sapper Archives (https://richardsapperdesign.com). **19br** Chris Willson / Alamy Stock Photo. **22** Peter Stone / Alamy Stock Photo. **23t** Apic / Getty Images. **23b** Realimage / Alamy Stock Photo. **24t&b** Photographs courtesy of Cherry Red Records Ltd. (www.cherryred.co.uk). **25** © Science Museum / Science & Society Picture Library. All rights reserved. **26** Marc Tielemans / Alamy Stock Photo. **27** Image © National Museums Scotland. **28** Snellings Museum © 2023 (www.snellingsmuseum.co.uk). **29** Photographs courtesy of Cambridge Audio (www.cambridgeaudio.com). **30–31** © Bang & Olufsen (www.bang-olufsen.com). **32** Library of Congress Prints and Photographs Division, Washington, D.C. 20540, USA. **33tl** Simon Robinson / Easy On The Eye / Alamy Stock Photo. **33tr** Pink Floyd 'A Saucerful Of Secrets' LP front cover artwork by Hipgnosis © Pink Floyd Music Ltd. **33bl** Buzzcocks 'A Different Kind of Tension' LP sleeve, 1979. Design by Malcolm Garrett (Assorted iMaGes). Photograph by Jill Furmanovsky. **33br** New Order, Power Corruption & Lies. Art direction Peter Saville. Design Peter Saville Associates. Featuring 'A Basket of Roses', Henri Fanton-Latour, 1890 (Courtesy of National Gallery, London). **34tr** Photograph courtesy of REHIFI.SE (www.rehifi.se). **34mr&br** Linn Products Ltd (www.linn.co.uk). **35** Gästriklands Auktionskammare, Gävle Sweden (www.gastriksak.se). **36** Christie's / Bridgeman Images. **37** DK Images / Science Photo Library. **38** Image courtesy of Dallas Museum of Art (https://dma.org). **39t** Christoph Sebastian / Ruhr Museum, Essen, Germany (https://ruhrmuseum.de). **39b** Tony Rusecki / Alamy Stock Photo. **40t&b** Cassina S.p.A. Copyright © CASSINA. All rights reserved. (www.cassina.com). **41** Cooper-Hewitt, Smithsonian Design Museum / Art Resource, NY / Scala, Florence. **42** Zenith Advertisement (Public Domain). **43** Photograph by Rick Vince. **44t&b** Cooper-Hewitt, Smithsonian Design Museum / Art Resource, NY / Scala, Florence. **45** Vicente Zorilla Palau. **46** Design Museum, London (https://designmuseum.org). **47** INTERFOTO / Alamy Stock Photo. **48t** Digital image, The Museum of Modern Art, New York / Scala, Florence. **48b** José G. Sánchez González. **49** José G. Sánchez González. **50** Paris Match Archive / Jack Garofalo / Getty Images. **51t** Panther Media GmbH / Alamy Stock Photo. **51bl** © Sony Group Corporation (www.sony.net). **51br** © Sony Group Corporation (www.sony.net). **52t** Courtesy of Richard Sapper Archives (https://richardsapperdesign.com). **52b** imageBROKER GmbH & Co. KG / Alamy Stock Photo. **53t,m&b** José G. Sánchez González. **54** Bukowski Auktioner AB, Sweden (www.bukowskis.com). **55** Science Museum Group Collection. © The Board of Trustees of the Science Museum. David Huntley. **56** INTERFOTO / Alamy Stock Photo. **57** Courtesy of Richard Sapper Archives (https://richardsapperdesign.com). **58** Panasonic (www.panasonic.com). **59t** Joe Haupt. **59b** Photograph by Gregory Botha. **60** INTERFOTO / Alamy Stock Photo. **61t** mark follon / Alamy Stock Photo. **61b** Indianapolis Museum of Art at Newfields / Getty Images. **62** Commissioned photography. **63** Commissioned photography. **64** Panasonic (www.panasonic.com). **65t** Mark Edelsberg, Future Forms (www.future-forms.com). **65b** Photograph courtesy of Felix Cartagena. **66** Panasonic (www.panasonic.com). **67t** Martin Bösch. **67b** Photograph courtesy of Martino Viviani, owner of BicBauc (bicbauc.etsy.com). **68** The Design Museum, London, England (https://designmuseum.org). **69** Snellings Museum © 2023 (www.snellingsmuseum.co.uk). **70** INTERFOTO / Alamy Stock Photo. **71** Panasonic (www.panasonic.com). **72** The Design Museum, London, England (https://designmuseum.org). **73** Science & Society Picture Library / Getty Images. **74** © Bang & Olufsen (www.bang-olufsen.com). **75** The Design Museum, London, England (https://designmuseum.org). **76** Digital image, The Museum of Modern Art, New York / Scala, Florence. **77** The Design Museum, London, England (https://designmuseum.org). **78** Pier Marco Tacca / Getty Images. **79t** Brionvega, Milan, Italy (www.brionvega.com). **79bl** eyenigelen / Getty Images. **79br** The Design Museum, London, England (https://designmuseum.org). **80** The Design Museum, London, England (https://designmuseum.org). **81** © QUITTENBAUM Kunstauktionen GmbH, 2023 München (www.quittenbaum.de). **82** © San Francisco Museum of Modern Art, Gift of Dr. Dietmar Vogt, Frechen, Germany. Photograph: Katherine Du Tiel. **83** David Price. **84t** Museum of Communication Foundation Trust (https://museumofcommunication.org.uk). **84b** Photograph courtesy of Crypto Museum (www.cryptomuseum.com). **85** Birgit Reitz-Hofmann / Shutterstock. **86** Audio Technology Switzerland (www.nagraaudio.com). Photograph by Michel Berard. **87** INTERFOTO / Alamy Stock Photo. **88l** Science & Society Picture Library. **88r** Science & Society Picture Library. **89** Russell McNeil. **90t** mark phillips / Alamy Stock Photo. **90b** Panasonic (www.panasonic.com). **91** INTERFOTO / Alamy Stock Photo. **92** Photograph courtesy of Anderson & Garland Ltd (www.andersonandgarland.com). **93** Cooper-Hewitt, Smithsonian Design Museum / Art Resource, NY / Scala, Florence. **94** Photograph by Gregory Botha. **95t&b** © Sony Group Corporation (www.sony.net). **96** Photograph courtesy of SkyFi Audio LLC (skyfiaudio.com). **97** © Sony Group Corporation (www.sony.net). **98** Mike V / Alamy Stock Photo. **99t** Photograph courtesy of TheLion (https://personalhifiblog.blogspot.com). **99b** Commissioned photography. **100t** Joseph McCullar / Shutterstock. **100b** Photograph by Glenn E Waters. **101t** evemilla / iStock. **101b** Voxx International (www.voxxintl.com). **102** Bruno Passigatti / Alamy Stock Photo. **103** Vudhikul Ocharoen / iStock. **104–105** Photograph courtesy of Rick Thorpe. **106** Thomas Mulsow. **107** Iconmac / Dreamstime. **108** National Museum of American History, Smithsonian Institution, USA. **109** The Design Museum, London, England (https://designmuseum.org). **111** Jack Esten / Getty Images. **112tr** Timothy Hellum / Alamy Stock Photo. **112ml** Science & Society Picture Library / Getty Images. **112br** Science & Society Picture Library / Bridgeman Images. **113t** Wikimedia Commons (Public Domain). **113mr** Polaroid Land Camera Model 95 and Polaroid Land Film Type 40. Polaroid Corporation records, Baker Library, Harvard Business School. Photographed by Susan Young. **113bm** Science & Society Picture Library / Getty Images. **114t** Library of Congress Prints and Photographs Division, Washington, D.C. 20540, USA/Public Domain. **114ml** Museums Victoria, Australia (https://museumsvictoria.com.au). **114br** Science & Society Picture Library / Getty Images. **115ml** Heritage Auctions, HA.com. **115bl** Bits and Splits / Shutterstock. **118t** Science & Society Picture Library / Getty Images. **118b** RG-vc / Shutterstock. **119** Onslow Auctions Limited / Mary Evans Picture Library. **120t** Polaroid Land Camera Model 95 and Polaroid Land Film Type 40. Polaroid Corporation records, Baker Library, Harvard Business School. Photographed by Susan Young. **120b** Photo Cafe (https://photocafe.bg). **121t** ImageBROKER.com GmbH & Co. KG / Alamy Stock Photo. **121b** Andrew Kitching / Alamy Stock Photo. **122t&b** Commissioned Photography. **123** Andrew Shorey / Alamy Stock Photo. **124t&b** Flints Auctions (www.flintsauctions.com). **125** Photograph courtesy of Remy Steller (www.BROWNIEcam.com). **126** Library of Congress Prints and Photographs Division, Washington, D.C. 20540, USA. **127t** George Rose / Getty Images. **127bl** Science & Society Picture Library / Getty Images. **127br** Jeffrey B. Banke / Shutterstock. **128** Indianapolis Museum of Art at Newfields / Getty Images. **129** Apic / Getty Images. **130t** Wikimedia Commons (Andriy Matusevich/Public Domain). **130b** ProximaCentauri1 / Shutterstock. **131** Wikimedia Commons (s58y/CC BY 2.0). **132tr&ml** Bill Truran / Alamy Stock Photo. **133** George Rose / Getty Images. **134** Wikimedia Commons (Jarek Tuszyński/CC BY-SA 4.0). **135t** Photograph courtesy of Crypto Museum (www.cryptomuseum.com). **135b** pio3 / Shutterstock. **136–137** German Spy Museum (www.deutsches-spionagemuseum.de). **138t&m** Jason Wood / Alamy Stock Photo. **139t** Joe Tree / Alamy Stock Photo. **139b** Jeremy Pembrey / Alamy Stock Photo. **140t** Ricoh Imaging Europe S.A.S. (https://ricoh-imaging.eu) / (https://pentax.eu). **140b** Ole Meduza / Shutterstock. **141** © Sony Group Corporation (www.sony.net). **142** Stephen Hyde / Alamy Stock Photo. **143t** Museums Victoria, Australia (https://museumsvictoria.com.au).

Quarto

First published in 2024 by Frances Lincoln Publishing
an imprint of The Quarto Group.
One Triptych Place, London, SE1 9SH
United Kingdom
T (0)20 7700 6700
www.Quarto.com

Every effort has been made to trace the copyright holders of material
quoted in this book. If application is made in writing to the publisher, any
omissions will be included in future editions.

This book was conceived, designed, and produced by
Quintessence Editions
One Triptych Place, London, SE1 9SH
United Kingdom

Senior Commissioning Editor: Eszter Karpati
Senior Editor: Emma Harverson
Assistant Editor: Ella Whiting
Design: Peter Dawson, with Ronja Ronning, www.gradedesign.com
Art Director: Gemma Wilson
Senior Art Editor: Rachel Cross
Picture Research: Susannah Jayes
Production Manager: David Graham
Associate Publisher: Eszter Karpati
Publisher: Lorraine Dickey

A catalogue record for this book is available from the British Library.

Printed in China

ISBN 978-0-71129-301-4

10 9 8 7 6 5 4 3 2 1